AF605950

THE PROSTHETIC PEDAGOGY OF ART

THE PROSTHETIC PEDAGOGY OF ART

Embodied Research and Practice

CHARLES R. GAROIAN

STATE UNIVERSITY OF NEW YORK PRESS

Printed in the United States of America

For information, contact
State University of New York Press, Albany, NY
www.sunypress.edu

Production, Laurie D. Searl
Marketing, Fran Keneston

Library of Congress Cataloging-in-Publication Data

Garoian, Charles R., 1943–
The prosthetic pedagogy of art : embodied research and practice / Charles R. Garoian.
pages cm
Includes bibliographical references and index.
ISBN 978-1-4384-4547-2 (hardcover : alk. paper)
1. Art—Study and teaching—Philosophy. 2. Art and society. I. Title.

N84.G37 2013
707—dc23 2012010768

10 9 8 7 6 5 4 3 2 1

CONTENTS

ILLUSTRATIONS

ACKNOWLEDGMENTS

It is with pleasure that I dedicate this book to Lilit Ayanian, who was born on May 31, 2011, during the final stages of my writing. Our first grandchild, she came into our lives in a year when so many of our close family and friends passed away, and in doing so, reminded us of the regeneration of life. What fascinates us about Lilit is her innocence, her inquisitiveness, and her limitless absorption of all things and happenings in her environment. Turning her head, twisting her body up and down, right and left, backward and forward, she hears and sees everything. She touches, holds, pulls, pushes, and taps all things within close proximity. Her learning is insatiable. Putting things into her mouth, she touches then tastes her world. Her wonderment at every movement and sound is infectious; it has effected an intensity and renewal in our lives, and confirmed the importance of what we do as parents and educators in the lives of our children.

I would like to thank the members of my family who embraced me with love and patience as I buried myself in the research process and the writing of this volume. Most specifically, Sherrie, who as my inspiration for the past forty-four years continually reawakens and reaffirms the importance of stepping outside of my academic frame of mind to see and experience the multiplicities and fullness that life has to offer. And, to Jason Garoian, and Stephanie and Garo Ayanian (Lilit's parents) who continue to inspire hope through their generosity, creativity, and loving hearts.

My research and writing of this book would not have been possible without the inspiration of my students and colleagues in the School of Visual Arts at Penn State University, and at universities across the United States and internationally. Their differing and peculiar ways of seeing and understanding has extended and expanded my scope of experiencing and valuing the world, and their boundless desire for making meaning through art research and practice continues to inspire my cultural work as a teacher, artist, and writer. Chris Staley, Yvonne Gaudelius, Dónal O'Donoghue, John Howell White, Christine Marmé Thompson, Kimberly Powell, Graeme Sullivan, Gail Boldt, Jorge Lucero, Chris Schulte, Joe Julian, Kevin Slivka, Olivia Gude, Jerome Hausman, Liora Bresler, Rita Irwin, Laura Trafí-Prats, B. Stephen Carpenter II, Elizabeth Garber, jan jagodzinski, James Hayward

Rolling Jr., Stephanie Springgay are but a few who continue to foment my thinking about the educational significance of art research and practice.

Thank you to the following individuals and agencies who provided permission to publish the images that are contained within the pages of this book: artists Tim Roda, Brian Franklin, Stephanie Springgay, Nico Muhly, Francis Alÿs, Dorothy Schultz, Louise Barry, Bryan Rogers, Rob Martin, Gene Cooper, Janine Antoni, and Chuck Close; art educators Montse Rifà, Laura Trafí-Prats, and Xavier Giménez; archivist Heather Monahan at The Pace Gallery in New York City; Daniel Cooney Fine Art in New York City, Heather Monahan, Artists Rights Society, Art Resource, Visual Arts and Galleries Association, California Raisin Marketing Board, University of Pennsylvania Archives, Missouri Botanical Gardens, and Dr. Joseph (Joe) Julian Jr.

Finally, I am grateful for the encouragement and funding support that I received from Dr. Graeme Sullivan, Director of the School of Visual Arts, and Dr. Bill Doan, Associate Dean of Administration, Research, and Graduate Studies in the College of Arts and Architecture for the research and completion of this book project. And, I would like to acknowledge the support of Beth M. Bouloukos, Acquisitions Editor, and Laurie Searl, Senior Production Editor, at The State University of New York Press without whose advice and encouragement the publication of this book would not have been possible.

ONE

INTRODUCTION

The Prosthetic Space of Art

Art does not reproduce the visible; rather, it makes visible.

—Paul Klee, *Schöpferische Konfession*

Gaps seem to give us somewhere to extend: space for our prosthetic devices.

—Marilyn Strathern, *Partial Connections*

I have often wondered about that canvas (Figure 1.1), that first canvas leaning against the wooden easel, the one that I stretched in the first, that beginning painting course in which I was enrolled years ago . . .

its 18" x 24" dimensions . . .

its pure, immaculate surface sealed with thick white gesso, reflecting bright light from an adjacent window, taut from drying and shrinking against the milled wooden bars upon which I had pulled and stapled its loose fabric . . .

its unbleached cotton duck, which upon drying and shrinking, and stretching, resonated the thunder of a kettledrum in response to the thump of my snapping finger . . .

its blank, empty space, suggesting a patch of skin from art history's body, loudly staring back daringly, returning my gaze . . .

Figure 1.1. Stretched canvas, 2011 (Courtesy Charles Garoian).

that canvas, on easel and ready for painterly action . . .

its space a lacuna, intimidating while inviting my leap into its open gap . . .

the art classroom like that canvas, equally paradoxical, spatially available yet awesome and indifferent . . .

Thanks to my unknowing teacher who invited my participation in the painting lesson, who enabled and encouraged me . . .

to begin a process, a trajectory of work . . .

to extend beyond . . .

to reach outside the demarcated space, the bounded, rectilinear, pictorial edge of the surface while applying paint he said, his words suggesting the confidence of Francis of Assisi . . .

to "start by doing what's necessary; then do what's possible, and suddenly you are doing the impossible" . . .

to transgress the walls of the classroom . . .

to disrupt its academic and institutional confines he said, by imagining, exploring, and creating in ways similar to the playful making, working, and living on the raisin vineyard and farm of my emigrant parents he said . . .

where my spatial parameters extended well beyond my parents' provisions of safety and home as I ventured out on foot or bicycle across and beyond Valentine Avenue and Whitesbridge Road . . .

or, as I floated away on inflated inner tubes with my brother, rafting the waters of Fresno County's irrigation ditch bordering our property, hacking our way through its congested jungle of Johnson Grass . . .

to and from the County Dump where heaps of cultural refuse and detritus awaited curiosity, our insatiable desire to sift, to dig through its ruins, and scavenge what remained in that ancient tell . . .

ours was an archeological disposition to search, perhaps genetically and historically determined, an eagerness to find buried fragments, broken and discarded objects that comprised the Dump's sedimentations . . .

a surfeit, an excess of visual and material culture that stirred the imagination (Figure 1.2), compelling our ambition as alchemists to turn lead into gold . . .

our bricoleur's fancy improvising, jerry rigging incongruous images and ideas, adding and subtracting, attaching and detaching, gluing

. . . bi/**cy**>cles, t/oy+s, **fu**⊕RN/I=ture, **a**uto<**MO**>tive, bo/o/*ks*, mag//a:**zines**, t:o:o:ls, LET=ters, w/oo/**d**, ste∅el, PA-↓per, card^**boa**/rd, clo{thes, ro:>**pe...**

Figure 1.2. . . . bi/cy>cles,t/oy+s, 2011 (Courtesy Charles Garoian).

and nailing, leaning and propping, in order to extend and expand their presumed functions *prosthetically*, linking the present with the past, the familiar with the strange, to see and understand the one through the other, back and forth, and again . . .

Such drifting of the imagination and facility with the hand, playful work, research for making meaning, coincided with our parents' fractured lives, their telling of persecutions and atrocities experienced as children, surviving the Armenian Genocide, forced from their homeland . . .

their exodus and displacement among a worldwide Diaspora . . .

their refuge and search for new beginnings and possibilities in America . . .

their newly adopted country, where memories of past oppressive regimes and representations of space could be transformed through the lived representational spaces of the raisin vineyard and farm—their new Armenia . . .

That, that is where my art teacher encouraged me to go on that day, to the space of memory and cultural history, that which I received from my parents, and to the unknown spaces beyond the haven of our vineyard, home, where I migrated as a child . . .

the County irrigation ditch, and the Dump where Mr. Lindsey was the tender, Mr. Bonnini's dairy, Zareh Balasanian's onion patch, across Valentine Avenue, on Whitesbridge Road, and the other emancipating, lived spaces of my youth, to re-member, re-configure them in relationship, one with the other, one through the other, to conflate them with the space of the art classroom where I was standing before that easel . . .

the space of that canvas . . .

the space of my body with paintbrush in hand, to explore, experiment, and improvise, to make possible their impossible associations, connections, and relationships . . .

the conceptual leaps from one cultural space to the other . . .

> . . . the contingent and ephemeral, yet profound interconnections between their complex and contradictory spaces, the empty canvas, the art classroom, the vineyard, the irrigation ditch, the dump, the dairy, Armenia, and the others . . .
>
> The creative impulse for difference, the curiosity and desire for seeing and understanding the world and others differently, in new and compassionate ways through art research and practice, was first introduced to me by that painting teacher, who suggested that the unknowing, fear, and anxiety that I experienced before the empty space of that canvas constituted opportunities for transformation; *if I dared to take a risk . . .*
>
> to reach impetuously beyond my limiting assumptions of self, art, and schooling . . .
>
> to begin a process of work where the materiality of the body and the materiality of the world interconnect and achieve a coextensive and interdependent relationship, and where their cultural spaces inform and challenge each other in order for new and immanent, furtive and fugitive spaces of knowing and understanding to emerge . . .

Pertaining to such materiality and embodiment, two decades later I was reading art historian Ursula Meyer's book *Conceptual Art* (1972, 34–41) in which she describes artist Robert Barry's *Inert Gas Series* (1969).[1] The single photograph that Meyer uses to represent Barry's series is a scene of the Mohave Desert in California containing what appear to be tumbleweed and sage grass in the foreground and a distant mountain range in the background. Curiously, she describes Barry's intended subject matter as other than the desert scene that actually appears in the photograph: two cubic feet of the inert gas helium (HE) that the artist released into the atmosphere from a metal cylinder while standing in front of the camera, then quickly moving out of view, its visual field, before its shutter was released.

Notwithstanding that the materiality of inert gas was nowhere to be seen in the photograph, what puzzled me most was Barry's adjoining text: "Indefinite Expansion." While contemplating his image/text disjunction, my inability to find any tangible, material evidence of indefinite expansion within the frame of the photograph roused curiosity that delayed any quick understanding or explanation on my part. Such delay provided opportunities for lingering on Barry's juxtaposition: in-between what was readily evident in his Mojave Desert scene; knowledge provided by Meyer that he had released helium into the atmosphere in front of the camera; and its indefinite expansion thereafter.

Contextual movements occurred during my lingering between and among Barry's disjunctive concepts; slippages of understanding and mis-understanding from which emerged a realization that the photograph of the supposed inert gas, its visual representation of an invisible lived action, the fact of its gaseous materiality expanding indefinitely, suggested the possibility that I had embodied and was actually living and breathing the Helium while viewing its photographic representation almost a decade after its release into the atmosphere; that I am breathing it in during this writing three decades later; that others will breathe it during subsequent readings of this volume; and beyond.

Hence, the presence of the Helium, and its indefinite expansion, actually and virtually existed and continues to exist in its absence, in my mind's eye and my imagination; that ambiguous generative space of my body that Barry aroused with his *Inert Gas Series*. As in my embodiment of Barry's enigmatic artwork, the aforementioned liminal and contingent spaces of my empty canvas, the art classroom, the vineyard, the County Dump, the dairy, and the others of my youth, enabled complex and contradictory experiences and understandings of differential materiality. The expansion and extension of my cultural space interconnecting with those of others indefinitely, represents the premise of this book: *The prosthetic space of art*.

In each of its chapters, I will argue that the research and practice of art does not merely reproduce spaces but creates them just as artist Paul Klee's (1920) maxim suggests in the first epigraph at the beginning of this chapter . . . that is, artists create and open spaces into which existing knowledge can extend, interrelate, coexist, and where new ideas and relationships can emerge prosthetically as suggested by anthropologist Marilyn Strathern (1991, 115) in the second epigraph. However, before I introduce the chapters in this volume, in what follows I examine and discuss philosopher Henri Lefebvre's (1991) conceptualization of social space within which to contextualize and distinguish the particularities of the prosthetic space of art: its liminal, contingent, and ephemeral operations.

In theorizing and advocating for a science of space Lefebvre claims that social space precedes, prescribes, and proscribes the body's activity. In other words, we are always already in it. The interpretation and understanding of social space only follows later, after its production. It was "produced before being read; nor was it produced in order to be read and grasped, but rather in order to be lived by people with bodies and lives in their own particular urban [suburban and rural] context" (143). According to Lefebvre, the production of space is constituted by an interconnected, interdependent, dialectical relationship among a triad of *perceived*, *conceived*, and *lived* social spaces. With this spatial triad, he focuses on a priori attributes and properties of social space, rather than what has been interpreted, produced, and exists within it. Perceived space is constituted by

> the *spatial practice* of a society [as it] secretes that society's space; it propounds and presupposes it, in a dialectical interaction; it produces it slowly and surely as it masters and appropriates it. From the analytic standpoint, the spatial practice of a society is revealed through the deciphering of its [perceived] space. (Lefebvre 1991, 38)

Accordingly, the *spatial practice of art* developed dialectically through an organic and incremental process of social necessity and advocacy. Its span of history secreted over time through the emulation of natural processes and the sifting and deciphering of everyday practice and routine; its value and purpose accrued according to the situations, locations, and spatial circumstances of the society from which it emerged. Considering the coexistence of its disparate characteristics, spatial practice is paradoxically cohesive, yet logically incoherent due to its differing social formulations and disjunctive associations. Aesthetician Herbert Read (1955) writes that the spatial practice and origins of art, its prehistory, may have initiated out of necessity as nomadic Paleolithic cave painters discovered, memorized, and mimicked processes of image production to orient and ensure their success in hunting, gathering, and their procreative practices for species survival while interacting with and emulating the unpredictable rhythms and processes of nature. As such, natural space preceded, prescribed, and proscribed cave painters' spatial practices of image making on the *found* walls and shelters of caves, which then preceded, prescribed, and proscribed the *prepared* spaces of Neolithic life. In other words, as the sedentary, social practices of Neolithic agriculture and animal husbandry cohered through study and the modification of nature's rhythms so were symbolic images created and designated in the form of architectural demarcations of space, the prepared, painted, and inscribed spaces of walls and pottery rather than upon the rock wall formations of caves. Such correlations between cohesive, yet logically incoherent spatial practices that emerge out of the practice of everyday life are evident throughout the history of Western civilization.

As spatial practices shift from disparate and idiosyncratic social circumstances in which they are perceived, their assimilation and codification are constituted as *conceived spaces*, which Lefebvre defines as

> *Representations of space*: conceptualized space, the space of scientists, planners, urbanists, technocratic subdividers and social engineers, as of a certain type of artist with a scientific bent—all of whom

> identify what is lived and what is perceived with what is conceived . . . this is the dominant space in any society (or mode of production). (Lefebvre 1991, 38–39)

Representations of space in art are constituted by intellectualized, codified spatial parameters and properties. In Western art history, for example, intellectualized spaces of art were developed and advocated by the artisan guilds, the Church, and the wealthy patrons of the Middle Ages and the Renaissance; the art academies of the seventeenth and eighteenth centuries; and artists' styles, gallerists' exhibition spaces, critics' reviews, historians' methodologies, museologists' collections, educators' curricula, and the practices of other art specialists since the nineteenth century. The social spaces that were conceived during these historical moments determined and transmitted the dominant academic, institutional, and corporate understandings and taste of Western European society. Lefebvre cites Classical perspective as an example where "representations of space have at times combined ideology and knowledge within (social-spatial) practice" (1991, 45). Similarly, the complex and contradictory characteristics of Modernist art and film as revealed through collage, montage, and assemblage are examples of how these genres disjunctive, ideological representations of space, while shifting from the spatial representations of the past, combined with the ideological forces and practices of industrialization and mechanized society.

Given that Lefebvre's concept of spatial practice is experienced and learned perceptually, and his representations of space are academically, institutionally, and/or corporately conceived, the third in his triad, "representational spaces," introduces the indeterminacy, contingency, and ephemerality of *lived* experiences in the production of social spaces.

> *Representational space*: space as directly *lived* through its associated images and symbols and hence the space of "inhabitants" and "users," but also of some artists and perhaps of those, such as a few writers and philosophers, who *describe* and aspire to do no more than describe. This is the dominated—and hence passively experienced—space which the imagination seeks to change and appropriate. It overlays physical space, making symbolic use of its objects. Thus representational spaces may be said, though again with certain exceptions to tend towards more or less coherent systems of non-verbal symbols and signs. (Lefebvre 1991, 38–39)

While Lefebvre calls for the interconnection and dialectical consideration of his spatial triad, it is the "directional, situational, or relational" possibilities of representational space, its "essentially qualitative, fluid, and dynamic" characteristics that dominates his formulations about socio-spatial production (42). The representational is the lived, emergent space of the body, of imagination, of dreams, and the ambiguities of play and improvisation. It is a liminal, in-between space where disjunctive images and ideas coexist contiguously and interact dialectically while resisting intellectual closure and concrescence. It is an open, passively experienced space of art production; a lived space of creative and intellectual possibility in contrast with the presumptive associations of conceived spatial representations.

Inasmuch as it constitutes the site of subjectivity, Lefebvre locates his triadic spatial dialectic in the body. Its membership and participation in spatial practice is presupposed by its perceptual capacity to learn and function within the everyday circumstances of the outside world. The body is conceived as a constructed and sedimented representation of space "derive[d] from accumulated scientific knowledge [about its material, physiological and aesthetic characteristics, and] disseminated with an admixture of ideology" (Lefebvre 1991, 40). Inversely, the representational space of the body is constituted by the complexities, peculiarities, and "illusory immediacy" of its memory and cultural history (40) in dialectical relationship with the present; "our time . . . this most essential part of lived experience . . . [which] is no longer visible to us, no longer intelligible . . . cannot be constructed . . . it is consumed, exhausted, and . . . it leaves no traces" (95). The interstices of Lefebvre's dialectical triad, its in-between spaces, are where poetry and art originate. Its "lethal zone," a "mixed space"[2] is where slippages between and among rarified meanings and understandings

> escape the embrace of lived experience, to detach itself [*sic*] from the fleshy body . . . [to] facilitate metaphorization—the transport, as it were, of the physical body outside of itself. This operation, inextricably magical and rational, sets up a strange interplay between (verbal) disembodiment and (empirical) re-embodiment, between uprooting and reimplantation, between spatialization in an abstract expanse and localization in a determinate expanse. (Lefebvre 1991, 203)

Lefebvre's conception of the representational space of the body, its reciprocal, rhythmic oscillation of disembodiment offset by re-embodiment[3] corresponds with the prosthetic space of art research and practice discussed in this book; within its liminality and contingency, where disparate, disjunctive images and ideas extend one to and through the other and in doing so suggest and inspire new and renewed possibilities for interpretation and understanding social space.[4] Unfettered and open, a prosthetic space of creative production, I argue, is where slippages of meaning and understanding between and among perceived and conceived images and ideas, and the ambiguities of lived experiences, postpone a reliance on assumptions and presuppositions to create an interstitial, reflexive delay[5] in the body. This embodied time and space of delay is where reciprocal, rhythmic repetitions of difference occur; where familiar and strange, new and old, self and other, private and public, provide opportunities to linger on and contemplate juxtaposition, and resist a rush to metaphoric closure.[6]

The reflexive oscillation and lingering of delay is intentional and apparent in artist Brian Franklin's *Fermata* (2008–09), which consists of a series of video loops and installations of athletes prior to bursting into action. A pause on a musical "note, chord, or rest that is sustained at the performer's discretion for a duration longer than the indicated time value" (Evangelista 2009), *fermata* in Franklin's work challenges viewers' enthrall, fixation, and consumption of spectacle, and in doing so, offers a delayed time and space within which to expose, examine, and critique the hypervelocity and schizophrenia of mass mediated images and ideologies. Fermata suggests metonymic adjunction rather than metaphoric conjunction; a contiguity of forms whose disjunctions and slippages resist synthesis and generalized representations. Franklin describes the paradox of fermata in his series as athletes' "moment of stillness and preparation right before a burst of climactic energy causes the scene to slip between stuttering tension incapable of release and soothing, yet mundane repetition" (Franklin, online). Delaware Center for the Contemporary Arts curator Carina Evangelista characterizes the "stuttering tension" in the Franklin's video loops in similar ways:

> Adjusting their foothold, buttressing their muscular pitch, and steeling both psychological and physical will, these moments are the preamble—taut with all that is invested in the pursuit of perfection—to full-throttle force. Expecting exquisite coordination, grace, speed, and exactness, we hold our breath. And as spectators, we share in the "fermata" of the moment. The video triptych played simultaneously on a loop renders the interminable suspension into a kind of purgatorial black hole of tense, unconsummated propulsion. (Evangelista 2009)

In one video projection entitled *Fermata: Jesse Owens*, 2009 (Figure 1.3), Franklin has appropriated and looped a very brief segment of footage from Leni Riefenstahl's Nazi propaganda film *Olympiad* (1938) so that it pauses attention on U.S. Olympian Jesse Owens in a starting position just prior to taking off and in anticipation of the historic 100-meter sprint to victory, which earned him one of four gold medals at the 1936 Olympics

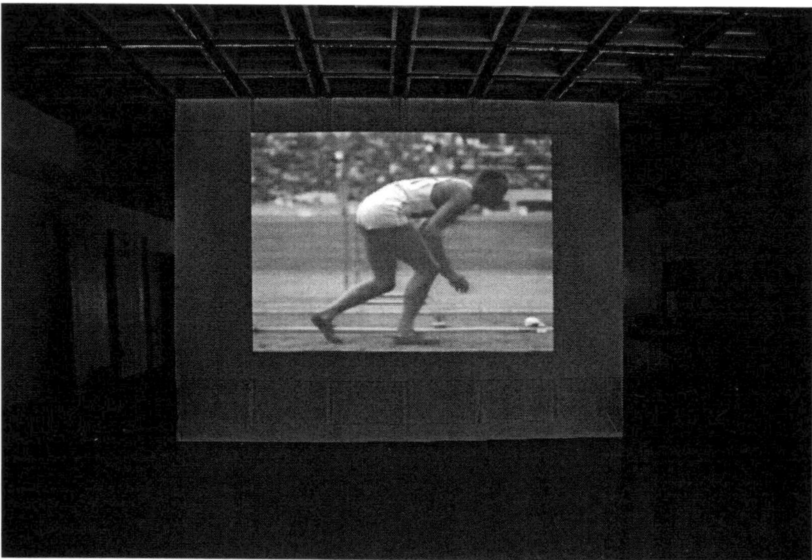

Figure 1.3. Brian Franklin, *Fermata: Jesse Owens*, 2009.

in Germany. While recognition of Riefenstahl's footage in Franklin's installation is immediate based on the film's modernist ubiquity and renown, the continuous and repetitive movement of Owens's endless rocking back and forth at the starting line of the race creates visual and conceptual pause that evokes tension, suspense, and anticipation in viewers.

Philosopher Gilles Deleuze (1994) argues that repetitive movement such as in *Fermata: Jesse Owens* should not be confused with the act of repeating for purposes of memorization, but the creation of a performative space within which "repetition is woven from one distinctive point [of difference] to another, including the differences within [the space] itself" (Deleuze 1994, 10). Similar to the lethal and mixed dialectics of Lefebvre's spatial triad, Deleuze characterizes the performative apparatus of repetition as "terrible power":

> We experience pure forces, dynamic lines in space which act without intermediary upon the spirit, and link it directly with nature and history, with a language which speaks before words, with gestures which develop before organized bodies, with masks before faces, with specters and phantoms before characters. (Deleuze 1994, 10)

The interminable and unconsummated forces that Evangelista describes about Franklin's repetitive video loops constitute the terrible power of *Fermata: Jesse Owens*, which allows for multiple readings, critiques, and disarticulations of Riefenstahl's spectacle of Nazi grandiosity, Adolf Hitler's hosting of the 1936 Olympics to extol Aryan superiority, and the Nazi propaganda machine that depicted African ethnicity as inferior. Pausing on the start of Owens's run also enables a double reading of "race"; namely, the object of the runner's participation in the track and field event on the one hand, and on the other, his racial identity as a non-Aryan, African American athlete, who, ironically, humiliated Hitler and Nazi hegemony while a citizen and member of an oppressed race back home in the United States.

Franklin's fermata of Jesse Owens's run also suggests correspondences with the pedagogical peculiarities of *currere*, a concept derived from its Latin origins and developed for educational purposes by educators William Pinar and Madeline Grumet (1976, 68–69). Currere blurs the boundaries between curriculum and pedagogy, teachers and students, so that they are mutually constituted. It refers to the *running* of a course; that is, the emancipation of learners to *run with* and assume responsibility for their own education and re-education through a self-reflexive process that connects their personal lived experiences with multiple, self-constituting learning opportunities that challenge the academic determinism of schools. Accordingly, Franklin's fermata series presents opportunities for currere; for engaging, running with, and disarticulating the sedimented pedagogies, ideologies, and representations of space, so that "thinking and doing come together in the transformative processes of art" research and practice (Eliasson 2010, 309).

The self-reflexive, self-constituting space of currere also corresponds with the compelling representational spaces created by artist Tim Roda, whose autobiographical photographs are inspired by memories of growing up in a working-class Italian immigrant family in rural Pennsylvania, and where his grandfather and father built their family home and garage using found and recycled materials, and where they slaughtered chickens and cows to put food on the table. Similar to Lefebvre's notion of spatial practice, the ethos of that originary, atavistic impulse is evident in Roda's harvest and bricolage[7] of eviscerated, disparate fragments of visual and material culture: paper, wood, tape, clay, mirrors, lamps, among other cultural detritus from his everyday environment. His approach to storytelling with a mix of disparate materials is improvisational and in keeping with his personal history. Like the eidetic imagery of Paleolithic cave dwellers,[8] there is urgency and transparency in his assemblage process as if to visualize and restore unity, presence, and liveness to memories and a cultural history that have past; to restore and unify within view of the camera what has been broken up and lost to modernity and our contemporary world of commodity fetishism, planned obsolescence, and mass mediated spectacle. Roda describes the function of his camera accordingly: "to record one moment in time that hovers between memories and constructed commentaries, yet is a documentation of 'real time' events for me, my wife, Allison, and son, Ethan" (online).

Indeed, Roda and his son and wife are directly involved in the creative process, as if to continue a tradition passed on by his grandfather and father in working to hold the family together and to restore its unity in the abstract, homogeneous space of contemporary society. While Tim, Evan, and Allison, all three participate in the creative process; she is usually the one outside the picture frame making pictorial adjustments and releasing the shutter of the camera. While father and son most often perform in front of the camera, Tim is the one who usually constructs and stages the tableau, always referring to the image in the viewfinder of the camera as his guidepost. Before Allison releases the shutter and fixes the composition in time, all three have had input into its final composition during discussions at family meals, which are usually held in the space of the installation. While most of the ideas and images are lifted from Tim's eccentric childhood, Allison and Evan bring their own experiences to constructing and reconstructing their family history. While Allison is represented in some

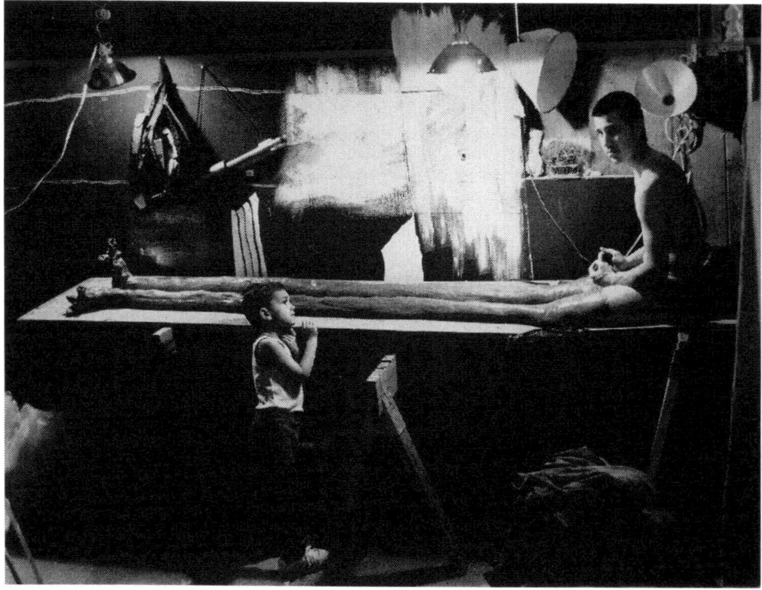

Figure 1.4. Tim Roda, *Untitled #27*, 2004, silver gelatin photograph on fiber matt paper, 22" x 28" (Courtesy Daniel Cooney Fine Art, New York, NY).

photographs, focus, nevertheless, is most often on the relationship between Tim and Ethan, father and son, and the shared history of their relationship.

That relationship is evident in Roda's *Untitled #27*, 2008 (Figure 1.4). Whereas the photograph is obviously staged, every aspect of its disjunctive composition seems improvised including the positioning of father and son. A makeshift table, consisting of an 8' plywood plank and supported by three sawhorses, runs across the width and bisects the photograph. Lamps are clipped on improvised armatures or loosely suspended from the ceiling with their cords dangling freely in space. What appear to be a backpack and some sort of tubular instrument are both hanging from nails on the back wall. The wall itself is entirely tacked with lengths of black paper, and in the area just behind the lamp that is suspended at the top center of the photograph, the black wall is roughly hand-painted white as if to emphasize and animate the radiating and reflecting glow of its light. It is within the noir of this Rauschenbergian combine[9] that we find Tim, in the top half of the photograph, dressed solely in black underwear and sitting at one end of the long plywood plank looking back at the camera with prosthetic legs formed crudely of clay stretching and protracting to the other end of the plank. Evan, standing in the foreground and bottom half of the photograph, looks up at his father as if in wonderment.

While the photograph's bifurcation suggests a generational divide between son and father, a familial tie extends by the trajectory of their gaze, and triangulates with Allison positioned behind the camera. In other words, the son's line of sight is directed toward the father, whose line of sight is aimed at the mother, whose line of sight, through the viewfinder of the camera, returns to the son. And, as viewers looking upon the scene, we too are implicated and conjoined with the Roda family. Within and among the spatial disparity of the photograph, it is the stretched, clay material of Tim's exposed prosthetic legs that draws, pauses, and extends our attention. In giving pause, they correspond with the biblical proverb *feet of clay*, a "fundamental weakness"[10] in the body, which in the case of Roda's work suggests a vulnerability and willingness to expose himself and protract his body into the flurried composition of the photograph and the complex relationships of family.

Like Lefebvre's social space, Roda's performative photographs precede, prescribe, and proscribe symbolic interpretations and understandings, which nevertheless will follow. In doing so, the ambiguities and incompleteness in his work, while inspired by his personal memory, offer a differential space where viewers can interconnect and perform their own memories and subjectivities. According to Pinar (n.d), "The significance of subjectivity [in this way] is not a solipsistic retreat from the public sphere . . . the significance of subjectivity is that it is inseparable from the social" (11). Apropos currere, performances of subjectivity and constructions of family history derived from personal memory, as in Roda's photographs, run with and challenge academic, institutional, and corporate representations of social space, and in doing so, they are simultaneously autobiographical and political. Hence, as the time and space of delay in art research and practice enables the performative running of currere, it emancipates subjectivity from normative, homogeneous conceptions of space, thus allowing it to stretch and extend beyond social and cultural sedimentations toward difference, and to reconsider them dialectically with furtive and fugitive lived experiences in a fluid and dynamic relationship. In doing so, possibilities exist of "disarticulating their constitutive elements, with the aim of establishing a different power configuration" (Mouffe 2010). Such slippages and movement toward and among disparate images and ideas within the emergent space of lived experience enables creative and intellectual anomalies that question and rub against the grain of paradigmatic representations of conceived space.[11]

As disparate, anomalous productions cohere into a critical mass, according to science historian and philosopher Thomas Kuhn (1970, 82), a "crisis" of knowledge occurs that shifts the spatial paradigm. This shift, which corresponds with the *history* of space, Lefebvre's fourth implication of spatial production, "is not to be confused either with the causal chain of 'historical' (i.e. dated) events, or with a sequence . . . [but] passage from one mode of production to another . . . [where] each mode of production has its own particular space . . . [and] the shift from one mode to another must entail the production of a new space" (46–47). Lefebvre's caution not to confuse historical passages of space with a chronology or sequence of events, suggests a contiguity of disjunctive spaces, old and new, familiar and strange, whose differences and particularities coexist and are extendable and connectible one to and through the other prosthetically. Rather than linear and universal, Lefebvre's conception of historical space is differential. Its coexistent and coextensive modes resist reductionism, codification, and immutability, and bring about interminable newness by restoring and unifying their differences and peculiarities. Accordingly, artists such as Franklin and Roda resist "produce[ing] a discourse and a reality adequate to the code" of historical representations of space (Lefebvre 1991,47) by creating fluid and dynamic differential spaces through their research and practice of art, where existing metaphors and assumptions of art practice, and canons of art history, are delayed allowing for eccentric oscillations and interplay between what is known and what is yet unknown and their empirical reembodiment. Such prosthetic interconnections, distortions, displacements, and mutual interactions within the representational space of art make creative and political agency possible within social space.

Apropos his commitment to exact a science of space, which precedes codified social formations, Lefebvre elaborates on historical space and distinguishes between its "absolute," "abstract," and "differential" attributes. "*Absolute space* [of history] was made up of fragments of nature located at sites which were chosen for their intrinsic qualities (cave, mountaintop, spring, river), but whose very consecration ended up by stripping them of their natural characteristics and uniqueness" (Lefebvre 1991, 48). As natural phenomena were discovered and essentialized as symbols, rites, and other magical properties during this primitive stage of social space, they were transferred and incorporated in religious and political practices accumulated and evolved as the absolute "bedrock of historical space and the basis of [and imperative for] representational spaces" (48). While absolute space retained many of the attributes of nature from which it originated, its eventual production and accumulation "smashed naturalness forever and upon its ruins established the space of accumulation . . . (knowledge, technology, money, precious objects, works of art and symbols)" (49). With the dependency on absolute space shattered, and accumulation established as the new social order, the production of space attained independence from natural life sustaining processes, giving rise to abstract forms of spatial production most commonly associated with the logic of corporate capitalism and its commodification of the individual body and the social body.

The *abstract space* of history is the space of homogeneity; it is space that consumes and colonizes local social practices and differences, and reconstitutes them into commodities for a global market. Its mass mediated, informational management systems and networks usurp social space, and replace productive and reproductive subjectivity with the false consciousness of consumption and commodity fetishism. It is a nostalgic realm dominated by master narratives, socially and historically constructed metaphors and codes, derived and distributed from academic, institutional, and corporate centers of production, wealth, and power; it thrives at the expense of nature and lived experience. Abstract space is bureaucratic and self-perpetuating, and it "endeavours to mould the spaces it dominates," according to Lefebvre (1991, 49).[12] Its hegemony coincides "neither with the abstraction of the sign, nor with that of the concept, it operates *negatively* . . . [and it] relates negatively to that which perceives and underpins it—namely, the historical and religio-political spheres" (50). Such negative abstraction is evident as artists' creative productions, subjectivities, and representational spaces are appropriated, commodified, and transformed into globalized strategies, brandings, and representations of space by the art market.[13]

Lefebvre identifies the inverse of negativity in abstract space, which "functions *positively* vis-à-vis its own implications: technology, applied sciences, and knowledge bound to power" (Lefebvre 1991, 50). Ironically, this positive function positions the subjectivity of academic, institutional, and corporate power, namely, its ability to extract natural and human resources for its own creative intentions and strategies for profit gain. Such imperious positivity constitutes "an apparent subject, an impersonal pseudo-subject, the abstract 'one' of modern social space . . . [an] awesome reductionistic force vis-à-vis 'lived' experience" (51). Accordingly, the body's impersonal desire and pseudo-subjectivity becomes apparent as lived experience and production of space is diminished, eradicated, supplanted, and bound to the pseudo-subjectivity and desire of academic, institutional, and corporate power. The positivity of abstract space is evident in the pseudo-altruism of post-Fordist appropriations of differentiated lived experiences, and its manufacture and commodification of purported democratic institutions. In his characterization of counterfeit choices offered vis-à-vis institutional ingenuity, art critic Tim Griffen writes: "Increasingly, we encounter a desire for more democratic institutions, and yet the participatory moments we are offered are choreographed very specifically, providing us with examples of democracy *as* quantities rather than *of* singularities" (Griffen 2010, 335). Within this quantified, pseudo-democratic space, the singularities of the body, its subjectivity is choreographed by power and perpetuated as false consciousness, desire, and compulsion to consume, which according to political theorist Chantal Mouffe (2010, 327) constitutes a form of participation that "commercializes and depoliticizes" social space. Hence, the voracious engine of abstract historical space operates negatively as it consumes and crushes differences and peculiarities of local, lived productions of space, and positively as it extorts and consumes knowledge to maintain and advance its position of social power. In doing so, it impedes the body's ability "to challenge either the dominant system's imperious architecture or its deployment of signs," and specific to adolescent bodies, "it is only by way of revolt that they have any prospect of recovering the world of differences—the natural, the sensory/sensual, sexuality and pleasure" (Lefebvre 1991, 50).

Notwithstanding its demoralizing force and consumption of lived experience, Lefebvre identifies the possibility of intellectual and creative agency within abstract space based on its insatiable need to feed and reinvent itself by generating new spaces of capital. To advance its dominant positioning, abstract space operates negatively by continuing to appropriate and colonize heterogeneous, lived productions of space, and positively by shuffling and reshuffling them with its existing operations of space. Ironically, as these fluid and dynamic operations of abstract space disengage to reconstitute, extend, and expand its reach of power, interstitial peculiarities emerge mixed and lethal, representational spaces that coincidentally materialize a *differential* space of opportunity and agency.

> [D]espite—or rather because of—its negativity, abstract space carries within itself the seeds of a new kind of space . . . [a] "differential

> space," because inasmuch as abstract space tends toward homogeneity, towards the elimination of existing differences or peculiarities, a new space cannot be born (produced) unless it accentuates differences. It [differential space] will also restore unity to what abstract space breaks up—to the functions, elements and moments of social practice. It will put an end to those localizations[,] which shatter the integrity of the individual body, the social body, the corpus of human needs, and the corpus of knowledge. (Lefebvre 1991, 52)

Whereas dissociated social fragments of abstract space are held in hostage by dominant, homogeneous ideologies, the social disjunctions of differential space restore and unify differences and peculiarities. Accordingly, the reconstruction and restoration of unity within differential space corresponds with the interconnections, distortions, displacements, and mutual interactions that constitute research and practice within the prosthetic space of art. Differential space is the space of possibility where prostheses can operate.[14] In other words, it is by way of differential possibilities, the seeds within abstract space, and its craving for extracting newness from social differences and peculiarities, for generating and regenerating new informational, technological, and mass mediated systems and networks to ensure profit gain, that the prosthesis of art research and practice comes into play. Rather than withdrawing from and deserting the homogeneity of abstract space, differential, prosthetic operations of art activate, reactivate, and advocate from within as underground interventions[15] that challenge and transform its hegemonic order (Mouffe 2010, 326).

As the collection of chapters in this book will show, the prosthetic space of art is an emergent space where socially and historically constructed, dissociated, and uncritical images and ideas of abstract space are brought together in a contiguous relationship for a lingering on their juxtapositions. Within the delay of that differential space, the social fragmentations and sedimented practices of academic, institutional, and corporate power can be exposed, examined, and critiqued, and their unity reconstructed and restored prosthetically. Such engagement within regimes of power is constituted by strategies of critical citizenship, according to Mouffe, which are "absolutely crucial for envisioning democratic politics today. We must acknowledge that what is called 'the social' is the realm of sedimented political practices—practices that conceal the originary acts of their contingent political institution—but recognize as well that such moments of political institution can always be [reinhabited and] reactivated" (Mouffe 2010, 326). Thus, the complexities and contradictions of differential space disengage sedimented political practices, and open interstitial, pedagogical opportunities for critical citizenship and possibilities for social democracy and, in doing so, break up the ideological hold of abstract space. Such transgressions and transformations of abstract space, its social canons and master narratives, through the creative play and improvisation of art research and practice recovers and restores the integrity of the individual body and the social body prosthetically.

In the second chapter of this volume, "Verge of Collapse: The Pros/thesis of Art Research," I explore *prosthesis* as a metaphor of embodiment in art-based research to challenge the utopian myth of wholeness and normality in art and the human body. Bearing in mind the correspondences between amputated bodies and the cultural dislocations of art, I propose *prosthetic epistemology* and *prosthetic ontology* as embodied knowing and being in the world to challenge the disabling, oppressive prosthetics of mass mediation, and to enable the creative and political agency of fragmented, limbless bodies. I discuss the historical origins of "prosthesis," its use as a rhetorical augmentation of language and technological augmentation of amputated bodies, to suggest that the visual language of art disrupts and extends beyond the dialectical closure of *thesis*, *antithesis*, and *synthesis* through the divergent interconnectivity of *prosthesis*. Within the context of art education, prosthetic pedagogy is characterized as performances of subjectivity that intersect, critique, and extend beyond academic, institutional, and corporate assumptions and sedimentations to enable the creation of new and diverse understandings through art practice.

In the third chapter, "The Prosthetic Pedagogy of the Ignorant Schoolmaster," I discuss the prosthetic space of subjectivity and identity as architectural metaphors based on the body's re-memberings and re-presentations of fragments from private memory and cultural history. I argue that such performances of subjectivity challenge socially and historically constructed public assumptions that are inscribed on the body. The liminality and contingency of prosthetic *space* is characterized as providing children with opportunities to expose, examine, and critique rarified academic, logical, rational, bureaucratized, institutionalized, and commodified *places* of schooling through art-making activities, which enable them to attain creative and political agency as critical citizens in contemporary culture. Within the prosthetic space of art research and practice, children's exploratory, experimental, and improvisational performances of subjectivity constitute critical interventions in overly determined school curricula, thus enabling their creative and intellectual growth. In defending the necessity for the ambiguities and indeterminacies of art practice, I invoke cultural theorist Michel de Certeau's (1988) dialectic of places and spaces, and the pedagogical possibilities of philosopher Jacques Rancière's (1991) concept of the ignorant schoolmaster. To support my claims about the prosthesis of art research and practice, I discuss the emergent and generative characteristics of cultural historian Alison Landsberg's concept of prosthetic memory. To complement theory with practice, I elaborate on the prosthetic pedagogy of art with a research project at the Universitat Autónoma de Barcelona, Spain, which involved emigrant children's autobiographical narratives in overcoming linguistic and cultural barriers as they responded to an exhibition of photographic essays at the Museu d'art contemporani de Barcelona.

Following the example of the Surrealists' parlor game *Exquisite Corpse*, chapter 4, "Precarious Leanings: The Prosthetic Research of Play in Art," contains four contiguous sections (folds) whose disjunctions and conjunctions challenge yet augment one another, which is characteristic of the play of images and ideas in art research and practice. I argue that the indeterminate slippages of meanings and understandings of *Exquisite Corpse* play are constituted by *prosthesis*, an emergent research process of exploration, experimentation, and improvisation that resists intellectual closure while supplementing and interconnecting disparate bodies of knowledge to one another. The visual and conceptual disjunctions and conjunctions that constitute the *Exquisite Corpse* process, like the play of prosthesis, open gaps, spaces of liminality where a multitude, an excess of meanings and understandings can be speculated and extended. While the chapter as a whole is collaged similar to *Exquisite Corpse*, one of its sections describes a specific curriculum for graduate students in art education to play at the folds, in-between personal memory and cultural history, art, theory, and pedagogy to conceptualize research metaphors based on the prosthetic play of *Exquisite Corpse*.

In "The Anxiety of Disequilibrium in the Museum," the fifth chapter of the book, I speculate about museums as liminal and contingent in nature, as prosthetic spaces of risk taking, spaces of intellectual tension, and creative anxiety. My purpose for evoking suspense and unease in this way is to stir questions about the privileging of art historical content in current museum education practices, and curiosity about the creative and intellectual possibilities that exist when learners' individual, private memories and cultural histories are allowed to intersect with the institutional, public memory and cultural histories of museum collections and exhibitions. My intention is not to confuse learning, but to complicate understandings about museum education, to argue that when the public memory of the museum is conjoined with the private memories of learners in prosthetic space, an anxiety of disequilibrium occurs at their border, an interstitial crisis of understanding, that allows for an immanent critique of their respective assumptions, and an interchange and augmentation of knowledge. Invoking the spatial concepts of philosophers Gilles Deleuze and Félix Guattari, I will discuss how prosthetic interconnections and slippages of understanding in-between museums' academic and institutional practices and learners' lived experiences constitute a generative, fluid, and dynamic educational environment. The imperative for disequilibrium brought about by risk taking in museums is also discussed and supported in this chapter from the scholarly perspectives of artist and critic Ron Jones, cultural critic Hal Foster, and others. Both Jones and Foster advocate for rigorous and reflective pedagogical approaches that evoke anxious curiosity through critical and creative risk taking. Within the context of museum education such approaches to teaching enable transcultural and transdisciplinary learning opportunities about collections and exhibitions that are dialectically charged and open to the cultural differences of learners.

In chapter 6, "~~Drawing Blinds~~: Art Practice as Prosthetic Visuality," I explore and conceptualize the anomalous spaces of perception and memory in art practice and research where experimental and alternative discourses and pedagogies can emerge. I argue that the instabilities and slippages between what is visible and invisible, known and unknown in these spaces enable insightful and multivalent ways of seeing and understanding the complexities of alterity and otherness. Furthermore, I discuss how the insights and revelations of art practice and research challenge socially and historically constructed ways of seeing and understanding and, in doing so, constitute the immanent and generative learning processes of prosthetic visuality.

In chapter 7, "Art-in-the-Flesh: The Materiality of Sensation and Embodiment," I explore and theorize the processes by which our bodies engage, perceive, and represent their relationship with the external world as prosthetic embodiment. The coexistence and coalescence of the opposing forces of the body and world constitutes the body as a virtual space of connectivity. As such, prosthesis is a perceptual predisposition that the body learns to use as it engages the corporeality of the world. "The body" in this sense is always already an object, a tool, and a cultural artifact; an ontological medium that we use to extend into the materiality of the world. I will argue that the prosthetic intertwining and enfleshment of the subject with the object of the body is made apparent through art research and practice; that is, bodies make artworks just as artworks make bodies. As the materiality of the body engages the corporeality of materials, tools, and objects through art making, manifold sensations, associations, and understandings extend one to and through the other prosthetically. In doing so, the sensate embodiment of art precedes and enables understanding embodiment *across* bodies, disciplines, and cultures. The theories of Merleau-Ponty, Massumi, Lyotard, Hayles, Dewey, and other scholars will be invoked to support my conceptualization of prosthetic that connects the flesh of the body and the flesh of the world felt in the body through art research and practice.

In chapter 8, "Art Research and Practice as Deleuzoguattarian Embodiment," I conceptualize the creative and political agency that is enabled through the prosthetic pedagogy of art from the theoretical perspectives of Deleuze and Guattari. I invoke the writings of these two philosophers as well as those of disability scholars who, in theorizing the body, have challenged the institutionalization and exclusivity of disability politics by arguing for an inclusive politics based on *impairment*, which advocates for the creative agency of all bodies regardless of their differences. Furthermore, I discuss the creative research and practice of artist Chuck Close and artist/scholar Petra Kuppers whose respective modes of addressing disability and impairment correspond with the rhizomatic assemblage of Deleuzoguattarian embodiment. I then end the chapter with excerpts of an interview with Joseph Julian Jr., MD (1986), whose creative teaching and rehabilitation accomplishments serve as an example of the rhizomatic assemblage of Deleuzoguattarian pedagogy. As a young neurologist, Dr. Julian spent one and a half years (1981–82) building and administering a comprehensive rehabilitation program for disabled Cambodian refugees at Khao I Dang, the largest of the Cambodian refugee camps on the Thai-Cambodian border.

Finally, as in the example at the beginning of this introduction, several of the chapters in this book begin with a disjunctive autobiographical narrative—fragments that I have remembered and reconstructed from personal memory and cultural history. My purpose in doing so is to create a differential, prosthetic space within which the particularities of my own lived experiences, and those of the artists, critics, historians, and theorists whose research and creative scholarship I invoke, can coexist contiguously and coextend dialectically one to and through the other. Nostalgia for the past is not my objective, but the audacity "to break up the past, and apply it [to the present], too, in order to live"; the dialectic of history espoused by philosopher Friedrich Nietzsche (1957, 21) from which possible futures can be envisioned. Further interstitiality throughout this volume is evident in-between the disjunctive ideas and images within my personal narratives; in-between my memory narratives at the beginning of each chapter, and my theoretical narratives that follow; and, in-between each of the chapters.

It is the premise of this book that a contiguous positioning of differential narratives within the prosthetic space of art research and practice will enable readers to run with, interconnect, and find correspondences between and among their own lived experiences and those of others. Such interminable criticality vis-à-vis cultural differences and peculiarities constitutes creative and political agency within social space, which brings about interminable newness to our understanding of others, and challenges the intellectual closure, reductionism, and immutability of academic, institutional, and corporate power.

TWO

VERGE OF COLLAPSE

The Pros/thesis of Art Research

> Knowledge about ourselves demands prostheses, which tie meanings and bodies together.
>
> —Morton Søby, "Collective Intelligence—Becoming Virtual"

As dead American GIs are returned home in body bags from the war in Iraq, the many wounded, a vast number of them amputees who in any previous wars would have died on the field of battle or on an operating table in a combat support hospital, have survived, their lives extended due to the most recent technological advances and surgical procedures in medical science.[1] These developments in medicine correspond with advances in the technologies of destructive weapons that are being deployed in the war.[2] Moreover, the mass mediation of the war is equally advanced as compared with previous conflicts due to sophisticated communication technologies[3] and the networks' deployment of embedded journalists who risk their lives to report and broadcast in real time the horrific battling in every sector of the war, including the gruesome wounding and killing of both military and civilian personnel. As *amputated* bodies of information, these journalists' disparate, truncated reports restrict the public's comprehensive and accurate understanding about the circumstances of the war, thus dismembering the body politic. As cultural critic Susan Sontag writes, "[T]he understanding of war among . . . [those of us] who have not experienced war is now chiefly a product of the impact of these [reports] and images" (Sontag 2003, 21).

These broadcastings have had global consequences as images of wounding, death, and dying are viewed every day through the various news networks and every hour on the half-hour through round-the-clock news reports from the likes of CNN, BBC, MSNBC, ABC, CBS, NBC, the Fox

Network, etc., not to mention continuous access via the Internet. What is localized in the zone of battle is then hypothesized and globalized through the apparatus of the mass media in every corner of the world . . . in bars and restaurants . . . in our living rooms and bedrooms . . . and now we have the ability to download the war onto our iPods™ and cell phones, which we carry in our pockets or attach to our bodies wherever we go. Ironically, while as cyborgs we are connected and experience the war virtually and vicariously through mass mediation systems, there are those in actual battle who are physically being disconnected of their limbs and losing their lives.

The corporeal horrors of the war in Iraq recall the pictorial amputations of the German Dadaists, namely Otto Dix, whose fragmented collages and montages represent the devastations to the body politic in Germany during and after World War I (Perry 2002, 76). According to art historian Brigid Doherty, Dix and the German Dadaists "look[ed] to the body as the repository of politics" (Doherty 1998, 77). Dix's oil and collage on canvas, *The Skat Players—Card Playing War Invalids*, 1920 (Figure 2.1), is a cynical

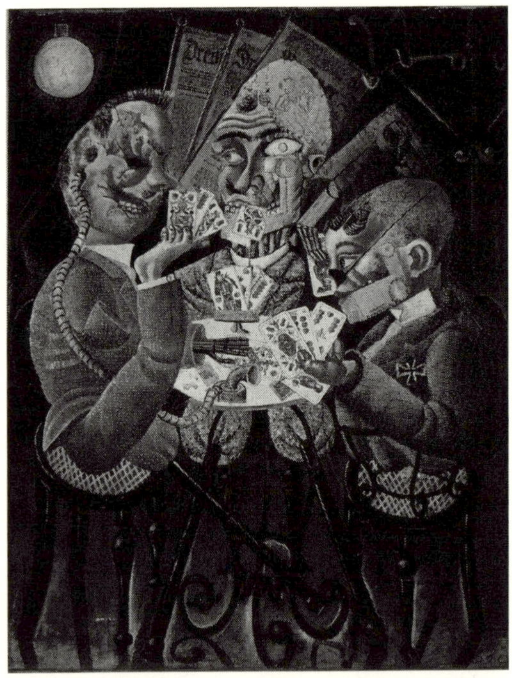

Figure 2.1. Otto Dix, *The Skat Players—Card Playing War Invalids*, 1920. Oil and collage on canvas. 110 x 87 cm. Nationalgalerie, Staatliche Museen, Berlin, Germany. © 2012 Artists Rights Society (ARS), New York/VG Bild-Kunst, Berlin. Photo credit: Erich Lessing/Art Resource, NY.

representation of how the human body is both the supplier and recipient of the scheming brutality of political power. A card game of tricks that involves three or four players, Dix's skat players, apparent veterans of World War I with official standing, multiple amputees fitted with multiple prosthetic body parts, having been tricked into believing that World War I would end all wars, engage in their own folly as they trick each other in the card game by using their prosthetics to stack the deck, deceive, and cheat one another. A parody of the utopian representations of Cézanne's and Picasso's card players, Dix transforms these artists' Postimpressionist and Cubist disfigurations, the formalism of their machine metaphors, into the amputations of collage and montage whose fragments represent bodily dismemberment on the one hand, while on the other hand serving as pictorial prostheses affixed to the canvas. As art historian Graham Bader argues, the fragmented anatomical representations of Dix and the Dadaists "suggest not an aesthetic strategy but an entire culture driven by an ongoing cycle of corporeal assault, inscription, experimentation, and decomposition" (Bader 2007, 229–30).

As a metaphor of the brutality of World War I, art historian Ernst Cohn-Wiener (1998) describes the 1920 Berlin Dada Fair as "an anatomical museum, in which you can behold yourself dissected, not just arm and leg, but head and heart. Not only your very own body, but that of all of you collectively" (cited in Doherty 1998, 75). The disfigurations of German Dadaist collage and montage parody politicians as "ridiculous machines made up of mismatched industrial and biological parts" (Doherty 1998, 77). Such technological metaphors, which represent the devastations to the body politic in Germany as a house of cards during and after World War I, echo the power politics of the war in Iraq. Both wars were waged with the most technologically advanced and destructive weapons of their time. Both wars benefited from the most technologically advanced and invasive surgical procedures and prosthetics to repair damaged bodies. Both wars were sensationalized through advances in mass mediation of their day and, in doing so, communications technology was used to confront the victims of war in order to freeze and reproduce their horror (79). In characterizing such technological correspondences between prosthetics and war, architectural theorist Mark Wigley writes: "Prosthetic technology alternated between producing substitutes for the body parts that military weapons had destroyed and producing these very weapons" (Wigley 1991, 23).

When it comes to devastations of war, history most certainly repeats itself. In fact, since the Iraq war began, an inordinate number of GIs, both women and men, having returned as amputees, such as Lieutenant Dawn Halfaker,[4] have been photographed, chronicled, and broadcast by means of print and electronic journalism. Halfaker lost her right arm when a rocket-propelled grenade exploded near her in the war in Iraq. Such ubiquitous exposure through the mass media essentializes and represents the maimed, limbless body as a rarified symbol of relentless sacrifice, heroism, and loss worthy of sympathy, while casting a *gaze of normality* that marks it as the spectacle of contemptible freakery, which is often ascribed to and experienced by amputees (Serlin 2002, 48–49, 53). Art historian Marquard Smith characterizes the essentializing and fetishizing of disability as "feed[ing] our culture's fascination with spectacles of difference" (Smith 2006, 59). Ironically, the voyeuristic regime of this fetishizing gaze represents a doubling of amputation, the first being the loss of the body's limb/s, the second that of being ostracized, cut off by the culture for the amputee's bodily difference. Considering that the body's knowledge, identity, and desires are technologically mediated, constructed, and augmented by academic, institutional, and corporate assumptions suggests that the embodiment of contemporary cultural life is always already disjunctive and dystopian; and that its wholeness constitutes a utopian myth, which dissociates, stereotypes, and stigmatizes the amputated body as dysfunctional, abnormal other (Jain 1999, 32). What constitutes normality anyway? Are we not all aberrant? Does not our horror and fascination with anomalous bodies in and of itself constitute a human anomaly? Given the cultural dislocations of our bodies, are we not all amputated in some form or another? Are we not all other?

In what follows, I will explore the correspondences between amputated, fragmented bodies and the disjunctive strategies of creative research, experimentation, and representation found in modernist and postmodernist artworks whose collage narratives can be described as "a cutting off, sectioning, segmenting [and juxtaposing]" of materials, processes, images, artworks, artists, viewers, and the cultural body (Lingis 2006, 75). Arguably the most important twentieth-century contribution to the history of art, the disjunctive narrative of collage has in common the jerry-rigging research of *bricolage*; that is, the improvisational dis-assembling, exchanging, and re-assembling of images, ideas, and objects in ways that they were not originally designed. In describing the undecidable and contingent subjectivity of this process, anthropologist Claude Lévi-Strauss writes: "The 'bricoleur' may not ever complete his [*sic*] purpose but he always puts something of himself into it" (Lévi-Strauss 1966, 21–22). What Lévi-Stauss is alluding to is that the bricoleur's performative subjectivity and creativity takes place in-between the cultural fragments, the detritus of his enterprise.

Moreover, I will conceptualize the robust, yet tenuous juxtapositions, interconnectivity, and criticality in-between and among the fragmented art bodies of collage narrative as *prostheses* that *supplement* displaced, disjunctive representations and understandings. In describing the disjunctive character of art research and representation, literary theorist David Wills writes:

> Such an idea of juxtaposition as coincidence is a function of *prosthesis*. It takes a fact of shared space, the contiguity of two or more

> differences, and narrates their relation as a coincidental event. But that shared space remains [unstable] impossible to delimit; for as long as every relation is a relation to difference, what is a close or distant relation cannot be rigorously determined. (Wills 1995, 42; italics added)

According to Wills, given the instability of images and ideas, their meanings and our understanding of them are contingent, they always exist in prosthetic relation to other images and ideas.

Philosopher Jacques Derrida's conceptualization of the logic of supplement as two opposing yet strangely unified significations corresponds with prosthetic interconnectivity. Based on his critical reading of Rousseauian texts, Derrida defines the first signification of the supplement as:

> A surplus, a plenitude enriching another plenitude, the *fullest measure* of presence. It cumulates and accumulates presence. It is thus that art, *technè*, image, representation, convention, etc., come as supplements to nature [originary and normalized knowledge] and are rich with this entire cumulating function. (Derrida 1976, 144–145)

Derrida then juxtaposes this "self-sufficient" signification of the supplement with that which "intervenes or insinuates itself in-the-place-of . . . as substitute . . . it produces no relief, its place is assigned in the structure by the mark of an emptiness" (145).

By juxtaposing these oppositions of the supplement, Derrida argues that its two significations "cannot be separated" from each other, and that each "is by turns effaced or becomes discreetly vague in the presence of the other" (Derrida 1976, 145). In doing so, Derrida suggests a paradox that reveals yet postpones the differences between the two significations to allow for a multiplicity of significations and understandings to occur. Apropos prosthetic interconnectivity, Derrida characterizes the connectivity of the supplement's two significations as being an exterior addition. In doing so, his logic of the supplement confirms that prosthesis functions both as a surplus and as filling a lack, which paradoxically represents the amputated body as both a "plentitude enriched by another plentitude" yet a "mark of emptiness."

Hence, bearing in mind the possible linkages between art-based research and the amputated body, I propose an embodied form of knowing and being in the world, a *prosthetic epistemology* and *prosthetic ontology*, that challenge the disabling, oppressive prosthetics of mass mediation, its gaze of normality. As critical theorist Donna Haraway suggests, mass mediation and other culturally constructed perceptual systems constitute prosthetized forms of vision and visuality. She writes:

> The "eyes" made available in modern technological sciences shatter any idea of passive vision; these prosthetic devices show us that all eyes, including our own organic ones, are active perceptual systems, building in translations and specific [constructed] ways of seeing, that is, ways of life. (Haraway 1991, 190)

Photographer Andreas Feininger's *The Photojournalist* (1951)[5] is consistent with Haraway's claim that prosthetic devices reveal perceptual systems. As the photojournalist in Feininger's photograph holds the camera to his face, its lens and viewfinder align with his eyes to suggest the prosthetic augmentation of his body's perceptual capabilities. In doing so the body is represented as cyborg, machine and meat interconnected. While body and camera seem incompatible, both represent interconnected perceptual systems, one organic the other technological, which complement and supplement one another. Moreover, as we viewers return the gaze of this photograph, we too are connected if not implicated in its perceptual regime and apparatus. As with Feininger's prosthetic embodiment, art-based research is an active process of critical examination and deconstruction of the gaze of normality, which enables the creative and political reconstruction and agency of fragmented, limbless bodies.

My aim here is not to minimize or trivialize the pain, suffering, and rehabilitation of those with amputated bodies, or to use the metaphor of prosthesis at the expense of those who live with artificial devices, because, as cultural critic Vivian Sobchack cautions, doing so ignores "the phenomenological—and quite different—structural, functional, and aesthetic terms of those who successfully *incorporate* and *subjectively live* the prosthetic and sense themselves neither as lacking something nor as walking around with some 'thing' that is added on their bodies" (Sobchack 2006, 22). Similarly, cultural theorist Sarah S. Jain warns against limiting the use of the prosthetic trope merely to argue in favor of or in opposition to technology when "the wounding ingredients of technological production [those academic, institutional, and corporate *proselytizing* offenses to the body committed through schooling, labor, and consumption] remain continually under ontological erasure" (Jain 1999, 49). Moreover, I want to avoid the abuse of disability tropes as "opportunistic metaphorical devices" suggested by literary theorists David T. Mitchell and Sharon L. Snyder, who conceptualize the fetishizing of disability in literature as *narrative prosthesis* "to indicate that disability has been [too easily] used throughout history as a crutch upon which literary [and other mass mediated] narratives lean for their representational power, disruptive potentiality, and analytical insight" (Mitchell and Snyder 2000, 49). Consequently, while healing and rehabilitation of the wounded body is imperative, art as therapy will not be addressed in this writing because positioning art research and creative work merely within clinical and pathological understandings often undervalues their enabling of amputees' creative and political agency for which Sobchack, Jain, and Mitchell and Snyder are advocating; especially in a culture that is compelled and consumed by the political economy of institutionalized and corporate medicine (Illich 1976; Foucault 1994).

Instead, my aim is to position art and prosthesis in a disjunctive, yet coterminous, dialectical relationship in order to expose and examine both their discursive and corporeal correspondences as embodied knowing. My intention in doing so is to examine alterity and how art research can enable the embodiment of cultural difference. As critical theorist Morton Søby points out, considering that, historically, the body has extended beyond its physical limits through the use of various kinds of tools, including orthopedic devices to enable the disabled body, "prosthesis has a restoring and normalizing function and it becomes an element in the great story of evolution and development of civilization" (Søby 2005, online). Based on the body's willful desire and ability to extend its limitations, psychologist Sigmund Freud argued:

> Man has, as it were, become a sort of prosthetic God. When he [*sic*] puts on all his auxiliary organs he is truly magnificent; but these organs have not grown entirely together with him and they still give him troubles at times. (Freud 1962, 38–39)

As Søby argues: "For Freud, prosthesis presents the boundary between that which is human and that which is cultural," suggesting that the "troubles" about which Freud writes call attention to the incompatibilities of nature/culture, body/machine, normal/abnormal, and other delimiting dualisms (Søby 2005, 6, online).

It is this troubling, incompatibility of prosthesis, which advocates *prosthetic pedagogy*, an embodied form of art research and teaching that challenges and resists both the disabling stereotypes and stigmas of the amputated as dysfunctional, and the fear and loathing of technological supplements that enable the body's agency. Indeed, there exists an interesting correlation between the fear of disabled bodies and their enabling through prosthetic technology insofar as the fear of technology is the consequence of denying the body's technological need, which in turn is a consequence of the body's presumption of wholeness and self-sufficiency. Critical theorist George P. Landow's example of technophobic academics and intellectuals is a case in point:

> Transferring the term *prosthesis* from the field of rehabilitation . . . gathers a fascinating, appalling congeries of emotion and need that accurately conveys the attitudes contemporary academics and intel-

> lectuals in the humanities hold toward technology. Resentment of the device one needs, resentment [and denial] at one's own need and guilt, and a Romantic dislike of the artificiality of the device that answers one's needs mark most humanists' attitudes toward technology, and these same factors appear in the traditional view of the single most important technology we possess—writing. These attitudes result, as Derrida has shown, in a millennia-long elevation of speech above writing, its supposedly unnatural [prosthetic] supplement.[6] (Landow 1992, 170–71)

Ironically, what Landow describes as Romantic idealization and bifurcation constitutes an amputation, which isolates the body from technology, and from the body politic the way Derrida suggests about attitudes toward speech and writing. What modern and contemporary artworks and amputated bodies have in common is that they constitute an irritant as their disjunctive, abstracted materiality rubs against the grain of viewers' assumptions and understandings of the totalized body. Corporeal abstractions either in the actual and virtual sense do not correspond or fit viewers' assumptions of what normal bodies should look like. Philosopher William Barrett's characterization of viewers' aversions to abstractions in modern art, like those of the Cubists, Fauvists, Surrealists, and Abstract Expressionists, corresponds with viewers' fear and loathing of amputated bodies. He writes:

> Modern art touches a sore spot, or several sore spots, in the ordinary citizen of which he [*sic*] is totally unaware. The more irritated he becomes at modern art the more he betrays the fact that he himself, and his civilization, are implicated in what the artist shows him. (Barrett 1962, 43)

Cultural theorist Rosemarie Garland Thomson's theory of anxiety surrounding "freak discourse" corresponds with Barrett's irritant. Thomson argues, "Because such ['exceptional'] bodies are rare, unique, material, and confounding of cultural categories, they function as magnets to which culture [projects and] secures its anxieties, questions, and needs at any given moment" (Thomson 1996, 2). Thus, according to Barrett and Thomson, as we experience and embody the visual and conceptual complexities and contradictions of modern art and exceptional bodies, we do so with horror and fascination because we discover and identify with those same "sore spots and irritants," as qualities and characteristics within ourselves. Contrary to the presumption of wholeness, such eccentric embodiment suggests that we are always already *disabled* in one form or another; amputated, fragmented, and in a mutable relationship with a technological world that requires constant placements, displacements, and replacements; in other words, we are *enabled* by virtue of prosthetic alterations and adjustments.

Considering the origins and history of its applications, the trope *prosthesis* is an apt representation of complementary and supplementary relationships between art and other forms of research found in the sciences and social sciences. According to Wills, the use of the word was first recorded in England in 1553 in Thomas Wilson's *Arte of Rhetorique*, which the author "borrowed directly from the Greek . . . in its rhetorical sense of the addition of a syllable [*pre*-fixed] to the beginning of a word" (Wills 1995, 218). In contemporary cyberculture, for example, the prefix *e* in *e-Learning* constitutes a prosthetic extension whereby *learning* is supplemented by the use of electronic devices such as computers. Pertaining to this writing, *art-based re-search* suggests *art* as a prosthetic supplement to stand on, and the prefix *re* as prosthesis to search back, examine again, and acquire knowledge anew.

The sixteenth century was a time when the Reformation reconstituted religious doctrine, when Gutenberg's press revolutionized the production and dissemination of print. There was a renaissance in medicine, science, and art when one body of knowledge replaced another—a time that has since been referred to as the beginning of the Age of Reason, the Enlightenment, and the Early Modern. It was a time when Wilson's rhetorical reintroduction of the word *prosthesis* coincided with Ambroise Paré's rediscovery of *ligature* in France in 1552. A surgical procedure that Paré attributed to Galen of Pergamon, the second-century Greek physician, ligature was the binding of arteries following amputation, thus replacing the practice of cauterization, which was more than likely to result in the patient "bleeding to death" (Wills 1995, 215–16). Paré's use of ligature, an artificial construction in its own right, made it possible to augment both the life of the limb and subsequently the patient. Ligature also made it possible to attach prosthetic devices to amputated limbs.

Wills writes: "For the French the medical sense of the word [*prosthesis*] would come first, but not until 1695 [143 years after Paré's rediscovery], about a decade before the rhetorical sense, which first appeared in French in 1704" (218). Wills further characterizes knowledge during this historical period of renaissance as not only "rearranged but prosthetized—broken apart and artificially reconstructed" (219). Historical placements and replacements are replete in his account of the trope *prosthesis* as it extends from its rhetorical use by the Classical Greeks to late-sixteenth-century England, then by yet another extension to the human body in early-eighteenth-century France. Through this trajectory, both body and text are discursively *prosthetized*, hence artificially supplementing one another and suggesting, by yet another extension, the possibility that art research represents *prosthetic* embodiment.

The prosthetic embodiments of metaphor and metonymy correspond epistemologically with the Hegelian dialectic of thesis, antithesis, and synthesis. Like metaphor, dialectical tension between thesis and antithesis is resolved by synthesis into a unified whole—a totalized understanding or representation. However, while synthesis enables movement beyond the initial dualism of thesis and antithesis, its dialectical closure constitutes a new thesis position disconnected from other complex and contradictory understandings and, in doing so, it has a tendency to stabilize as yet another art/body paradigm. Critical theorist Jean-François Lyotard reminds us: "Research that takes place under the aegis of a paradigm tends to stabilize . . . [and exploit creative and political agency]" (Lyotard 1999, 61).

The rhizomatic augmentations of prosthetic criticality constitute cyborgian epistemology, claim cultural theorists Chris Hables Gray, Heidi J. Figueroa-Sarriera, and Steven Mentor:

> Once, most people thought that artificial-natural, human-machine, organic and constructed, were dualities just as central to living, but the figure of the cyborg has revealed that it isn't so. And perhaps this will cast some light on the general permanence and importance of these dualities. After all the cyborg lives only through the symbiosis of ostensible opposites always in tension. We know, from our bodies and from our machines, that tension is a great source of pleasure and power . . . [As such, the cyborg metaphor challenges and moves beyond] dualistic epistemologies to the epistemology of cyborg: *thesis, antithesis, synthesis, prosthesis.* And again . . . (Gray, Figueroa-Sarriera, and Mentor 1995, 13; emphasis added)

Hence, as these scholars suggest, thesis/antithesis/synthesis/prosthesis represents a fourfold open and mutable epistemology that enables oppositional discourse beginning with the dialogic of thesis/antithesis, followed by a resolving of its tension through synthesis, then indeterminate flights of understanding that extend beyond our bodies and symbiotically interconnect with others and broaden our capacity to understand and accept difference in the world. This indeterminacy of prosthesis is constituted by disjunctive, incongruous fragments of images and ideas, knowledge and understandings, whose complex, irreducible slippages of meaning resist synthetic closure similar to the ways in which collage narrative resists concrescence (Kuspit 1983, 127). In doing so, prosthesis represents excess, a surplus knowledge and understanding, which is unapparent or unknown yet supplements the dialogical framework of thesis/antithesis/synthesis through an ongoing process of becoming.

In her response to post-9/11 global politics, terrorism, and war, critical theorist Judith Butler regards "vulnerability" and "recognition" as important aspects of resisting synthetic closure when responding to others in times of violence and mourning. For Butler, vulnerability "dislocates us from our positions, our subject-positions" and allows us to recognize one another not "as we already are, as we have always been, as we were constituted prior to the encounter itself . . . [but] to solicit a becoming, to instigate a transformation, to petition the future *always* in relation to the Other" (Butler 2004, 44; italics added). Such deliberate and ongoing solicitation of becoming and petitioning of future relations with others constitutes a hopeful version of the Hegelian dialectic, "but it is also a departure, since [as Butler explains] I will not discover myself as the same as the 'you' on which I depend in order to be" (44). The vulnerability, recognition, and deliberate becoming called for by Butler correspond with the characteristics of prosthesis that resist concrescence—the synthetic closure of one's subject position in relation with the other.

The precarious, teetering materiality of artist Robert Rauschenberg's *combines* is consistent with the motility of prosthesis. Rauschenberg coined the term *combine* to characterize his bridging of painterly and sculptural processes; his combining of found visual and material culture; and, his desire for the viewer's embodiment of his art through their respective materiality. The disjunctions between and among the detritus and quotidian materials and objects that are found in Rauschenberg's combines "materialize the image, to make a representation read as though it were a corporeal thing," writes art historian Rosalind Krauss (1964, 39). Krauss continues:

> When the "images" are actual objects . . . [as in the example of Rauschenberg's combine, *Canyon*, 1959 (Figure 2.2),[7] affixed with oil, paper, fabric, metal, cardboard box, printed paper, printed reproductions, a photograph, wood, paint tube, and mirror on canvas, with oil on a stuffed bald eagle, string, and pillow], the sense of identification between material objects and "images" is heightened in every way. (39)

Krauss's conceptualization of Rauschenberg's materiality constitutes prosthetic embodiment; a connectivity between the representation of an object and the actual object itself; the object and its connectivity with other objects in the combine; the objects and their connectivity with the contexts from which they were transferred; and, the combine's material connectivity with viewers' bodies as its attached objects physically and conceptually extend beyond the frame of the combine. Invoking the Derridean

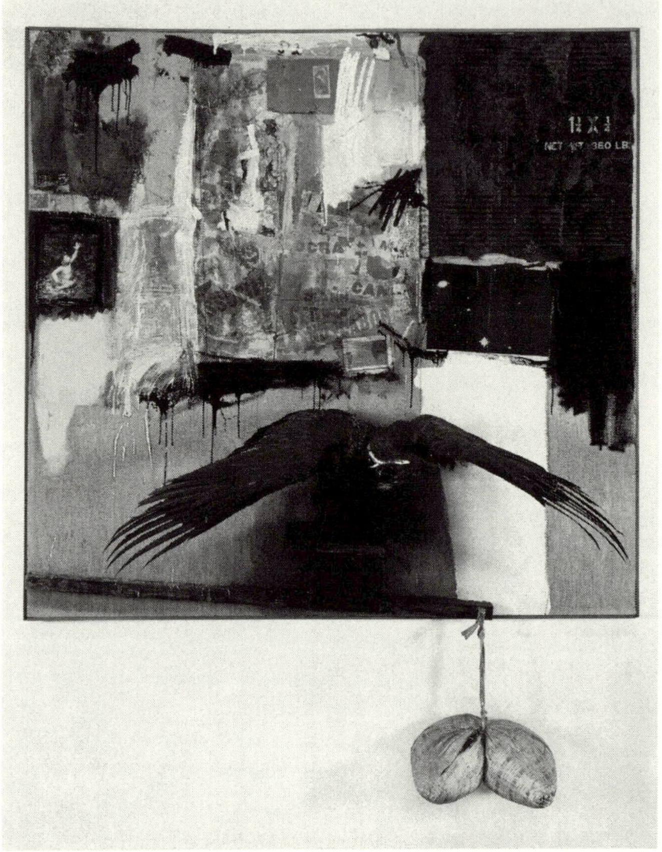

FIgure 2.2. Robert Rauschenberg, *Canyon*, 1959 (Courtesy Sonnabend Collection, New York). Art © Estate of Robert Rauschenberg/Licensed by VAGA, New York, NY.

concepts of "recognition and misrecognition," Wills describes the viewers' extending beyond the frame of their understanding to embody works of art as "reading[s] informed by prosthesis" (Wills 1995, 59).

> In reading or analyzing the work of art one recognizes the work of the author; but in the same movement, one inevitably requires that the author stands aside, that she yield some space for the [misrecognized] discourse of the spectator. (59–60)

Art critic and historian Branden W. Joseph characterizes Rauschenberg's materialization of images in the combines as a transgression that goes against the framing edge of historical, rectilinear representations of pictorial space. Such "framing contingency" is consistent with the destabilizing yet enabling facility of prosthesis as it "implies both separation and continuity, both a seamless relation to the world outside itself and a cut, break, a gap, or bifurcation from it, what might be called a contingent framing edge as opposed to a formalist one" (Joseph 2006, 62, 66). Krauss argues,

> In Rauschenberg's work the image is not about an object transformed. It is a matter, rather, of an object transferred. An object is taken out of the space of the world [de-territorialized] and embedded [re-territorialized] into the surface of a painting, never at the sacrifice of its density as material. (Krauss 1974, 40)

Furthermore, Rauschenberg's title *Canyon* ironically suggests a gap or impasse that is traversed when an object such as the stuffed bald eagle has been de-territorialized and transferred from its natural habitat and the taxidermist's studio, and re-territorialized within the context of the combine and, from its perch, projected out toward the viewer. Such prosthetic extension affirms Rauschenberg's well-known declaration: "Painting relates to both art and life. Neither can be made. (I try to act in that gap between the two.)" (Perreault 2006, online).

While modernists such as Rauschenberg confined their prosthetic criticality within the formalistic boundaries of the art world, a generation of contemporary postmodern artists has created radical works of art that openly and directly challenge the oppressive socially and historically constructed assumptions and conventions that exist within the broader context of contemporary cultural life. Thus, by extension, the prosthetic materiality and framing contingency associated with Rauschenberg's combines are evident in the radical critiques of artists such as Judy Chicago[8] whose collaborative, community-based installations challenge gender politics, the painted quilts of Faith Ringgold[9] and paintings of Robert Colescott[10] that critique racial injustice, Merle Laderman Ukeles's[11] ecological performances, and Cindy Sherman's[12] uncanny photographic impersonations that raise questions about the marked body and its construction of identity by the spectacle of mass mediated culture. Unlike the modernists, the prosthetic criticality of these and other contemporary postmodern artists constitutes examples of critical citizenship and radical democracy.

Unlike the Heideggerian understanding of *difference*, which posits prosthetic technologies as disembodied amputations and erasures of the body's capabilities, prosthesis, argued from a Derridian perspective of *différance*, constitutes an embodied supplement. Derrida's is a prosthetized word, *différance*, in which a meaning that differs is grafted onto a meaning that is deferred, thus rendering language and understanding undecidable, indeterminate, and mutable (in Ulmer 1985, 46–47). A graft, according to Derrida, is a linguistic structure that contains two distinct concepts situated side-by-side, yet separated by parenthetic, apostrophic, or hyphenated punctuation marks, ( ), /, [ ], { }, " ", and —, which he describes as "passing a knife between two texts" (Wills 1995, 295; Derrida 1986, 64). Similarly, Wills argues, the "recontextualization that defines citationality through the use of punctuation marks in text bodies . . . allows for the operations of excision and insertion, removal and replacement . . . [constitutes] prosthesis" (Wills 1995, 296). Excised yet sutured together, disparate texts and in the case of art, images are prosthetically co-dependent. While their separate meanings expose and critique their differences, their co-dependence exposes and defers metaphysical closures. Thus, the paradoxical logic of *différance* constitutes not merely a "playing with words . . . [but a] betting with words, employing them strategically with an eye on larger stakes," argues critical theorist Jonathan Culler (1982, 146).

Within the body of art education, Derrida's prosthetic grafting of *différance* is evident in the art-based research, writings, and theories of art education scholars Rita Irwin and Alex de Cosson, and Graeme Sullivan. By adjoining the first letter in each word, *a*rt, *r*esearch, and *t*eaching, then "passing" the "knife" of a slash between them, Irwin and de Cosson prosthetize these cultural practices into the neologism *a/r/tography* to suggest their linguistic and epistemological differences and correspondences. Indeed, the word *métis* (for an indigenous Canadian of mixed race), its appropriation from the French *métissage*, and Irwin and de Cosson's re-contextualization within a/r/tography consists of a dis-membering and re-membering process based in the epistemology of prosthesis. These scholars characterize métissage as "an act of interdisciplinarity. It hyphenates, bridges, slashes, and creates [interstitial spaces that enable] exploration, translation, and understanding in deeper and more enhanced ways of meaning making" (Irwin and de Cosson 2004, 30–31). Educators Cynthia Chambers, Dwayne Donald, and Erika Hasebe-Ludt further define métissage as

> [a] site for writing and surviving in the interval between different cultures and languages; a way of merging and blurring genres, texts and identities; an active literary stance, political strategy and pedagogical praxis. As Métis has been appropriated from its original and negative meaning "half-breed," . . . métissage [is appropriated] from its original meaning "mixed-blood" to become

> a creative strategy for the braiding of gender, race, language and place into autobiographical texts. (Chambers, Donald, and Hasebe-Ludt 2002, online)

In her installation *The Body Knowing*, 2004 (Figure 2.3)[13] a/r/tographer Stephanie Springgay assembles several small oil paintings, rose petal panels, and a dress to collage an autobiographical narrative that "alludes metaphorically and metonymically to gender, sexuality, and desire, and to issues pertaining to the shifting identity of woman, artist, and scholar in the academy" (Springgay 2004, 62). In doing so, the collage fragments in Springgay's installation constitute an "archive of body memories" that are braided together and stand in, prosthetically, for the body's identity, knowledge, and understanding (62–63).

Irwin's and de Cosson's conceptualization of a/r/tography as métissage parallels Derrida's grafting of *différance* and the fourfold epistemology of thesis/antithesis/synthesis/prosthesis discussed previously in this chapter. By dis-membering and re-membering *a*rt, *r*esearch, and *t*eaching, they argue for their interconnectivity, interchangeability, and interdependency.

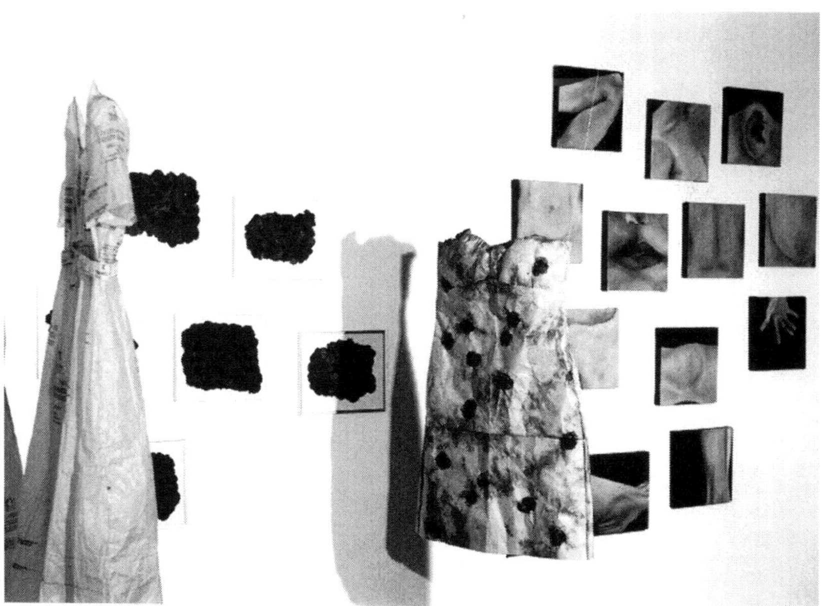

Figure 2.3. Stephanie Springgay, *The Body Knowing*, 2004 (Courtesy the artist).

> In these [three] interlingual acts, there is at once an acceptance of playing with particular categories and a refusal to be aligned with any one category. Where two would be inclined to dialogic opposition [thesis/antithesis] a third space offers a point of convergence [synthesis]—yet respect for divergence [prosthesis]—where differences and similarities are woven [sutured] together. (Irwin and de Cosson 2004, 28–29)

Hence, with the adverbial phrase, "yet respect for divergence," Irwin and de Cosson prosthetize dialogical convergence and, in doing so, they advocate its extension and interconnection with a diversity of interpretations and understandings, and again, and again . . .

Like Irwin and de Cosson, Sullivan's conceptualizations of art research are also based on prosthetic *différance*. His "artist-theorist," for example, metaphorically juxtaposes the "artist" with the "theorist" to reveal their differences, while suggesting their metonymic contiguity, which is coterminous, interconnected. Sullivan's prosthetizing of art and theory is further made evident through his detailed illustrations of frameworks, or mappings of diverse research trajectories and intersections that art making enables. Each framework represents for Sullivan strands of inquiry that when flexibly folded upon, around, and under one another prosthetically, create complex yet complementary "dimensions of theory" and "domains of inquiry" (Sullivan 2005, 98–99). He argues, "[A]lthough [the] conceptual barriers [of these strands] help to define areas of interest, they are *permeable barriers that allow ideas to flow back and forth*" (94; italics added). Sullivan writes about this permeability and flow in his characterization of installation artist Jayne Dyer's[14] art research:

> Dyer's art suggests that where and how we locate ourselves requires an acceptance that our relationship with place is neither stable nor able to be coded. Rather, it constantly shifts [allowing ideas to flow back and forth] in the space between the tangible and the transient. (Sullivan 2005, 134)

For Sullivan, such flexible folding constitutes a "braiding" process in which the differentiated strands of art research function as separate and distinct, yet intertwined lines of inquiry, thus prosthetizing a robust network of perspectives and understandings to occur (105).

What Irwin and de Cosson's a/r/tography and Sullivan's artist-theorist have in common is art research that extends and augments academic, institutional, and corporate understandings through performances of subjectivity, community, and the embodied knowing of critical prosthesis. These scholars' notions of "permeable barriers," "flexible folding," "braiding," "merging and blurring" of cultural boundaries enable the interconnections and interdependencies of prosthetic criticality where slippages of knowledge and understanding resist reified and rarified assumptions, representations, and enable creative and political agency.

Unlike quantitative researches in the sciences and social sciences, the prosthesis of art research "again and again," as Gray, Figueroa-Sarriera, and Mentor (1995) suggest, extends beyond the dualism of thesis/antithesis, and the absolute closure of synthesis, as personal memory supplements public memory (Lury, 1998; Landsberg, 2004). And again, such *prosthetic memory* is interconnected with *linguistic prosthesis* as metaphor and metonymy mutably amputate, graft, and augment visual and verbal language to create and re-create new meanings and representations. And again, the prosthetics of memory and linguistics are interconnected with *perceptual prosthesis* as the vision and visuality of art research challenges oppressive regimes of looking, seeing and understanding. And again, the prosthetics of memory, linguistics, and perception are interconnected with *cognitive prostheses* as the rhizomatic thought processes of art research challenge and augment the limitations of dualistic and dialectical thinking. And again, the prostheses of memory, linguistics, perception, and cognition are interconnected with *epistemological prostheses*, which challenge through art research oppressive, socially and historically, constructed assumptions and representations and enable new images and ideas to occur. And again, the prostheses of memory, linguistics, perception, cognition, and epistemology are interconnected with *ontological prostheses* as the body and identity are reclaimed from the objectifying regimes of academic, institutional, and corporate systems and re-presented through its own creative and political subjectivity. And again, the prostheses of memory, linguistics, perception, cognition, epistemology, and ontology are interconnected with the *phenomenological prosthesis* of the body, its breaking out of the frame of its materiality, its skin to extend and interconnect with the material world. And again, the prostheses of memory, linguistics, perception, cognition, epistemology, ontology, and phenomenology of the body are interconnected with *technological prostheses*, which augment and supplement the materiality of the body with tools that enable its facilitation of the world. Supported by the imperatives of vulnerability, recognition, and deliberate becoming, as Butler (2004) suggests, these prosthetic eccentricities of the body resist synthetic closure and enable open and mutable positions of subjectivity with the other. Doing so raises the hope that the brutality and devastations of war, and the gaze of normality, discussed earlier can be averted.

And again, and again . . .

While in this ending I have differentiated the prosthetic eccentricities of the body, it is their correspondences and interconnections, and with those of other bodies, those of community, and of the body politic that oppressive socially and historically constructed assumptions and representations of social injustice and violence are exposed, examined, and the creative and political agency of the body is continually enabled.

And again . . .

THREE

THE PROSTHETIC PEDAGOGY OF THE IGNORANT SCHOOLMASTER

Whoever teaches without emancipating stultifies.

—Jacques Rancière, "The Emancipated Spectator"

Handful of nails, pounding hammer (Figure 3.1), *th-h-hu-ud, th-h-hu-ud, th-h-hu-ud,* another nail, again, a hammer pounding, *th-h-hu-ud,* and again, another nail, poundings of a hammer, *th-h-hu-ud, th-h-hu-ud,* and again and again. . . . Because of his very young age I would not allow him up in the tree with me, to build the tree house that I was building for him with proper building tools, tools and materials, tools, materials, and procedures, milled lumber, exact measurements, plumbed verticals, level horizontal planes, tightly fitted joints, sturdy foundation, and a buttressed roof. . . . Having lost hope of climbing up into the tree with me, he left, then soon returned, dragging disparate geometric and biomorphic shaped pieces of wood from the refuse heap on the other side of the yard to where I was working up in the tree. . . . There, below me, he erected his tree-house-on-the-ground, its craggy edifice, a hodgepodge leaning against the backyard fence and rising up roughly four feet in the opposite direction toward where I was balancing myself ten feet off the ground in-between two large branches. . . . While I constructed a presumptuous, unassailable *place* for him to play in the tree, his was a modest, contingent, de Certeauian *space* open to all sorts of possibilities. . . . His earlier, childhood architectural achievements consisted of tent shelters that he would improvise with all that was present at hand, stretching his blankets and bed sheets over one piece of furniture to the next in the living room, from the upright piano near the front window to the floor lamp on the opposite corner of the room, fastening them with clothespins. . . . Unlike the modernism of Walter Gropius, Le Corbusier,

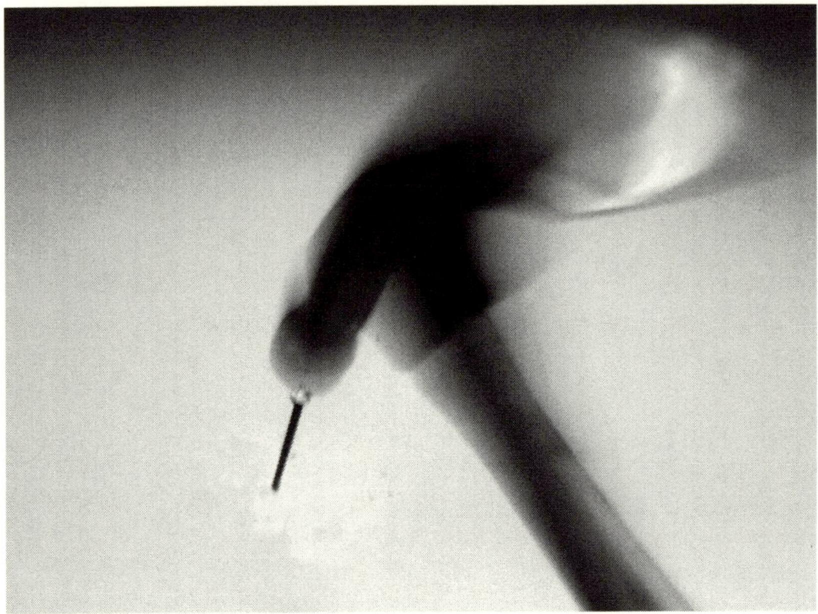

Figure 3.1. Hammer and nail, 2011 (Courtesy Charles Garoian).

Mies van der Rohe, Philip Johnson, and I. M. Pei, his was a schizophrenic, nomadic construction that Deleuze and Guattari would have admired, complex and contradictory, and ready at an instant to disassemble, transport, and then reassemble, feeling at home on the move through an eccentric blueprinting of architectural play. . . . His was not a structure that reinforced and protected existing theories of architecture. . . . Board-by-board, he hauled those dismembered pieces of lumber, the ruins of memory, across the yard. . . . Board-by-board, he dropped them helter-skelter, scattered amputations next to the backyard fence. . . . Board-by-board, he lifted, then gently propped them against each other defying gravity. . . . Board-by-board, nail-by-nail, he erected a bricoleur's shanty, a re-membered, precarious house of cards on the verge of collapse. . . . Nail-by-nail, he leaned the jumbled, baroque mass against the wooden fence to ensure stability. . . . Nail-by-nail, he declared his assemblage a "house," a "tree-house," a "tree-house-on-the-ground-against-the-backyard-fence". . . . Nail-by-nail, like the teetering accomplishments of his labor, this naming, a "tree-house-on-the-ground-against-the-backyard-fence," s-t-a-mmered, s-t-a-mmered, s-t-a-mm-ered, s-t-a-mmer-ed, hence stumping my academic architectural understandings, then reconstructing them anew. . . . What could he know at age nine? How did he come to know it? What had he experienced? His bedroom, our house, his classrooms at school, Prince's doghouse, the domestic spaces of his friends, neighbors, his grandparents, aunts, and uncles, where else would he have learned about built environments? His architectural history also consisted of a toy workbench and tool set, the wooden building blocks, that he played with dedication in his early years. . . . His youthful, playful memory yielded a post and lintel structure, however, disjointed, gone awry, with gaping holes in-between the oddly shaped assembled pieces of weathered wood unbefitting a shelter, yet able to hold the weight of a roof overhead, for his body to feel a sense of security inside, a prosthetic skin protecting him from the outside, for him to move to and fro, to play in and out and around it with his friends, a "tree-house-on-the-ground-against-the-backyard-fence". . . . His was a fearless labor, the result of emancipated obsession, one that his father, me, could only inhibit, stultify with my socially and historically constructed assumptions, unless, unless, unless, of course, I maintained an ignorance of what I thought he should know, ignorance of what I thought he had already experienced, ignorance of what I thought he already understood, ignorance of what I thought he was already capable, ignorance of what I thought he should do, ignorance constituted by a willful unknowing and a curiosity open to elements of surprise that hold presumption and prescription at bay. . . . He on the ground, me in the tree, building adjacent to one another, the space between us liminal, contingent and dialectically charged, working toward the same goal yet from different frames of mind, his risk-taking efforts, mine safe, our separate projects standing in opposition yet prosthetically contiguous, his "tree-house-on-the-ground-against-the-backyard-fence," and the one I built for him in the tree that he inhabited only from the vantage point of an emancipated spectator. . . .

The narrative that you have just read is about a remarkable experience that I had with my son Jason when he was nine years of age. It consists of re-membered fragments of my memory—disparate images in my mind's eye—of that event in 1979, and their re-construction in the form of a collage narrative whose disjunctive associations correspond with the precarious architecture of Jason's "tree-house-on-the-ground-against-the-backyard-fence." His building ingenuity and facility fascinated me. As he worked on the ground, I watched attentively from above as I worked on my own project where I was perched in the tree. I remained a silent observer. His disjunctive construction, a mimetic architectural response to my building a stable treehouse for him has, in turn, inspired my response in the mimetic narrative construction of this chapter.

In what follows, I will conceptualize the performance of subjectivity and construction of identity as artifice, an architectural metaphor based on the re-memberings and re-presentations of fragments from private memory and cultural history in order to challenge those socially and historically constructed public assumptions that are inscribed on the body. As an artist and teacher, I advocate in art classrooms the creation of de Certeau's (1988) notion of liminal and contingent *spaces*[1] where children are presented with opportunities to expose, examine, and critique the rarified academic, logical, rational, bureaucratized, institutionalized, and commodified *places* [2] of schooling through their art making activities and, in doing so, to attain creative and political agency as critical citizens in contemporary culture.

To initiate and encourage such critical interventions in the schools, the responsibility of art teachers is to foster children's play, their improvisations, explorations, and expressions through art, which can imbue their academic understandings in school with the ambiguity and incompleteness that is necessary for their creative and intellectual development. Accordingly, how can teachers maintain such radical openness considering the conditions of overly determined curricula in schools? What are the relational characteristics between teacher and student, between the discipline of art and the larger context of schooling within which it is situated? What role do these relationships play in enabling children's creative and political agency? What role does private memory and cultural history play in the attainment of such agency? What do I mean by my son Jason's mimesis inspiring my mimesis? What constitutes an ignorant schoolmaster and emancipated spectator, and how do they impact each other educationally? In what follows, I will address these questions and construct an argument for a critical art pedagogy that opens rather than closes possibilities for democratic discourse.

At the risk of being provocative, I am against romanticizing children's artistic development. When doing so, we art educators tend to venerate, essentialize, and protect children's innocence and their creative impulses from the world in which they are growing up; the one that continually manufactures their desires and inscribes their bodies and constructs their identities. Such cultural isolation and protectionism leads to children's emotional and intellectual desolation as it delimits their ability to respond critically and creatively to the cultural circumstances of their lives.

In his characterization of the ignorant schoolmaster, philosopher Jacques Rancière writes about the extraordinary pedagogical adventure of Joseph Jacotot, a nineteenth-century lecturer in French literature at the University of Louvain who when faced with a group of eager students found that they did not speak French just as he did not speak Flemish. The pedagogical conundrum that ensued from that encounter did not deter Jacotot or his Flemish students from creating ways of overcoming their cultural isolation and differences from each other.

> [Jacotot] had given no explanation to his "students" on the first elements of language. He had not explained spelling or conjugations to them. They had looked for the French words that corresponded to words they knew and the reasons for their grammatical endings by themselves. They learned to put them together to make, in turn, French sentences by themselves: sentences whose spelling and grammar became more and more exact as they progressed through the book [that he had assigned]. (Rancière 1991, 3–4)

What Jacotot found in the students' resourcefulness to learn was that they did not abide by the pedagogical myth of inequality that bifurcates "inferior intelligence" from "superior intelligence."

> [Inferior intelligence] registers perceptions by chance, retains them, interprets and repeats them empirically, within the closed circle of habit and need. This is the intelligence of the young child and the common man. The superior intelligence knows things by reason, proceeds by method, from the simple to the complex, from the part to the whole. It is this intelligence that allows the master to transmit his [*sic*] knowledge by adapting it to the intellectual capacities of the student and allows him [*sic*] to verify that the student has satisfactorily understood what he learned [Jacotot refers to this explicative pedagogy as *enforced stultification*]. (Rancière 1991, 7)

According to Rancière, Jacotot's unwitting ignorance as schoolmaster left his enthusiastic Flemish students to fend for themselves, to explore and discover the chance associations between the Flemish and French languages, and to construct their own understandings empirically. Such emancipation from explicative pedagogies blurs class boundaries, which divide the privileged that are in the know from those who are not. Based on Jacotot's revelations, Rancière writes: "one can teach what one doesn't know" (101), which suggests that teachers consciously position themselves in the classroom as ignorant schoolmasters not to abdicate their pedagogical responsibilities, but to postpone their predetermined, academic teachings and allow for their students' playful observations, explorations, and improvisations. Insofar as students' learning processes are enabled in this way, the positioning of ignorance constitutes a pedagogical strategy whereby both teacher and students are emancipated to learn from and about each other. Under these circumstances, Rancière claims that the ignorant, whether schoolmaster or student, "need not be ignorant."

> He [*sic*] need only dissociate his knowledge from his mastery. He does not teach his knowledge to the students. He commands them [as emancipated spectators] to venture forth in the forest, to report what they see, what they think of what they have seen, to verify it, and so on. What he ignores is the gap between two intelligences. It is the [prosthetic] linkage between the knowledge of the knowledgeable and the ignorance of the ignorant. Any distance is a matter of happenstance. Each intellectual act weaves a casual thread between a form of ignorance and a form of knowledge. No kind of social hierarchy can be predicated on this sense of distance. (Rancière 2007, 275)

Hence, for Rancière, the example of the ignorant schoolmaster represents the possibility that the knowledge and understandings that students and teachers bring to the classroom are not in a hierarchical relationship, but are interdependent and necessary for their mutual creative and intellectual development.

Rancière's notion of the emancipated spectator corresponds with the experiential learning concepts of philosopher John Dewey, who writes: "Since freedom resides in the operations of intelligent observation and judgment by which a purpose is developed, guidance given by the teacher to the exercise of the pupils' intelligence is an aid to freedom, not a restriction upon it" (Dewey 1938, 71). Such freedom experienced by children through the empirical research and making of art constitutes what Dewey refers to as "learning by doing" (Dewey 1944, 184), which supports his concept of a spiraling curriculum where the teacher attends equally to two things:

> First, that the problem grows out of the conditions of [is contingent upon] the experience being had in the present, and that it is within the range of the capacity of the students; and secondly, that it is such that it arouses in the learner an active quest for information and for production of new ideas. The new facts and new ideas thus obtained become the ground for further experiences in which new problems are presented. The process is a continuous spiral. The inescapable linkage of the present with the past is a principle whose application is not restricted to a study of history. (Dewey 1938, 79)

Rancière's concept of "linkage" and Dewey's "linkage of the present with the past" suggests that children's' memories and cultural histories, the knowledge and understandings that they bring to school from their respective families, neighborhoods, and communities, augments their academic learning.

Landsberg refers to such augmentations as "prosthetic memory," which "emerges at the interface between a person and a historical narrative about the past, at an experiential site such as a movie theater or museum. In this moment of contact, an experience occurs through which the person sutures himself or herself into a larger [memory and] history" (Landsberg 2004, 2). Landsberg differentiates between the "prosthetic" characteristics of larger public forms of memory and those "authentic" memories that we acquire from our immediate, private lives. Her reasoning for the use of the "prosthesis" trope for memory is as follows:

> [prosthetic memories] are not natural, not the product of lived experience . . . but are derived from engagement with a mediated representation (see a film, visiting a museum, watching a television miniseries).
>
> These [prosthetic] memories, like an artificial limb, are actually worn on the body; these are sensuous memories produced by an *experience* of mass-mediated representations.
>
> Calling them "prosthetic" signals their interchangeability and exchangeability and underscores their commodified form.
>
> [Landsberg] call[s] these memories prosthetic to underscore their usefulness. Because they feel real, they help condition how a person thinks about the world and might be instrumental in articulating an ethical relation to the other. (Landsberg 2004, 20–21)

And I would add a fifth rationale for conceptualizing memory as prosthesis, namely, that any linkage of children's private memories with public ones, while "worn on the body" as Landsberg claims, are prone to prosthetic slippage and as such they resist the concrescence of cultural absolutes and enable children's heterogeneous understandings and representations. In doing so, the slippage of their cultural discontinuities and dislocations evokes excess knowledge that exceeds Hegelian dialectical understandings where the conceptual tension between thesis and antithesis is resolved in synthetic closure. Hence, thesis, antithesis, and synthesis are supplemented and extended by the heterogeneity of prosthesis, and again, again, again. . . . (Gray, Figueroa-Sarriera, and Mentor 1995, 13).

Related to Dewey's spiraling curriculum, Landsberg's theory of prosthetic memory suggests linkages even beyond the four examples that she has delineated, that is, what children learn through empirical processes making art has the potential for multiple sutures: their private memories and cultural histories; with those of their classmates; with the public memory of schooling, museums, films, and other cultural representations; and the public memory of the mass media and the Internet. Landsberg's prosthetic trope is provocative, as it suggests metonymic contiguity, in other words, the interdependence of private, public, and differing forms of memory whose interconnections are prone to slippage, hence resisting formations of rarified assumptions and oppressive stereotypes, and allowing for ambiguity and incompleteness to exist as important outcomes of creative inquiry and critical citizenship.

Literary theorist Homi Bhabha refers to the ambiguity and incompleteness of prosthetic slippage as "metonymic interruption," which exposes an agonistic "third space of enunciation" (Bhabha 1994, 37) where a "supplement" of discourses and cultural identities are insinuated, in-the-place-of [3] in-between pedagogical (Rancière's "explicative") and performative modes of address. Like a pun or double entendre, the supplement carries the double meaning of both the pedagogical and performative, hence maintaining an undecideable position. Bhabha writes: "The supplementary strategy suggests that adding 'to' need not 'add up' but may disturb the calculation [between the pedagogical and performative]" (155). Hence, like Landsberg's prosthetic memory and Rancière's ignorant schoolmaster, the metonymic slippage, or interruption of the supplement's double meaning occurs in-between the socially and historically constructed assumptions of pedagogical explicatives and the performative subjectivities of students' private lives and, in doing so, it enables prosthetic discourses and understandings through which cultural identities can emerge (Bhabha 1994, 154).

Analogous to Rancière's "weaving of ignorance and knowledge," and Bhabha's doubling of the supplement, Landsberg's prosthetic memory constitutes a suturing of what children already know from the context of their memories and cultural histories with what they do not yet know from the historical and cultural context of the other. Landsberg's concept of prosthetic memory, Bhabha's supplement, and Rancière's weaving of two intelligences parallel psychologist Lev Vygotsky's "zone of proximal development" (Vygotsky 1978, 85–90), which exists between what the child has learned independently as an emancipated spectator and the aid of a more knowledgeable other. Vygotsky writes: "[The zone of proximal development] is the distance between the actual development level [of the child] as determined by independent problem solving and the level of potential development as determined through problem solving under adult guidance or in collaboration with more capable peers" (86).

This "scaffolding" process (Wood, Bruner, and Ross 1976; Berk and Winsler 1995), a prosthetic pedagogy, enables children to learn what they do not yet know through the guidance of teachers by building on what they already know from their personal memories and cultural histories. Hence, Vygotsky's zone of proximal development constitutes a critical pedagogical space where children's "retrospective" and "prospective" knowledge are brought together in a dialogical relationship (Vygotsky 1978, 86–87). Apropos prosthetic pedagogy, educator Beth Kemp Benson suggests, "if scaffolding is properly administered, it will act as an enabler, not a disabler" (Benson 1997, 126).

Both the zone of proximal development and scaffolding have commonality with radical educator Peter McLaren's concept of the "teacher-as-liminal-servant," an intellectual provocateur who, like Rancière's ignorant schoolmaster, holds academic mastery in abeyance to encourage students' performances of subjectivity in the classroom as vital content in their becoming critical citizens and participating in a cultural democracy. According to McLaren,

> The liminal servant understands teaching to be essentially an improvised drama. To fully understand the subtext of the student, the liminal servant must "become" the student as part of the dramatic encounter. While in the thrall of such a drama, the liminal servant knows that the results will often be unpredictable; that understanding, like play, has a spirit of its own. (McLaren 1993, 117)

Similar to the contingent pedagogy of McLaren's teacher-as-liminal-servant, art educators Brent Wilson and Marjorie Wilson (1982, 64) have long challenged the romanticization of children's art by arguing that children's expressions do not occur in a cultural vacuum, but are in response to the knowledge and understandings that they receive through various cultural experiences such as family, schooling, and visual and popular culture. Contrary to the neo-Rousseauianism of Progressive educators early in the twentieth century who argued that adults teaching children art would stifle their innate creativity, Brent Wilson situates children's art education in three distinct pedagogical sites: First, like Rancière's emancipated spectator, the child engages in art making through exploratory and experimental play based on their personal memories, desires, and motivations; second, like Landsberg's prosthetic memory, children link their private memories with learning from public institutions such as schools and museums; and, Wilson's third pedagogical site is comparable to Bhabha's third space where McLaren's teacher-as-liminal-servant assumes a position of ignorance to create a zone of proximal development, and where they and their students can learn from one another as emancipated spectators. In characterizing his third pedagogical site Wilson writes:

> Teachers and students make connections between formal schooling and kids' self-initiated arts activities. In other words, the third site links individuals' interests [prosthetically] with institutional prerogatives. It's in this third site where webs of adult-motivated school-world and art-world related interests, values, and content have the possibility of being [prosthetically] connected to kid-motivated visual cultural interests, values, and content. [What Wilson is] pointing to

> [are] pedagogical transactions, which usually begin after a teacher has noticed and encouraged kids to expand upon and continue to create visual culture—on their own time and in their own spaces. (Wilson 2007, 920)

What Wilson is proposing by "pedagogical transactions" is a process of radical imitation, or *prosthetic mimesis*, whereby children and teachers learn and build upon each other's knowledge and understandings through emulation and invention. Unlike the Platonic objection [4] that posits mimesis as alienating children from reality by relying solely on imitation, Aristotelian thought characterizes the acquisition of knowledge as fundamentally mimetic.

In Wilson's third pedagogical site the teacher and learner interact dialogically, one learning from the other, and in doing so both are engaged in eccentric learning, to-and-fro between ignorant schoolmaster and emancipated spectator. In his reevaluation of imitation (mimesis) in learning, Vygotsky de-romanticizes children's innate learning and argues imitative activity as an important factor in their mental development. In debunking the myth of imitation as "purely mechanical processes," he writes: "children can imitate a variety of actions that go well beyond the limits of their own capabilities" (Vygotsky 1978, 87–88).

In her book about cultural theorist Walter Benjamin's *Arcades Project*, social theorist Susan Buck-Morss characterizes his defense of children's mimetic practices as a significant form of cultural practice: "[C]hildren instinctively mimic objects as a means of mastering their experiential world" (Buck-Morss 1989, 268). According to Buck-Morss, mimesis represented for Benjamin a "defense against the trauma of industrialization" and a "counterforce" that could reconstruct what had been shattered by it (268).

For Benjamin, Charlie Chaplin's mechanical gestures in *Modern Times* (1936) [5] represented a form of countermimicry where, as Buck-Morss claims, the actor "rescued the capacity for experience by mimicking the fragmentation that threatened it . . . [suggesting that] to recreate the new reality of technology mimetically (—to bring to human speech its expressive potential—) is not to submit to its given forms, but to anticipate the human reappropriation of its power" (Buck-Morss 1989, 270). What Benjamin and Buck-Morss are differentiating between is *mimetic contemplation* that "submits to given forms," and *mimetic action*, which opens spaces where children's creative and political agency are possible.[6]

Art educators Laura Trafí and Montse Rifà's (2007) research at the Universitat Autónoma de Barcelona on children's production of visual narratives provides an example of the power of mimetic action. In an inner city primary school with a classroom of fourth and sixth grade children 98 percent of whom were from differing immigrant backgrounds (i.e., Pakistan,

Bangladesh, China, Morocco, Rumania, Dominican Republic, Colombia, Ecuador, and Brazil), Trafí and Rifà witnessed children overcoming linguistic and cultural barriers as they responded to an exhibition of Robert Frank's photographic essays at the Museu d'art contemporani de Barcelona (MACBA) (Figure 3.2).

A peripatetic storyteller, the narratives in Frank's photographic essays are told from the perspective of his personal memory and cultural history as a world traveler in search of freedom from secure, familiar places. Considering the parallels between Frank's and the children's journeyed experiences, the museum visit was centered on "reconstructing [their] identities through the production of visual narratives based on [their] emotions and migrations" (Trafí and Rifà 2007). From their observations, conversations, and interpretations of Frank's autobiographical narratives, the children created stories based on their own immigrant experiences.

In one part of their museum visit, the children were invited to consider the objects in Frank's *My Father's Coat* (2001),[7] a three-part autobiographical essay of digital prints made from Polaroid photographs. In the background of

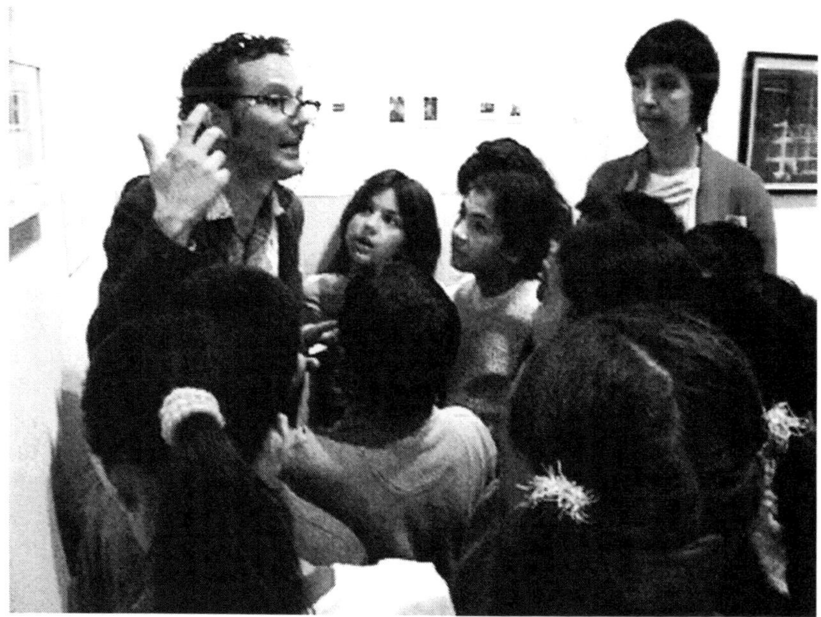

Figure 3.2. Xavier Giménez discussing Robert Frank with children at MACBA, 2004–07 (Courtesy Montse Rifà, Laura Trafí, & Xavier Giménez).

the first print, Frank's father's overcoat hangs against a wall beside a bright sunlit window and, in the foreground, a potted Aloe Vera plant sits on a table; the second print is a close-up of the plant's fleshy leaves in the foreground overlapping the overcoat in the background; and, the third print in the series is of a close-up of a star medallion pinned on the overcoat's lapel. Below each of the three digital prints, Frank has handwritten "my fathers [*sic*] coat." Like a collage of photographs in a family album, "*My Father's Coat* shows [disjunctive] objects which are linked in the artist's mind: [He writes:] 'I hung up the coat in a small room in our house—with all my film cans on the window sill and an Aloe plant (needs a little water). . . . The writing under the photograph is like sending a postcard—the medal on the coat an imaginary past; the plant is alive and waiting and growing . . . and I am getting old'" (Tate Modern online). Hence, Frank's use of tropes such as "sending a postcard," "an imaginary past," "alive," "waiting," "growing," "getting old," suggest the space/time representations of migratory existence.

What Trafí and Rifà found was that the students saw things in *My Father's Coat* that evoked their own cultural perspectives and immigrant memories rather than the conventional, academic understandings that their teacher expected of them. The children were able to narrate their immigrant memories through Robert Frank's photographs and the objects that were represented in them.

In a post-museum experience, the children emulated Frank's three-part autobiographical essay by constructing "their own [Polaroid narratives and] scenarios, using objects, pictures, songs and backgrounds that they . . . brought from their homes (Figure 3.3). In some cases, their parents helped them to remember a situation or a story. Mostly, they revisited their own family pictures by using the lenses of Robert Frank's family and memory pictures" (Trafí and Rifà 2007).

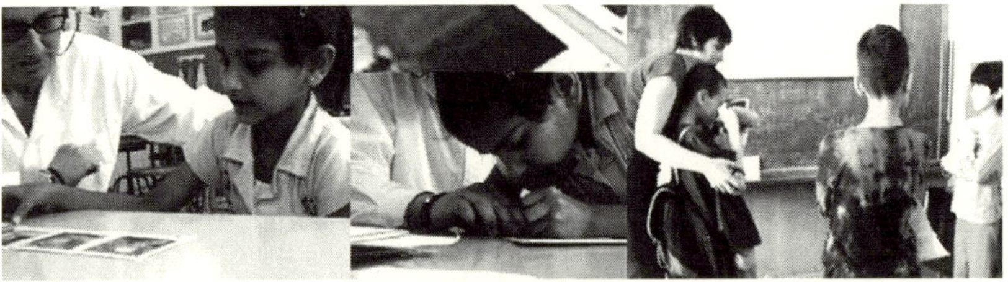

Figure 3.3. Narratives de la infància. Biografies, llocs (comunitats), visualitats, Escola Collaso i Gil, Barcelona, 2004–07 (Courtesy Montse Rifà, Laura Trafí, and Xavier Giménez).

Art historian Jennifer A. González refers to the evocation of memory through the use of material culture, such as *My Father's Coat*, the Polaroids of the children, and the objects represented in them, as *autotopographies* (Figure 3.4), a form of self-expression whereby "the material world is called upon [mnemonically] to present a physical map of memory, history, and belief" (González 1995, 134). Given their ability to evoke memory and signify identity, González argues that autotopographies function as "prosthetic device[s]: an addition, a trace, and a replacement for the intangible aspects of desire, identification, and social relations" (134). Compared with historical representations that reify and codify the past, memories that are aided by autotopographic prostheses

> undermine history's seamless narratives by providing the material traces of a shifting symbolic and sacred relationship to things. More important, memory implies, as against history, that there are multiple stories to be told in an overlapping layering of signification that does not take place in a linear, linguistic, or necessarily coherent manner. (González 1995, 139)

Similarly, by way of their discussions and Polaroid interpretations of *My Father's Coat* the children's autotopographies (Figure 3.5) positioned and linked their immigrant memories in a metonymic, contiguous relationship with Robert Frank's memories and with each other's. As prosthetic mimesis, their contiguous linkages enabled them to emulate, not replicate, Frank's

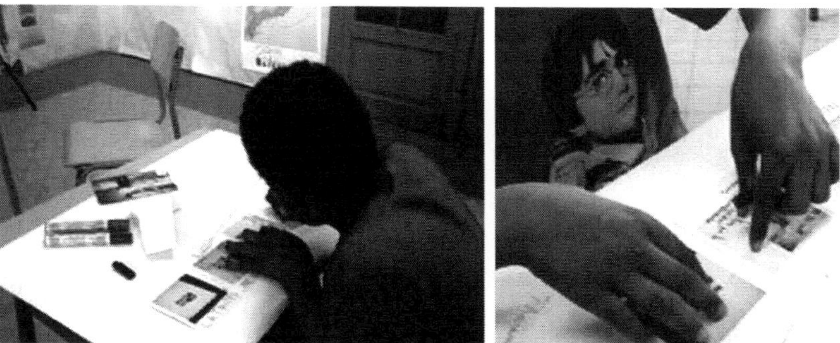

Figure 3.4. Narratives de la infància. Biografies, llocs (comunitats), visualitats, Escola Collaso i Gil, Barcelona, 2004–07 (Courtesy Montse Rifà, Laura Trafí, and Xavier Giménez).

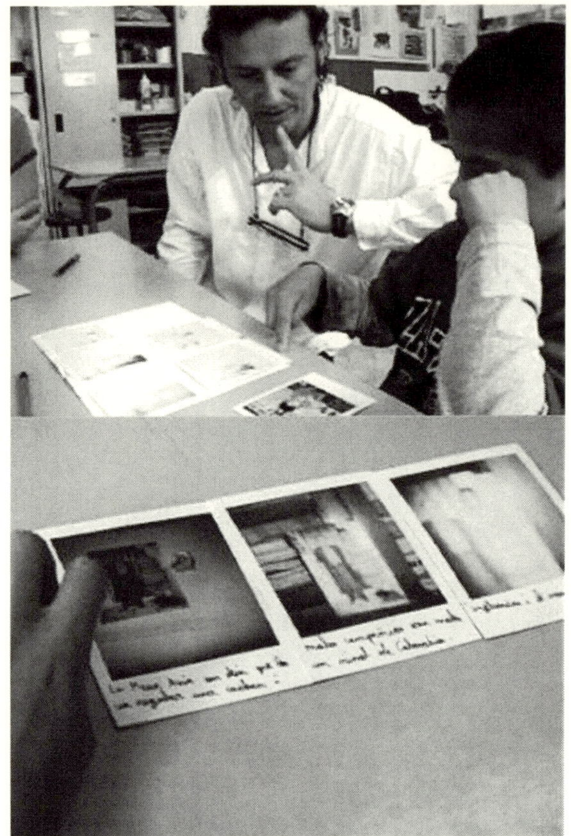

Figure 3.5. Narratives de la infància. Biografies, llocs (comunitats), visualitats, Escola Collaso i Gil, Barcelona, 2004–07 (Courtesy Montse Rifà, Laura Trafí, and Xavier Giménez).

and each others' storytelling. In performing subjectivity in this way, they materialized their own stories, from personal memory and cultural history.

In mimicking my son Jason's rickety tree-house-on-the-ground-against-the-backyard-fence, in this chapter I have juxtaposed Jacques Rancière's ignorant schoolmaster, with John Dewey's spiraling curriculum, with Alison Landsberg's prosthetic memory, with Homi Bhabha's third space, with Peter McLaren's teacher-as-liminal-servant, with Walter Benjamin's countermimicry, with Brent Wilson's third pedagogical site, with Robert Frank's peripatetic narrative, and with Jennifer A. González's autotopographies. In doing so, I have constructed a contiguous and precarious architecture with my writing to expose and examine their prosthetic linkages with those of children's heterogeneous memories and cultural histories, and with those of the academic pedagogies of schooling.

Like the geometric proportioning of the body and its associations with the natural world in Leonardo's *Vitruvian Man*,[8] Wigley argues that the body and the knowledge and understandings that constitute its identity represent prosthetic constructions. He writes: "In a strange way, the body depends upon the foreign elements that transform it. It is reconstituted and propped up on the 'supporting limbs' that extend it. Indeed, it becomes a side effect of its extensions. The prosthesis reconstructs the body, transforming its limits, at once extending and convoluting its borders. The body itself becomes artifice" (Wigley 1991, 8–9). Like Jason's construction of his tree-house-on-the-ground-against-the-backyard-fence, and the fourth and fifth graders' Polaroid responses to Robert Frank's photographic narratives in Trafí and Rifà's study, the critical pedagogical architecture of prosthetic mimesis enables children to build dialogical linkages between their academic learning in schools and the knowledge that they acquire through their independent, playful observations, explorations, and experimentations. Their performances of subjectivity in the art classroom provide students with the necessary creative and political agency to construct a heterogeneous body politic, and to challenge, extend, and convolute the academic, institutional, and corporate understandings that constitute the homogeneity of globalization.

FOUR

PRECARIOUS LEANINGS

The Prosthetic Research of Play in Art

Play is the supreme *bricoleur* of frail transient constructions.

—Victor Turner, "Body, Brain, and Culture"

The tool kit of any culture can be described as a set of prosthetic devices by which human beings can exceed or even redefine the "natural limits" of human functioning.

—Jerome Bruner, *Acts of Meaning*

A PLAYING

. . . disasters, *Disasters of War,* war paintings, the poster read outside the gallery door, the open door through which I walked in, into the gallery where, except for the several large-scale paintings exhibited on the walls, no one else was in sight, no other bodies in the gallery, I walked in, a place unlike I'd ever been before, now, all by myself, never seen such dark, imposing, difficult compositions, never such abstraction, dark nonobjective abstractions, images composed of raw, forceful brushstrokes, raw, jagged shapes, jagged, gritty, protruding textures, somber tones of color . . . the push and pull of their profound, compelling forms . . . on the one hand, prostheses appearing to jut from the canvas, leaning toward me, while, on the other hand, their gravitational fields, black holes engulfing and pulling my anxious body into their vortices . . . these paintings' raw images, their dismembered, amputated imagery playing with disaster . . . something, something about them seemed familiar, something, even though I'd never experienced abstract art, art that was unrecognizable as art, art that was not concrete and realistic, art that didn't do all that I expected it to do, all that I knew and already understood . . . daring misunderstanding their unfamiliarity complicated perception yet drew me closer . . . these strange paintings' forceful brushstrokes, their precarious provocations intimidating yet liberating, evoking a compulsion in me to run, to escape from their forceful abstractions . . . maintaining composure, I observed, explored, and wondered about their significance . . . avoiding hasty interpretations, imprudent judgments, I found delight in the strange familiarity of my experience . . . I had crossed a threshold into a zone, an interstitial zone, a liminal in-between space, not the gallery per se, but not-not a gallery, between knowing and not knowing and not-not knowing, where seeing and not seeing and not-not seeing were playing simultaneously . . . my hyper-mediated, hyper-academic, hyper-rational cultural history, my personal understandings about disasters of war, the horrors of forgotten genocide, the familiar "i-a-n" in the artist's Armenian surname being played by ludic disruptions and dislocations, a play among the ruins of memory and the disasters of these paintings' raw fragmentations . . . how unusual such uncertainties representing such gruesome realities, suggesting such dismembered bodies, amputated limbs, pictorial abstractions, being played back-and-forth, to-and-fro, between what is comfortable and risky, chance worth taking, leaping into Kristeva's (1982) horrific realm of the abject, where crisis of knowledge enables the power to create and augment new understandings as the ambiguity and incompleteness of these gritty paintings intersect with memories of historical pain and suffering, sensing a necessity for survival, with nothing to lose, the freedom *of play*, the freedom *to play*, to move on, with nothing to lose and everything to gain, projecting myself into these abstractions empathically, to expose and experience complexities and contradictions in my own life, the prosthetic play, slippage between my memories and those of these images, being played by them as Gadamer (2006) would have it, constituting a reflexive, ontological investigation, seeing and understanding one's self through the sensibilities of the Other as in the permeable economy of Lyotard's (2004) *libidinal body* and Merleau-Ponty's (1968) *chiasm*, corporeal materiality interconnecting the body's interior architecture with the materiality of the external world, technology with the body, machine and meat, how, how else the unusual connections in how the crises of these paintings' abstractions played my passions, a playing that years later I was re-minded, re-played by Arnheim's[1] playful telling of Rubinstein's piano virtuosity, the excess of his improvisational transgressions, his e-lusive *playing with the notes*, compared with the banal precision of technical musicianship dispassionately *playing the notes*, the latter seeking synthetic closure, fearful intimacy with the indeterminacy of play and being played . . . undecidable characters at play, ideas, images, words, these words like those paintings' images befuddling yet compelling participation, knowing nothing more than what they inform me . . . the freedom of Huizinga's (1955) play, an emancipation that disrupts, transgresses, transforms understandings by way of a pre-rational playing along with play in order to be played by play wherein the undecidable, in-between to-and-fro ontology of play plays the body . . . the prosthesis of play corresponds with the play of prosthesis . . . the ontology of play constitutes the body's prosthetic augmentation, it is both *not* the body and not-not the body . . . as of this writing, I'm not-not in the gallery, yet I may always be . . .

INTRODUCTION: THE PLAY OF PROSTHESIS

In the previous narrative, the one that you the reader just read, the one that precedes this sentence, in this paragraph, the one that you are now reading, there is a playing with words, images, and ideas that I constructed from the fragments of memory about an incident, prior to my becoming an art student many years ago, where I found myself awestricken by a stunning exhibition of pictorial abstractions representing disasters, disasters of war, during my first visit to an art gallery in my youth. I recall that the only thing that I had in common with those paintings was that the artist who painted them, Varaz Samuelian, was Armenian, like me, and that we shared a tragic cultural history. As the first-born son of emigrants, refugees who had survived the Armenian Genocide, I identified with the artist's ethnicity and with the horrific theme of the exhibition. Those two links, the "prosthetic devices of my cultural toolkit,"[2] compelled me to remain, to take a stand in the gallery. As the intersections of ethnicity, Genocide, disaster, and the abstract paintings played me, I felt a compulsion to risk everything, to go beyond what I already understood about art and my life. It was the difficulty of those images, the crisis of knowledge invoked by their visual and conceptual abstractions that compelled me to challenge myself, my ignorance and to lean on them in order to research, to learn more about them, learn through them, about myself, who I was, where I had come from, and where I was going in my life. In actuality, the ontological play of those paintings aroused my raison d'être, which is why I'm not-not in the gallery, and I may always be . . .

What is play? What is prosthesis? What do they have in common and how do they represent art research? What are the performative correspondences between play and art, play and prosthesis, prosthesis and art? How are creative research and the practice of art making constituted by the ontology of play? What does the play of art have in common with the play of prosthesis? How does the indeterminacy of these processes affect subjectivity, and creative and political agency? How is critical pedagogy in art education constituted by prosthetic epistemology? In addressing these and other questions throughout this chapter, I will invoke the play theories of Hans-Georg Gadamer (2006), Victor Turner (1990), Richard Schechner (1985), Brian Sutton-Smith (1997), Jerome Bruner (1986; 1990); the prosthetic theories of David Wills (1995), Gray, Figueroa-Sarriera, and Mentor (1995), Celia Lury (1998); and the conceptual play in the research and creative work of artists Marcel Duchamp, René Magritte, Nico Muhly, and Francis Alÿs.

Considering my ongoing fascination with being *played by art*, I began this chapter with a narrative entitled "A Playing" to take into account my personal memory and cultural history, and to affirm such performances of subjectivity as significant content for research in art education, which I will elaborate on later. In the next section of the chapter, entitled "Theorizing Prosthesis as Research Metaphor," I will use the *prosthesis* trope to conceptualize the play of art, its slippage and indeterminacy, as prosthetic cognition and prosthetic epistemology, emergent research processes that resist intellectual closure to supplement and interconnect the interiority of the body with the exteriority of cultural knowledge that is other than its own.[3] I will further argue that the creative and intellectual supplementations and interconnections enabled through the prosthesis of play represent a critical pedagogy of possibility in art education.

In the section entitled "The Prosthetic Play of *Exquisite Corpse*," I will again *disrupt* the flow of my text like I did after my personal narrative at the beginning of the chapter, and *interject* a curricular approach that introduces and enables graduate students in art education to play in-between personal memory and cultural history, art, theory, and pedagogy in conceptualizing research metaphors based on the 1920s Surrealists' parlor game, *Exquisite Corpse* (Cadavre Exquis). The visual and conceptual disjunctions and conjunctions that constitute the *Exquisite Corpse* process, like the play of prosthesis, open gaps, spaces of liminality where a multitude, an excess of meanings and understandings can be speculated and extended. Finally, by disrupting my text yet again and interjecting the third section of this chapter, "Researching Pedagogy Through Art and Theory," I will provide examples of how the separate yet permeable boundaries in-between personal memory and cultural history, art, theory, and pedagogy enable a playing and intersecting of ideas and images in constituting art-based research. Hence, the four contiguous parts of the chapter are composed in a metonymic relationship similar to *Exquisite Corpse* with overlapping concepts while maintaining their separate characteristics. The purpose in doing so is to show correspondences between the *Exquisite Corpse* research processes that I have conceptualized in section three and how I have constructed this chapter as a whole.

THEORIZING PROSTHESIS AS RESEARCH METAPHOR

Philosopher Hans-Georg Gadamer suggests prosthetic slippage in his conceptualization of play as the ontology of art: "When we speak of play in reference to the experience of art, this means neither the orientation nor even the state of mind of the creator or of those enjoying the work of art, nor the freedom of subjectivity engaged in play, but the mode of being of the work of art" (Gadamer 2006, 102). Given that the ontology of art is paradoxically determined by the indeterminacy of play, independent of the subjectivity of the artist, suggests art as prosthesis and the play of art as prosthetic slippage. In arguing the independent subjectivity of art play, Gadamer writes:

> The work of art is not an object that stands over against a subject for itself. Instead the work of art has its true being in the fact that it becomes an experience that changes the person who experiences it. The "subject" of the experience of art, that which remains and endures, is not the subjectivity of the person who experiences it but the work itself . . . play [like art] has its own essence, independent of the consciousness of those who play. (103)

While conventional wisdom assumes that the play of art is constituted by the artist's subjectivity, namely, that the play of art is performed by the artist, in actuality the assumptions that encompass the artist's subjectivity hinder the contingency and indeterminacy of play by affecting or predetermining its outcome. Gadamer claims that "play is not to be understood as something a person does" (104); it is the subjectivity of the work of art that plays and "changes the person who experiences it."

The surrealist-biologist Roger Caillois's theory of play corresponds with and confirms Gadamer's ontological characterization of play and art. Caillois writes: "In strongly opposing the world of play to that of reality, and in stressing that play is essentially a side activity, the inference is drawn that any contamination by ordinary life runs the risk of corrupting and destroying its very nature" (Caillois 2001, 43). What Caillois is suggesting about the contamination of play by ordinary life is consistent with the artist's subjectivity, her/his cultural history, impeding the indeterminate, undecidable being of play. Play theorist Brian Sutton-Smith agrees with Gadamer and Caillois regarding subjectivity. He writes that the pleasure of playing resides in the fact that it frees the player from her/his subjectivity to be played by the subjectivity of play; "It frees you from one self by binding you [prosthetically] to another . . . [the] 'being' of play . . . is outside oneself rather than inside oneself" (Sutton-Smith 1997, 183). Hence, by being played by the ontology of play in art the interiority and exteriority of the body, the body and other, coexist and are coextensive.

Moreover, the indeterminacy of art is constituted by play through a precarious "to-and-fro movement that is not tied to any goal that would bring it to an end . . . rather, it renews itself in constant repetition" (Gadamer 2006, 105). This emergent, repetitive renewal of the to-and-fro movement of play corresponds with the slippages and indeterminate research logic of prosthesis, which I am here arguing as the propositional adjunction of the Hegelian dialectic (thesis and antithesis), the outcome of which is synthetic closure. In other words, the to-and-fro movement of play, in delaying concrescence and resisting closure, challenges binary logic by creating openings, imaginary in-between spaces[4] where multiple speculations, and understandings, can emerge and extend prosthetically beyond synthesis (Figure 4.1), again and again (Gray, Figueroa-Sarriera, and Mentor 1995; Lury 1998).

In challenging the intellectual closure of interpretation, for example, Sontag wrote: "By reducing the work of art to its content and then interpreting that, one tames the work of art. Interpretation makes art manage-

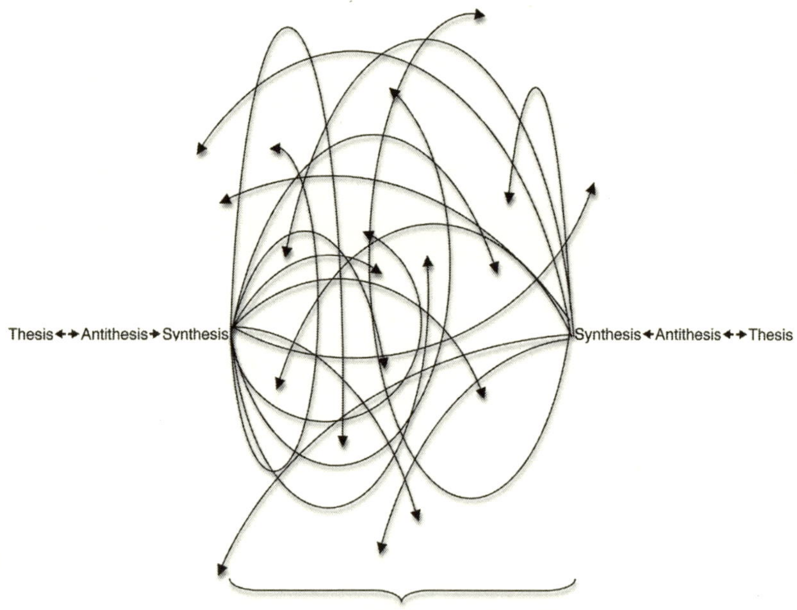

Figure 4.1. Lines of flight #1, 2011 (Courtesy Charles Garoian).

able, comformable [*sic*] (Sontag 1966, 8). Similarly, the dialectical closure of thesis and antithesis in synthesis is resisted through the slippages and unlimited possibilities for deferral in prosthesis. Consequently, the to-and-fro prosthetic play of art is consistent with *research* considering that in addition to its primary definition "to study or investigate closely," research is also defined: "to search again or repeatedly" (*OED*, online). This repeated play of research in art resists the synthetic reduction of art through interpretation, according to Sontag: "To avoid interpretation, art may become parody. Or it may become abstract. Or it may become ('merely') decorative. Or it may become non-art" (Sontag 1966, 10).

The parodic play of art research, the prosthetic slippage of its visual forms, ideas, and images, which are independent of the artist's subjectivity, is readily evident in the readymades of Marcel Duchamp.[5] While all visual works of art are constituted by the ontology of play, it was Duchamp who exposed the conceptual workings of that ontology. With his legendary readymade, *Fountain*, which he exhibited at the Society of Independent Artists in 1917, Duchamp purposefully circumvented what he referred to as the "retinal" preoccupation of visual art in order to focus on how art provokes and plays the "gray matter" or cognition (Krauss 1993, 108). In other words, what he challenged was the privileging of the eye, of art that was preoccupied with visual representation. In response to his problematizing of visual representation, Meyer writes, "All art (after Duchamp) is conceptual (in nature) because art only exists conceptually" (Meyer 1972, 162). Likewise, in pointing out the differences between the significant contributions of Pablo Picasso and Duchamp to twentieth-century art, poet Octavio Paz points to Picasso "by what he affirms, by his discoveries [of visual form] . . . [and Duchamp] by what he negates, by his [conceptual] explorations" (Paz 1978, 3). *Fountain*, an ordinary porcelain urinal that the artist purchased from a plumbing supply shop, was met with public consternation when it was exhibited. Duchamp's provocative gesture challenged social and historical assumptions of art, artist, and art making as it raised questions about functionality, namely the relationship of art with that of the gallery, with art history, questions about what constitutes art making, and the labor of the artist in society. Indeed, happenings, conceptual art, performance art, body art, and installation art that followed were profoundly influenced by the readymades; hence, they were rooted in the Duchampian social aesthetic, which exposed the limits and possibilities of artistic labor and productive labor (Roberts 2007, 25).

Author and cultural critic Arthur Koestler's characterization of bisociative thinking corresponds with Duchamp's conceptual play in particular,[6] and the prosthetic bipolarities of art play in general. According to Koestler, "bisociation," like dream cognition, occurs when two or more concepts *coexist* within the same space of the mind. Contrary to the synthetic closure of dialectical thinking and the binary logic of dualistic thought, the coexistence of "habitually incompatible matrices [in bisociation] results in an abrupt transfer of train of thought from one associative context to another . . . [as such, the] bisociative act [of the artist] is a *juxtaposition* of these planes or aspects of experience, not their *fusion* in an intellectual synthesis—to which, by their very nature, they do not lend themselves" (Koestler 1975, 59, 352). Koestler further describes the incompatible matrices of bisociation and its resistance to fusion in the following ways:

> the *pun*: two strings of thought tied together by a purely acoustic knot;
>
> the *optical pun*: one visual form bisociated with two functional contexts;
>
> the phenomenon of *displacement* or shift of attention to a previously unnoticed feature;
>
> the *concretization* of abstract and general ideas in a particular image; and vice versa, the use of concrete images as *symbols* for nascent, unverbalized concepts;
>
> the *condensation* in the same link-idea of several associative contexts;
>
> the unearthing of *hidden analogies*;
>
> *impersonation* and double identity—being oneself and something else at the same time . . . (179)

In each of these thought patterns, which Koestler refers to as "underground games," ideas and images interplay, their logic playfully reversing and transferring from one context to another, and resisting "fusion," thus corresponding with the prosthetic slippage of play in art research and practice.[7] The "purely acoustic knot" to which Koestler refers in characterizing the cognition of punning, for example, is analogous to the tenuous yet resonant interconnectivity and interdependence of prosthesis.

THE PROSTHETIC PLAY OF *EXQUISITE CORPSE*

The Surrealists' parlor game, *Exquisite Corpse* (Cadavre Exquis), corresponds with the prosthetic interplay of Koestler's underground games. A sheet of blank paper is folded three times, or as many times as there are players (Figure 4.2). Beginning with the first in the sequence of folds in the paper, a player renders a composition and extends it slightly into the next fold. The first player then folds the completed composition over and out of view of the second player who then contributes a second composition continuing from where the first player's ended. The third player, having been presented with the end of the second person's hidden contribution, then adds a third composition. After all the folds of the paper have been rendered it is then unfolded to reveal a composite three-part figure that resists fusion as its disjunctions and conjunctions play against each other.[8] This to-and-fro prosthetic play of *Exquisite Corpse* serves as a compelling metaphor for teaching graduate research in art education where students' create live performances in which they radically juxtapose their personal memories and cultural histories, with other artworks, with critical theories, with significant pedagogies; to bring them into question with each other, and to facilitate openings, in-between spaces where multiple researches can occur. The disjunctive, performative structure and sequence in the following fourfold (Figure 4.3)[9] approach to teaching art-based research is modeled after the prosthetic play of the *Exquisite Corpse*.

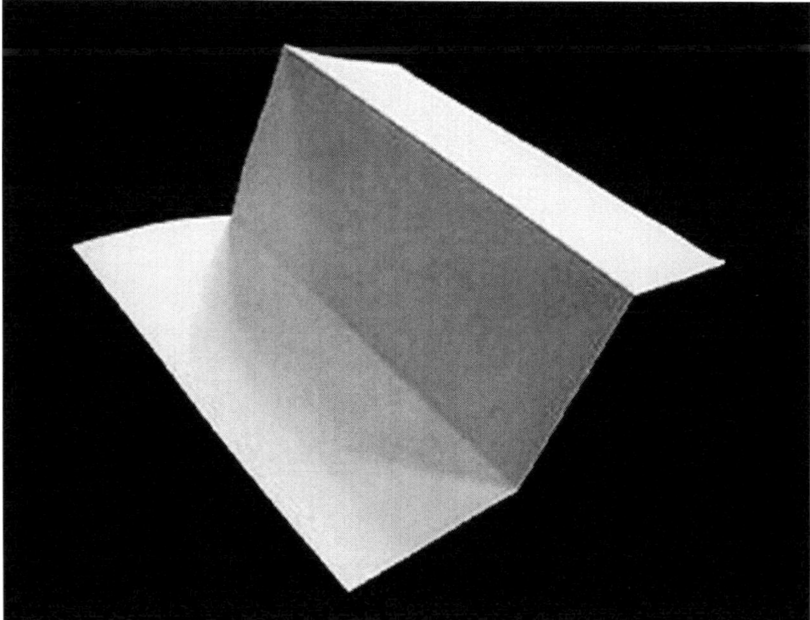

Figure 4.2. Folding/unfolding paper, 2011 (Courtesy Charles Garoian).

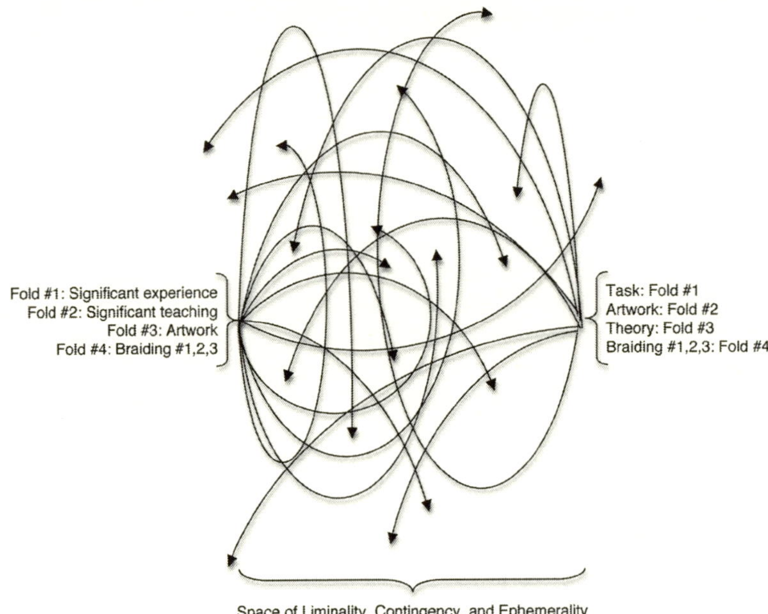

Figure 4.3. Lines of flight #2, 2011 (Courtesy Charles Garoian).

Fold #1: Performing the Embodied Research of Subjectivity

In the first part of this performance exercise, students write a two- to three-page detailed autobiographical narrative that tells about the most significant, memorable experience in their lives. This personal narrative affirms and brings into play students' memories and cultural histories as relevant content for theorizing art research, practice, and pedagogy. The purpose for writing the narrative is threefold: so that students are provided an opportunity to recall, reflect upon, and compose the salient details of their significant experience; to initiate and adapt to a practice of writing, which will serve their future research projects; and, to experience how performances of personal memory and cultural history challenge and augment public forms of memory (Lury 1998).

For the second part of the performance, students identify a task, any physical undertaking at which they have achieved some degree of proficiency with their bodies. Tasks may range from ordinary, everyday activities to those that students have attained virtuosity, from chopping carrots or hammering nails to playing a musical instrument or performing a dance. Like the significant experience part of the exercise, the students decide what task to perform and in doing so introduce yet another aspect of their personal memories and cultural histories. To achieve disjunctions and conjunctions similar to *Exquisite Corpse*, an important condition of this exercise is that the students' tasks must not relate to or illustrate any part of their narratives. After having decided on their tasks, students are then asked to bring all materials, tools, and equipment that are necessary to perform them in class.

The third part of the exercise consists of students' live performances of subjectivity. Each student is given a three- to five-minute timeframe within which to perform their individual narratives and tasks *simultaneously*; that is, they tell of their most significant experience extemporaneously while performing their task in front of their classmates. While students are performing, the disjunctions and conjunctions in-between their narratives and tasks become apparent thus opening a contingent and liminal space for exploratory, experimental, and improvisational research where multiple associations and understandings are possible.[10]

In addition to valuing students' performances of subjectivity, their memories and cultural histories, also important in this exercise is the research that takes place as they explore, examine, and critique the various signifiers that are revealed in-between the disjunctive associations of each other's performances. Science philosopher Robert Crease conceptualizes the creative and intellectual play that occurs in-between incompatible images, ideas, and actions as "argumentative analogies." Lyotard refers to such disjunctions in art research and practice as "incompossibilities," in other words, *impossible* associations occurring in the same time and space that make *possible*, paradoxically, manifold readings, interpretations, and understandings.

This first research performance enables students to foreground how art and cultural experiences are embodied, and to begin exploring, experimenting, and improvising metaphorical connections and associations between and among disparate images, ideas, and actions in their lives; a bisociative process of research similar to *Exquisite Corpse* that can later enable their conceptualizations of art and pedagogical theory. Performing research in this way begins with students' personal narratives and tasks, and sets the stage for creating theoretical associations between art making and art teaching, and how one informs the other.

Fold #2: Performing Art Research as Curricular Metaphor

In this second exercise students begin by writing a three- to four-page narrative that describes in detail their most significant experience teaching art.[11] If graduate students from other disciplines are enrolled in the course, they are encouraged to consider a teaching experience related to their respective fields of study. What were the interactions like between you and your students? What was the art lesson that you assigned to your students? What did your students create in response? What was said during the critique session? What happened? What do you remember most about the experience? These and other such questions constitute possible ways of eliciting students' significant teaching experiences for this exercise.

Separate and unrelated to the first part of this exercise, students identify a historical or contemporary work of art, in any genre, and write in detail the various ways that its form and content signify. Again, similar to *Exquisite Corpse*, an important condition of this exercise is for students to delay making associations between their significant teaching experience and their selected artworks. To assist in researching and excavating thick, abundant content from their selected artworks, students can be introduced to "Thirteen Ways of Looking at a Blackbird," art critic Thomas McEvilley's list of content attributes in works of art:

> Content that arises from the aspect of the artwork that is understood as representational.
> Content arising from verbal supplements supplied by the artist.
> Content arising from the genre or medium of the artwork.
> Content arising from the material of which the artwork is made.
> Content arising from the scale of the artwork.
> Content arising from the temporal duration of the artwork.
> Content arising from the context of the work.
> Content arising from the work's relationship with art history.
> Content that accrues to the work of art as it progressively reveals its destiny through persisting in time.
> Content arising from participation in a specific iconographic tradition.
> Content arising directly from the formal properties of the work.
> Content arising from attitudinal gestures (wit, irony, parody, and so on) that may appear as qualifiers of any of the categories already mentioned.
> Content rooted in biological or physiological responses, or cognitive awareness of them. (McEvilley 1991, 70)

With these content attributes, McEvilley provides multiple sources for research that students can explore to conceptualize how the works of art, which they have selected for this part of the exercise, signify.

When writing about their teaching experiences and their selected artworks, students are encouraged to take note of anthropologist Clifford

Geertz's ethnographic imperative "thick description." Conceptualizing art and teaching in this way exposes and foregrounds the complexities and contradictions of those experiences. According to Geertz, when writing with thick description the ethnographer does so with "a multiplicity of complex conceptual structures, many of them superimposed upon or knotted into one another, which are at once strange, irregular, and inexplicit, and which he [*sic*] must contrive somehow first to grasp and then to render" (Geertz 1973, 10). Hence, a thick description of art or teaching would not limit those experiences merely to passive recognition of their elements based on predetermined cultural assumptions. Doing so would arrest the complexities of perception "before it has a chance to develop freely," claims Dewey (1934, p. 52). Instead, thick description provides students with narrative form and content similar to the impossible performance in Fold #1 where disjunctions and conjunctions, in to-and-fro movement, yield in-between spaces where manifold interrogations and interpretations can extend prosthetically.

Once students have completed the thick descriptions of their significant teaching experience and their selected work of art, they perform this research before their classmates in the form of a public reading. In choosing the order of their reading, they may decide on their significant teaching experience first, in which case the image of their selected artwork is projected on a large screen so that their classmates can begin taking note of and creating associations in-between what they hear in the reading and their observations on the screen. The second reading provides classmates with thick, additional knowledge about the selected artwork with which to construct theoretical correspondences and understandings between its content attributes and those of the significant teaching experience. Should students decide to begin their performance with a reading of their selected artwork, the image of the art is again projected as a backdrop followed by the reading of their significant teaching experience. In either case, classmates would experience their attention shifting through a rhythm of continuity and discontinuity, to-and-fro from one context to the other similar to the playful, disjunctive narrative of *Exquisite Corpse*.

Fold #3: Performing Art Research as Theoretical Metaphor

For the next exercise in the sequence, students build on their research findings, the thick descriptions of their selected artworks from the previous exercise. Here they conduct further study of their artwork, to continue writing about them using McEvilley's thirteen areas of content. After attaining a thick, complex understanding of the artwork, they then identify and select a theoretical construct from the arts, humanities, or education that piques their curiosity. After researching their selected theory, students write a five-page essay articulating its most significant characteristics. Now, with thick descriptions and characterizations of their selected artwork and theory in hand, students begin creating metaphorical associations and a compelling reciprocity of ideas and images in-between their selected artwork and theory. In doing so, artwork and theory are intertwined and in dialectical tension. As one is seen and understood through the other manifold new theoretical associations are made possible. Similar to the previous exercise, the sequence of readings is left to the choice of the student. Regardless of whether or not the selected theoretical reading precedes the reading of the selected artwork, the image of the artwork is visibly present throughout the performance so that classmates can explore, experiment, and improvise associations between art and theory.

Fold #4: Performing Art Research at the Intersections of Subjectivity, Art, Teaching, and Theory

Like the play of disjunctive images unfolded in the *Exquisite Corpse*, this final research performance reveals playful associations in-between the previous three exercises and possible intersections of subjectivity, art, teaching, and theory (Figure 4.3). In a cumulative scholarly writing exercise, students braid these four areas of research together to comprise a comprehensive understanding about the prosthetic play of art-based research where discovery is immanent, and as art critic and philosopher Donald Kuspit (1983) claims, uncertainty is a method of creation (129).

RESEARCHING PEDAGOGY THROUGH ART AND THEORY

Similar to Koestler's bisociative thinking and Kuspit's method of creation, art theorist Suzi Gablik conceptualizes the object of visual and conceptual uncertainty in the paintings of René Magritte as the artist's means of deferring interpretation of his images to ensure that "painting was not an end in itself" (Gablik 1973, 124). Gablik describes the incongruent cognitive operations that are at play in Magritte's paintings in the following ways:

> Isolation. An object, once situated outside the field of its own power and removed to a paradoxically energetic field, will be freed of its expected role.
>
> Modification. Some aspect of the object is altered . . . or, conversely, a property normally associated with an object is withdrawn.
>
> Hybridization. Two familiar objects are combined to produce a third "bewildering" one.

> A change in scale, position or substance creates an incongruity.
> The provocation of accidental encounters.
> The double image as a form of visual pun.
> Paradox. The use of intellectual antitheses as in . . . delicately balanced contradictions.
> Conceptual bipolarity. The use of interpenetrating images where two situations . . . are observed from a single viewpoint, modifying spatio-temporal experience. (124–25)

Magritte's 1926 painting entitled *Ceci n'est pas une pipe* (This is not a pipe)[12] is an example of his playful conundrums. The painting, on canvas, contains a representation of a pipe with the text of what appears as its title inscribed below it in French. The operative word in the text is the use of the pronoun "this" raising an array of questions and improbabilities about which it is referring; whether the pronoun "this" is referring to the pipe, in which case it is only an image of a pipe; whether the pronoun is referring to itself ("this" is not a pipe); whether it is referring to the sentence in which it is situated ("this is not a pipe" is not a pipe); or, whether the pronoun "this" is referring to the canvas upon which it is inscribed (the canvas is not a pipe).

According to philosopher-historian Michel Foucault, Magritte's *Ceci n'est pas une pipe* moves to-and-fro as "similitude" and "resemblance" are dissociated and brought into play against each other. For Foucault, "resemblance serves representation, which rules over it; similitude serves repetition, which ranges across it" (Foucault 1982, 44). Like Magritte in *Ceci n'est pas une pipe*, Foucault is also arguing the arbitrariness of signs and a horizon of diverse associations that are possible in similitude.[13] If the image of a pipe resembles its referent, the actual pipe that is being represented, then the latter, the actual pipe, assumes dominance as the original, prescriptive model. In doing so, semiotic hierarchy is established where the signifier is subordinated by the signified. What Magritte has done, however, is to distract attention from and postpone reference from the actual pipe by means of similitude, which "circulates the simulacrum as an indefinite and reversible [to-and-fro] relation of the similar to the similar" (Foucault 1982, 44). This ranging repetition of similitude occurs as Magritte's image of the pipe, his text *Ceci n'est pas une pipe*, his use of the pronoun "this," and the canvas upon which they are painted, "multiplies different affirmations, which dance together, tilting and tumbling over one another" (46). Like Gadamer's to-and-fro movement of play, Foucault has described how Magritte's images play against each other and, in doing so, resist intellectual synthesis and remain undecidable.

Hence, the range of possible yet unstable interpretations that is constituted by similitude in *Ceci n'est pas une pipe* is "restored to itself—unfolding from itself and folding back upon itself. It is no longer the finger pointing out from the canvas in order to refer to something else. It inaugurates a play of transferences that run, proliferate, propagate, and correspond within the layout of the painting, affirming and representing nothing" (Foucault 1982, 49). This play of similitude to which Foucault is referring represents the contingent and liminal research of art making whereby a range of possible understandings exceeds the limiting assumptions of binary logic (52). In doing so, the play of art research constitutes an associative intelligence, which frees the artist from the limiting assumptions of linear thought, and opens thresholds to liminal spaces where a range of ideas and images, and their prosthetic associations are possible.[14]

The liminal, where prosthetic emergence and play in art occurs, constitutes a virtual, in-between space where knowledge and understanding is prone to slippage, ambiguity, and indeterminacy. For anthropologist Victor Turner, liminality is "in the subjunctive mood of culture."

> The mood of maybe, might-be, as-if, hypothesis, fantasy, conjecture, desire depending on which of the trinity of cognition, affect, and conation (thought, feeling, or intention) is situationally dominant. . . . Ordinary day-to-day life is in the indicative mood, where we expect the invariant operation of cause-and-effect, of rationality and commonsense. Liminality can perhaps be described as a fructile [*sic*] chaos, a fertile nothingness, a storehouse of possibilities, not by any means a random assemblage but a striving after new forms and structure, a gestation process, a fetation of modes appropriate to and anticipating postliminal existence. (Turner 1990, 11–12)

The "postliminal existence" to which Turner is referring is the creative and political agency, which is enabled through the subjunctivizing play and prosthesis of art. As I previously stated, as prosthesis resists and exceeds the limitations of synthetic closure through similitude, it enables a range of arbitrary visual and conceptual emergences and convergences in the subjunctive mood.

Prosthetic emergences and convergences are evident in the eccentric and eclectic research processes of contemporary American composer Nico Muhly (Figure 4.4). Author Rebecca Mead describes Muhly's process for composing musical scores: "The last thing he thinks about is the actual notes that musicians will play. He begins with books and documents, YouTube videos and illuminated manuscripts" (Mead 2008, 75). While Muhly himself claims inspiration "'by, like, Morse Code and the AIDS crisis,' [Mead goes on to characterize his] extra-musical interests and obsessions . . . [as] an associative intelligence that is [prosthetically] facilitated by Google and iTunes" (75–76). For Muhly, the eccentric play of these contiguous and

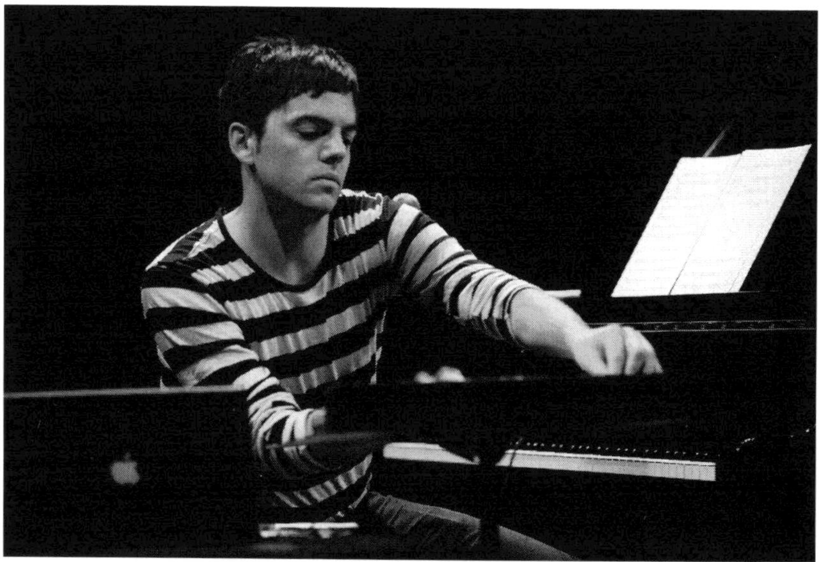

Figure 4.4. Nico Muhly Live at The Southern Theater, Minneapolis, MN, 2009 (Courtesy Nico Muhly and Eric Melzer, photographer).

coexisting eclectic cultural and historical contexts defers intellectual closure indefinitely and, in doing so, enables the diverse, extensive leanings and linkages of prosthesis.

According to cognitive psychologist Jerome Bruner, "To be in the subjunctive mode [like Muhly] is, then, to be trafficking in human possibilities rather than in settled certainties" (Bruner 1986, 26). By suspending the known, the certainties of musical notations at the beginning of his creative process, Muhly migrates toward and explores cultural resources that are unfamiliar; they are strange to the social and historical assumptions of music; his eclectic sources are *not* only *not*-notations, they are also *not-not*-notations.[15] Which is to say that his sources may not be notations, but how he uses them suggestively constitutes them as notations. Through this prosthetic double negativity, Muhly allows a host of possible resources to play him, and with which to play, in composing his scores that may or may not exclude historical forms of music. It is by way of his eclectic and eccentric outsourcing, and through his arbitrary, tenuous prosthetic associations that he creates new music. Thus, Muhly's imagined subjunctivity constitutes a renewed sense of resourcefulness that enables him to import and prosthetically suture his hypothetical consideration of eclectic materials, as "as-if" notations, to his life as composer and to historical and contemporary music (Hedtke and Winslade, online).

Performance theorist Richard Schechner (1985) writes about the profound research potential of double negativity, of *not-not*, in the workshop process of performance rehearsals. Indeed, for Schechner the exploratory, experimental, and improvisational character of workshop-rehearsals is as important, if not more important, than the final performance. Its antistructural process, corresponding with Turner's and Bruner's notions of subjunctive mood, is where hypothetical and prospective images, ideas, and actions, teeter and lean on each other, and whose similitude suggest multiple possibilities for play (Schechner 1988, 5, 11). So, for Schechner, the agonistic process of rehearsals builds until it is on the verge of collapse:

> The antistructure that is performance swells until it threatens to burst. The trick is to extend it to the bursting point but no further. It is the ambition of all performances to expand this field until it includes all beings, things, and relations. This can't happen. The field is precarious because it is subjunctive, liminal, transitional: *it rests* [prosthetically] *not on how things are but on how things are not*; its existence depends on agreements kept among all participants, including the audience. The field is the embodiment of the potential, of the virtual, the imaginative, the fictive, the negative, the not-not. (113; emphasis added)

Accordingly, and in reference to my previous examples of prosthetic slippage of play in art, Duchamp's *Fountain* is not an art object, but within the context of the art gallery, it is not-not an art object; an art object is not a urinal, but it is not-not a urinal; the gallery is not a men's restroom, but it is not-not a men's restroom; and, a men's restroom is not an art gallery, but it is not-not an art gallery. Similarly, Magritte's representation of a pipe is not a pipe, but it is not-not a pipe; his text *Ceci n'est pas une pipe,* is not a pipe, but it is not-not a pipe; the pronoun "this" in the text is not a pipe, but it is not-not a pipe; and the canvas upon which the representation of the pipe is painted and the text *Ceci n'est pas une pipe* is inscribed is not a pipe, but the canvas too is not-not a pipe. Finally, in the example of Muhly's eccentric use of eclectic cultural forms and objects, they are not musical notations, but they are *not* resources that can*not* constitute musical notations.

Schechner suggests that the to-and-fro characteristics of the double negative correspond with the exploratory, experimental, and improvisational processes of children's play as it "deconstructs actuality in a 'not me . . . not not me' way. The hierarchies that usually set off actuality as [resembling the] 'real' and fantasy as 'not real' are dissolved for the 'time being' [through a range of similitude]" (Schechner 1985, 110). The transformations that are made possible through the subjunctivity of Schechner's workshop-rehearsal process correspond with the contingent, hypothetical, and prospective narrative process of contemporary artist Francis Alÿs.

Alÿs is a peripatetic artist for whom *rehearsal* is the organizing premise and the consummation of his creative projects. He performs live, and also exhibits his research process by means of video, and scores of sketches, e-mails, faxes, books, notes, doodles, Post-its, clippings, and other bits and pieces of ephemera, which have been exhibited in archival installations on museum walls, floors, table tops, and vitrines throughout the world. In his 2008 exhibition entitled "Politics of Rehearsal" at the Hammer Museum in Los Angeles, Alÿs included documentation videos of *Rehearsal I (Ensayo I)* and *Rehearsal II (Ensayo II)*, the first two parts of a performance trilogy, in which subjunctivity and the prosthetic slippage of intellectual synthesis is evident.

In Alÿs's video *Rehearsal I*, 1999–2001 (Figures 4.5, 4.6, and 4.7), produced in Tijuana, Mexico, an old red Volkswagen Beetle attempts to drive up a steep hill on a narrow dirt road. As the VW climbs the hill, its movement is synchronized with the recording of a rowdy rock band whose members are rehearsing a song. As the band is playing, the car, driven by Alÿs, ascends gradually up the hill. Then, as it approaches the crest of the hill, it comes to a complete stop, then rolls back down in reverse when

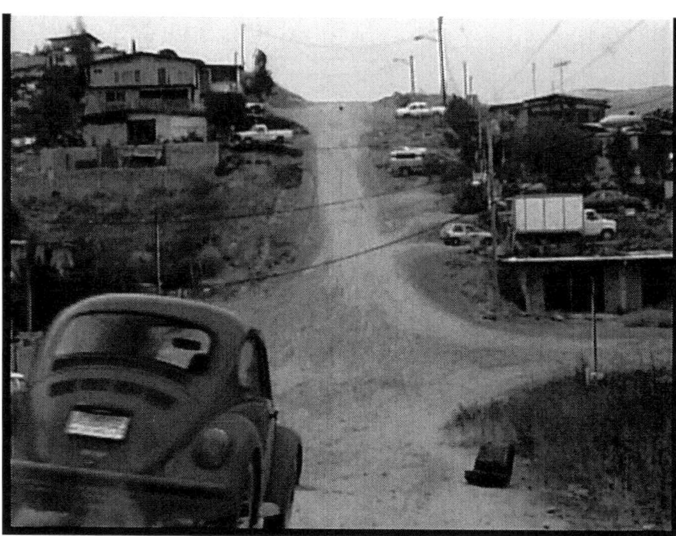

Figure 4.5. Francis Alÿs, *Rehearsal I (Ensayo), Tijuana*, 1999–2001 (Courtesy David Zwirner, New York).

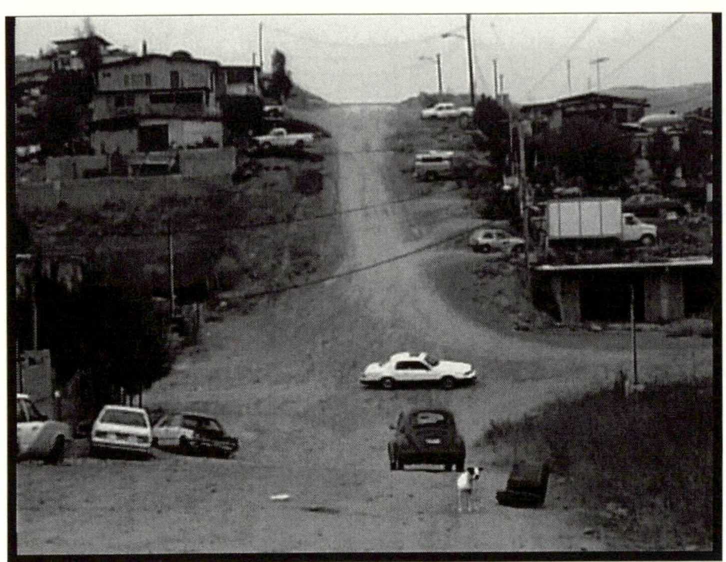

Figure 4.6. Francis Alÿs, *Rehearsal I (Ensayo), Tijuana*, 1999–2001 (Courtesy David Zwirner, New York).

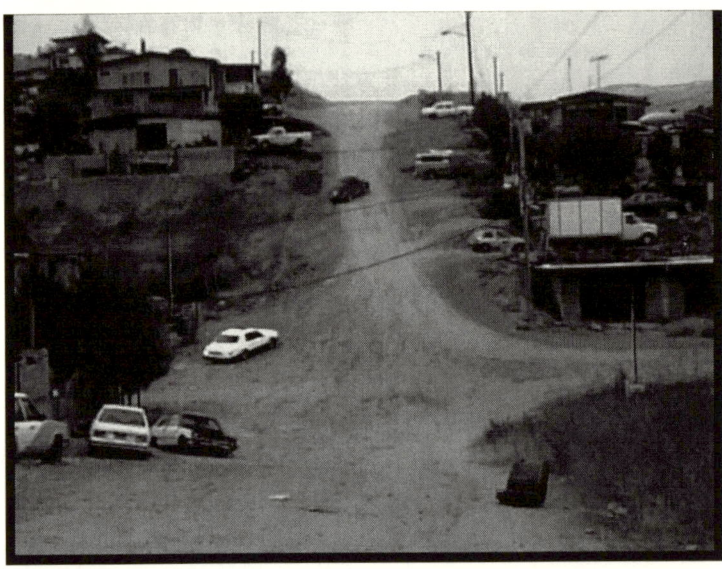

Figure 4.7. Francis Alÿs, *Rehearsal I (Ensayo), Tijuana*, 1999–2001 (Courtesy David Zwirner, New York).

the band stops playing to make rehearsal adjustments. In a series of missed attempts, or *mis-takes*, the VW mimics the coherence of the band's rehearsal by attempting to drive up the hill, then rolling back down the hill as the band's rehearsal breaks up . . . these mis-takes continue again and again, hence disappointing the viewer's expectation for concrescence. . . . Finally, after half an hour of trying Sisyphus-like, the VW is seen backing out of the frame of the video, yielding any further attempt at getting to the top of the hill (Kwon 2008, 280–82).

The mis-takes of a rehearsal process also appear in Alÿs's video *Rehearsal II*, 2001–06 (Figure 4.8), which corresponds sequel-like with those of the VW and the rock band in *Rehearsal I*. In *Rehearsal II*, again we find Alÿs dissociating and playing one action against the other, to-and-fro like Foucault's movement of similitude and resemblance mentioned previously. A striptease dancer undresses on a stage before a gaudy red curtain to the recording of a singer and piano accompanist rehearsing a melancholy song by composer Franz Schubert. Again and again, like the disruption of the VW's climb up the hill by the rock band recording, the starting and stopping of the singer and pianist's rehearsal disjoint the coherence of the stripper's performance. The stripper starts undressing, stops, starts dressing, stops, starts

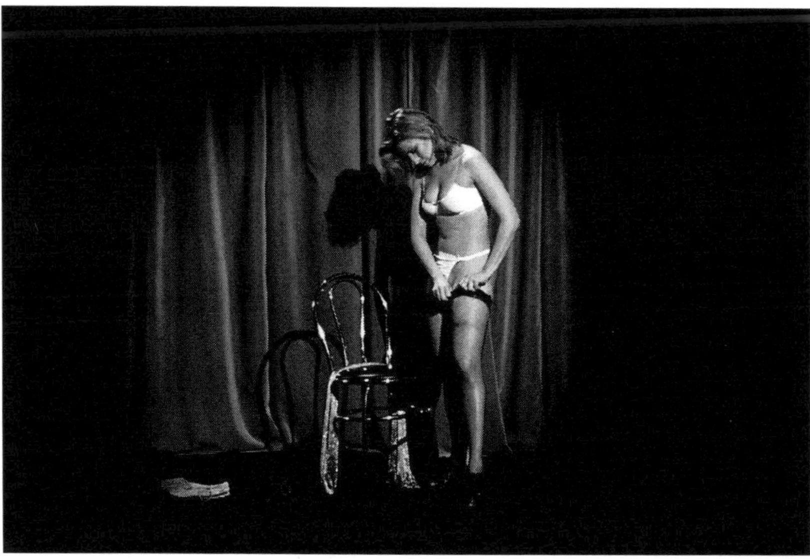

Figure 4.8. Francis Alÿs, *Rehearsal II, Mexico City and New York*, 2001–06 (Courtesy David Zwirner, New York).

undressing, stops, starts dressing, stops, starts undressing, and so on, which, according to art historian Miwon Kwon constitutes "a process involving multiple delays that frustrates the anticipated reward of beholding her fully naked body" (Kwon 2008, 280). In her conceptualization of Alÿs's body of work, Kwon writes:

> To propose a work of art, or even a museum exhibition, as a rehearsal, then, is not simply to refuse conclusions and completions in favor of impermanent forms or open-ended experimentation as an aesthetic preference. It also does more than challenge the conventional hierarchy of value that attends process (low) versus product (high). It questions the very nature of making a work, the struggle to accomplish something, anything. (282)

The refusal of conclusions, the incompleteness, and "the struggle to accomplish something, anything," that Kwon suggests about Alÿs's rehearsal projects, constitute the prosthetic slippages of subjunctivity in the play of art. The artist's use of quotidian objects, materials, and actions in his liminal, contingent, and ephemeral rehearsal projects shifts, defers, and plays with our assumptions, expectations, and understandings of socially and historically constructed culture through the conceptual bipolarities of his making the familiar strange.

The prosthetic slippages that occur in-between the familiar and strange contexts in Alÿs's work, such as *Rehearsal I* and *II*, correspond with Koestler's bisociation mentioned previously; Gilles Deleuze and Félix Guattari's (1987, 54–55) concept of deterritorialization and reterritorialization; and the hypothesizing process of art research theorized by critical theorist V. Shklovsky, "[which is] to impart the sensation of things as they are perceived and not as they are known. The technique of art is to make objects 'unfamiliar,' to make forms difficult, to increase difficulty and length of perception because *the process of perception is an aesthetic end in itself and must be prolonged*" (Shklovsky 1965, 12; emphasis added). I would argue that perception is prolonged, as Shklovsky suggestions, as we are played by and play with the questions that Alÿs raises with his "Politics of Rehearsal" exhibition about "the very nature of making a work, [and that] the struggle to accomplish something, anything," that Kwon describes, constitutes basic research that enables creative and political agency.

The "tilting and tumbling" of contexts "over one another" that Foucault describes about similitude, cited previously, is consistent with Alÿs's rehearsal process, and it evokes Bruner's theory of narrative construction and slippage in a liminal, subjunctive space where inconclusiveness and incompleteness rouse and invite the play of prosthetic cognition and epistemology through which the reader researches and rehearses the hypothetical possibilities of storytelling. Bruner uses the second definition of the "subjunctive," which is cited in the *Oxford English Dictionary*: "b. Designating a mood (L. *modus subjunctivus*, Gr.) the forms of which are employed to denote an action or a state as conceived (and not as a fact) and therefore used to express a wish, command, exhortation, or a contingent, hypothetical, or prospective event" (Bruner 1986, 26, *OED*, online). Alÿs's rehearsal projects and events, for example, are contingent, hypothetical, and prospective. The familiar strange ontology of play that goes on in the liminal, interstitial spaces that he creates has a reality of its own that "rescue[s our understandings] from obviousness, fill[ing them] with gaps that call upon the reader to become a writer, a composer of a virtual [prosthetic] text in response to the actual [one]" (Bruner, 24).

It is through the ontological play of rehearsal in Alÿs's artwork that an "ontological step" is taken by the reader, and that, according to Bruner (37), "the reader asks that crucial interpretive question, 'What's it all about?'" Bruner writes:

> But what "it" is, of course, is not the actual text—however great its literary power—but the text that the reader has constructed under its sway. And that is why the actual text needs the subjunctivity that makes it possible for a reader to create a world of his [*sic*] own. Like [critical theorist Roland] Barthes, I [Bruner] believe that the writer's greatest gift to a reader is to help him [*sic*] become a writer. (Bruner, 37; Barthes 1974, 4)

This writerly reading to which Bruner and Barthes are referring restores the vigor of the text, which was once present but is no longer there, as the subjectivity of the reader is performed. In doing so, Schechner argues, "[This] restored [or twice behaved] behavior is 'out there,' distant from 'me.' It is separate and therefore can be 'worked on,' changed, even though it has 'already happened'. . . . [It] includes a vast range of actions . . . [and it] is symbolic and reflexive: not empty but loaded behavior multivocally broadcasting significances" (Schechner 1985, 36). Hence, in Alÿs's rehearsal work the virtual, writerly texts, which the reader brings to the readings of the actual texts of *Rehearsal I* and *II* respectively, serve as prosthetic supplements that restore the vigor of the text as twice-behaved behavior. In doing so, the actual "writing" of Alÿs and the virtual "writing" of the reader coexist in a contiguous and subjunctive relationship that is contingent, hypothetical, and prospective.

In ending, I return again to the narrative with which I started this chapter, the story about the disasters of war paintings, the one in which I tell of how I was befuddled yet profoundly impacted by the perceptual play of the paintings' images and the conceptual play of ideas, which they evoked in my mind, and the ontological questions that they stirred about my life. Like the play of Duchamp's readymades, Magritte's paradoxical images, the Surrealists' eccentricities in *Exquisite Corpse*, and the rehearsal projects of Alÿs; their play played me in such a way that corresponds with the prosthetic cognition and epistemology of Koestler's bisociation; the conceptual bipolarities whereby the ambiguities and incompleteness of play in art allow a range of possibilities for seeing and understanding through the similitude argued by Foucault; and where the contingent, hypothetical, and prospective characteristics of Turner's, Bruner's, and Schechner's conceptions of subjunctive play in art are restored similar to Barthes's virtual writerly text of the reader. Like the to-and-fro exercises of the *Exquisite Corpse* curriculum, the pedagogies of bisociation, similitude, and subjunctivity enable creative and political agency as their eccentric modes of address open liminal and contingent spaces where socially and historically constructed knowledge can be researched, contested, and augmented with new and renewed understandings of art, theory, and teaching. Herein lies the significance of this chapter in providing alternative and expansive possibilities for research based on the prosthetic pedagogy of art through which critical perspectives, new knowledge, and critical citizenship can emerge.

FIVE

THE ANXIETY OF DISEQUILIBRIUM IN THE MUSEUM

> We need a Ministry of Disturbance, a regulated source of annoyance; a destroyer of routine; an underminer of complacency.
>
> —John Dewey, *Reconstruction in Philosophy*[1]

> [T]here are exchanges and relays between the past and the present that cannot be charted simply in terms of style and form. The relation is one of continual displacement, revision, and subsumption. But I do insist . . . that for all kinds of reasons we need models of historical connection as well as historical rupture.
>
> —Hal Foster, "Trauma Studies and the Interdisciplinary"

For me, culture has always been a prosthetic experience, not to compensate for a lack or to replace disparate fragments of my body of knowledge, but from curiosity and desire to explore and extrapolate from their dislocations new meanings and understandings. The images, ideas, and attitudes that surrounded me during my youth had a double aspect that was complex and often contradictory in nature. My father and mother, refugees of the Armenian Genocide, immigrated to the United States. They had a small vineyard in Fresno, California (Figure 5.1). My father was a raisin grower, yet he worked in a fig packing plant to make ends meet. My mother was a homemaker yet she took in work as a seamstress to bring in extra cash. My job as their oldest son was to do well in all my classes, yet after school I worked until past dark in the vineyard before doing my homework. Deprived of an education, my parents sent me to school to learn the American way of life, yet at home we only spoke Armenian, ate Armenian food, and socialized within the Armenian community. Mine was a bifurcated life.

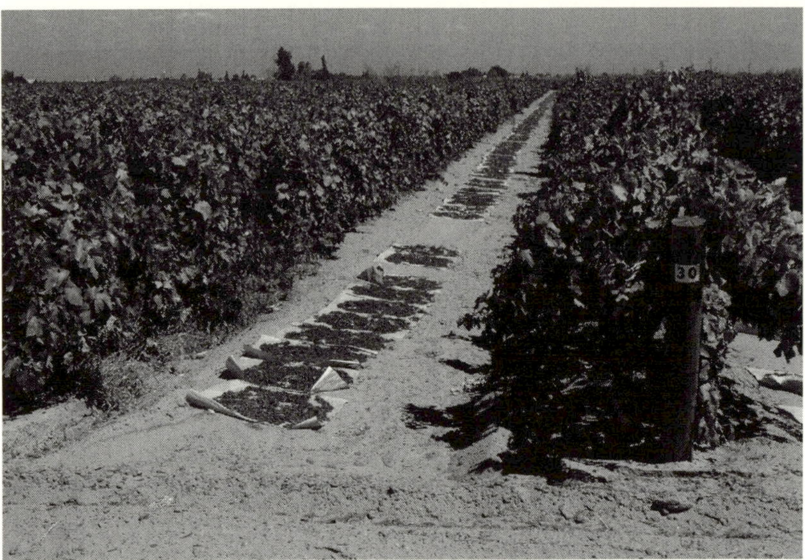

Figure 5.1. Raisins drying in a vineyard row, 2011 (Courtesy California Raisin Marketing Board).

Our economic status was such that what we could not afford to buy we improvised and made our own using found and discarded materials and parts; tools and implements to work the vineyard, household utensils and the repair of appliances, the clothes on our backs, and toys for my siblings and me. In that way we learned to intertwine work and play. Sad memories about our family's past, along with humorous storytelling, word play, singing and dancing went hand in hand with working in the vineyard. This playful research, contrasted with the regimentation of schooling where my attention was fixed on academics: math, science, English, and history, subjects in which I was expected to excel. Given my creative environment at home, one day, out of curiosity, I visited the art classroom in my high school. There I observed students crafting leather wallets as if in a factory. I pondered enrolling in the class, but since I already had a wallet it did not seem necessary to do so.

Upon leaving home after high school for college, I found myself drifting from one academic program to another. Even though I was a decent student, it was the playful and improvisational activities at the vineyard that occupied my thoughts; activities that only later I realized encompassed my early art education. Wanting to pursue a discipline where those activities are valued, I enrolled in a beginning art course. Horrified about what to do for an open painting assignment during the first week of class, I sat in fearful anxiety, staring at my empty canvas. Seeing that I was having difficulty getting started, my teacher approached and asked about my surname, whether it was Armenian.

"Yes," I responded, but I did not understand the purpose for such a question in school—let alone an art classroom. It seemed inappropriate and out of context. He then asked, "Do you know the history of your people?" Having been caught in an off-guard moment, with measured response I retold about my parents' horrific experiences and memories of the Genocide; the stories they had shared with my siblings and me, over and over again; testimonies that helped them purge their trauma and guilt as survivors. While as children it was difficult to fathom our parents' heartbreak, we somehow understood the imperative to keep the memory of lost loved ones alive, to never forget what had happened, for fear of the past repeating itself.

I lost track of time during that conversation with my teacher. I felt relief as the words released effortlessly from my mouth, although our exchange seemed strange and out of context. Prior to this, no teacher had ever asked or cared about my cultural history. I had assumed that the purpose of schooling was to learn how to be a proper American. I assumed that these and the other aspects of my split identity were irreconcilable. Nevertheless, the next thing he said to me changed my life. He encouraged me to take brush in hand and experiment with my pigments; to explore, to improvise, to paint images on the canvas that I had placed on my easel; images that represented what I had heard my parents tell about the Genocide, he said.

His words stirred my thoughts and affected me emotionally. They conjured all sorts of possible associations between my playful working at the vineyard, my parents' haunting stories, my schooling, and the many other experiences in my life that I had learned to compartmentalize. As I struggled technically during the remainder of that first formal art lesson, to do as my teacher suggested, I had an epiphany. All the fragments of my memory and cultural history came together, colliding, intersecting. That realization was emancipating, transformative; it enabled me, intuitively, to understand the disjunctions, the complexities and contradictions of my background in an associative, prosthetic relationship. The disequilibrium and slippages of meaning that were now possible in-between the disparate fragments of my cultural understandings roused creative anxiety and political agency in me as a young art student. . . .

My purpose in telling this story from my youth is twofold. First, I want to accentuate the liminal and contingent characteristics of art making, namely, its enabling learners to expose, examine, and critique academic, institutional, and corporate assumptions through performances of subjectivity based on their personal memories and cultural histories. Learners' subjectivities are constituted by cultural experiences, which they attain from their families, neighborhoods, communities, schools, television, movies, the Internet, and other forms of mediated culture; all of which are readily accessible to them in one form or another. When they enter institutions of learning, they bring that knowledge with them. The personal is political, as the feminists used to say, political as it rubs against the grain of socially and historically constructed understandings of learners' respective cultural environments. The criticality of subjectivity through art practice is constituted by creative and intellectual curiosity and risk taking; namely, the willingness to step outside of one's comfort zone, to cross the boundaries that separate the familiar and known from the strange and unknown.[2] In this way, transgressing cultural assumptions and absolutes through art practice, the transformation of creative and political agency is made possible.

The second reason for my story is to evoke suspense, an anxious curiosity about how the associative, yet indeterminate relationship between our individual, private memories and the corporate, public memory of the museum is constituted by prosthetic pedagogy. My intention is not to confuse, but to complicate our understanding of museum education, to argue that when the public memory of the museum is conjoined with the private memories of learners an anxiety of disequilibrium occurs at their border, a crisis of understanding that augments their respective regimes of knowledge. In doing so the disjunctions between museum knowledge and learners' knowledge are prosthetically enabled through their interconnections and interdependencies. What significance does the autobiographical content of private memory have in the museum? What role can private memory and cultural history serve within the public memory and curriculum of the museum? What constitutes an associative, relational pedagogy and why is it transformative? Why are disequilibrium and slippages of meaning important to transformative learning? How does the interconnectivity and interdisciplinarity of relational pedagogy constitute prosthetic research, and what impact can it have on learning in the museum? Prosthetic pedagogy? What do I mean by prosthetic pedagogy? What does this concept have to do with museum education? In what follows, I will address these and other questions to conceptualize a museum education that fosters learners' creative, intellectual, and political curiosity and agency.

I introduce the prosthesis trope here to challenge the immutability of academic, corporate, and institutional representations such as those that are commonly associated with schools and museums. In doing so, I assume that learners' performances of subjectivity transform schools and museums into liminal, negotiated spaces where their disjunctions constitute prosthetic embodiment through which knowledge and understanding are rendered mutable and prone to slippages of meaning.

In his characterization of prosthetic embodiment, literary theorist Harry Berger Jr. distinguishes between compensatory devices and additive devices. For Berger, compensatory prostheses such as eyeglasses, artificial limbs, hearing aides, make up for a lack, a deficiency in the body; whereas additive prostheses are those that "increase the power of human functions by extending them from the limits of the organic body to the instruments or media of communication, labor, transportation, perception, and representation" (Berger 2000, 104). In what follows, I will use Berger's additive definition of prosthesis to conceptualize art pedagogy that extends knowledge through art practice and museum experiences.

Literary theorist Will Fisher characterizes "prosthesis as a classic post-structural item that does not fit easily into the binary rubrics that structure much of our thinking about identity formation and subjectivity; it is neither clearly nature or culture, essential or constructed, body or artifact, self or other, inside or other" (Fisher 2006, 26). Fisher's misfitting properties of prosthesis suggests a complex mutability that resists the synthetic closure of the Hegelian dialectic. For Gray, Figueroa-Sarriera, and Mentor such mutability represents Cyborgian epistemology: *thesis, antithesis, synthesis, prosthesis, and again* (1995, 13). In other words, the dialectical associations and tensions between differing regimes of knowledge, in resisting closure, remain unstable and unresolved and as such, multivalent interpretations and understandings are made possible. Gray writes:

> Epistemology is . . . based on assumptions about how the world works on its deep levels. It isn't static, for example. And because we can't apprehend every cause and effect, we know it isn't a simple dynamic, such as the dialectic in any flavor, Hegelian idealist or Marxian materialist. [Cyborg epistemology] is open-ended, it shows how some things come directly from previous actions and yet other things come from outside the cause and effect we are noticing. The systems we are part of are too complex to map perfectly or to predict infallibly. (Gray 2002, online)

According to literary theorist Allon White, prostheses "occupy and occlude a disturbing middle ground, disrupting the clear mediation of subject and object. Ontologically unstable, they can be definitively claimed neither by the body nor the world and they thereby violate the coherence and integrity of the body-image. They are the very stuff of abjection" (White 1993, 173). By associating prostheses with abjection, White challenges our notions about wholeness and the totalization of knowledge; instead suggesting a space of embodied transgression; a third, in-between, interstitial space where understanding is contingent, fragmented, strange, unknown, grotesque, indeterminate, and undecideable.

The disruption of subject-object mediation to which White refers is evident in conceptual artist Joseph Kosuth's installation, *One and Three Chairs*, 1965 (Figure 5.2). In this work, Kosuth has juxtaposed a photograph of a wooden folding chair, the actual chair, and the text of the dictionary definition of a chair thus raising questions about representation, functionality, and the nature of art. Ironically, all three of Kosuth's "chairs" are representations of a single chair yet they differ in functionality. The photograph is after all not a chair nor is the text of the dictionary definition. Moreover, the actual chair, it can be argued, is also not a chair. Having been recontextualized in an artwork, the assumed sitting function of the actual chair is denied within the Museum of Modern Art where the guards will not permit sitting on artworks. With *One and Three Chairs*, Kosuth has created a "disturbing middle ground" where prosthetic disequilibrium challenges and resists absolute interpretations and understandings of what constitutes the functionality of a chair and the functionality of an artwork.

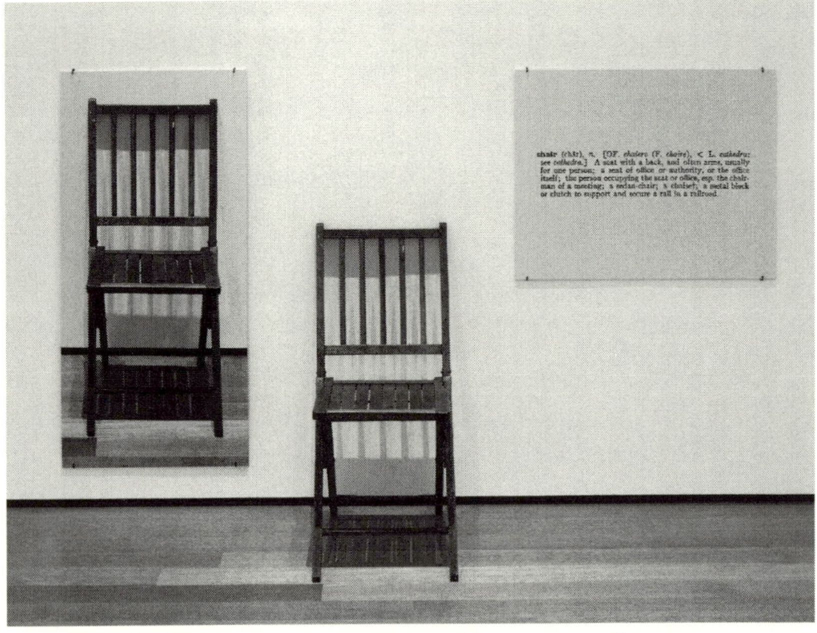

Figure 5.2. Joseph Kosuth, *One and Three Chairs*, 1965, The Museum of Modern Art, New York, NY, © 2012 Artists Rights Society (ARS), New York.

This third space of slippage, argues Homi Bhabha, is "unrepresentable in itself, [that it] constitutes the discursive conditions of enunciation that ensure that the meaning and symbols of culture have no primordial unity or fixity; that even the same signs can be appropriated, translated, rehistoricized and read anew" (Bhabha 1994, 37). The ambiguity and incompleteness of Bhabha's third space constitute the discursive conditions of prosthetic pedagogy where the totalized bodies of knowledge in schools and museums are brought into question. By presuming sole authorship and ownership of knowledge, these institutions practice what architectural theorist Robert Harbison refers to as the "museumifying" of memory and cultural history (Harbison 1977, 145).

The dialectic of prosthesis is constituted by transgressive and transformative embodiment. Its radical epistemology is predicated on abjection: the horror of disparate, foreign bodies of knowledge, and the contiguity and conjoining of the familiar with the strange, the known with the unknown, and the self with the other. Literary critic Julia Kristeva writes, "We may call it a border; [yet] abjection is above all ambiguity. Because, while releasing a hold, it does not radically cut off the subject from what threatens it—on the contrary, abjection acknowledges it to be in *perpetual danger*" (Kristeva 1982, 9; italics added). The associative power of prosthetic knowing and understanding is always already prone to slippage, teetering, and on the verge of collapse. Its multivalent, precarious characteristics are constituted by "perpetual dangers" that ensure mutability between and among differing categories of knowledge and understanding. Its epistemological eccentricity is released through hazarding a risk, through creative and intellectual exploration, experimentation, and improvisation: the research potential of art practice in schools and museums.

In characterizing the abject, ambiguous relationship of prosthetic embodiment, literary theorist Clark Hulse distinguishes between the "visual technology" of reading an artwork and the "verbal technology [of interpretation] . . . [which] operates in some parasitic relation to the artifact which is the host" (Hulse 2000, 148).

> We may imagine [for example] that reading a portrait [of a boy] proceeds toward the making of verbal meaning but does not stop there. It proceeds from significance to the aesthetic, from the aesthetic to the prosthetic, that is, from the [image of the] boy to its significance, from the significance to the recognition that when meaning is joined to the body it becomes more meaningful; then to scorn for the unperfected body which needed such verbal additions; and then to the realization that the verbal addition of meaning is itself "merely" a [parasitic] technology, which leads at least to a

> revulsion against reading, a return to the body. The technology of reading may begin in the semiotic impulse [of signification], but it ends in a reversal of semiotics; its movement is cyclical, from *the body as word to the word as body*. (151; italics added)

For Hulse, prosthetic embodiment occurs in-between the opposing technologies of visual reading and verbal interpretation. While meaning "becomes more meaningful" through prosthetic accrual, it nevertheless suggests a lack, as if meaning was always already present, yet appears absent from the body. This awareness of the body's hypothetical imperfection, which is due to its *accrual of meaning* in the form of verbal technology, leads to a "revulsion against reading" similar to Kristeva's notion of the horror of abjection, at which point attention turns away from the verbal and returns to the body. This to-and-fro slippage between the body and its verbal supplement constitutes prosthetic movement.

The risk of perpetual danger in the practice of art research creates an anxiety of disequilibrium; a prosthetic perturbation in museum education as it transgresses and extends beyond the limits of its collections and exhibitions toward differing, unrelated systems of knowledge. Premised on the constructivist notion that knowledge scaffolds previous knowledge, the anxiety of disequilibrium, according to genetic epistemologist Jean Piaget, occurs when learners encounter new experiences and knowledge that are unfamiliar and do not fit their preexisting frameworks. The perpetual danger of disequilibrium creates a crisis of understanding, Piaget argues, that causes deeper levels of learning, where learners' preexisting schemas are challenged, expanded, and reorganized (Sidman-Taveau and Milner-Bolotin, online). This prosthetic movement of disequilibrium evokes transformative learning that corresponds with the divergent energy of the work of art characterized by Rosalind Krauss.

> [T]he work of art . . . is a fragment—the partial articulation of an extended field of signs, one of the terms in a system of differences. The energy of the work of art is therefore seen as centrifugal, rather than reductive. It drives the perceiver's attention outward, away from itself into the vast institution of language systems that have made it possible and to which it refers. (Krauss 1998, 51–52)

Krauss's concept of the centrifugal movement of the work of art as "the partial articulation of an extended field of signs" corresponds with prosthetic pedagogy, which challenges the reductive positioning of artworks in museum education as it moves knowledge toward unrelated systems of understanding. Similarly, Kristeva claims the trajectory of such divergent movement occurs along a "diagonal axis"; an oblique, indirect line of motion that she attributes to interdisciplinary theory and practice. She argues,

> Interdisciplinarity is always a site where expressions of resistance are latent . . . [academic and institutional] specialists are often too protective of their own prerogatives, do not actually work with other colleagues, and therefore do not teach their students to construct a *diagonal axis* in their [research] methodology. . . . One can only benefit from interdisciplinary practices if researchers meet other researchers whilst learning how to discuss both their competencies and the outcome of their interaction; therefore contributing to the exposure of risks inherent in an interdisciplinary practice. (Kristeva 1998, 6–7; italics added)

Similar to White's notion of the "middle ground" and Bhabha's "third space," the indirectness of Kristeva's "diagonal axis" opens in-between spaces where critical discourse and creative and political intervention are possible. Skeptical about whether there exists willingness in current art practice and academic debate to undertake the risks of interdisciplinary collaboration, architectural theorist Jane Rendell first qualifies then reinforces Kristeva's concept of the diagonal axis:

> Thinking [in-]between demands that we call into question what we normally take for granted, that we question our methodologies, the ways we do things, and our terminologies, what we call what we do. The construction of a diagonal axis is necessarily, then, a difficult business . . . [it is] for this reason that I am also a passionate advocate for interdisciplinarity, because at best this is a difficult and transformative way of working—rigorous and reflective, creative and critical. (Rendell, online).

The correspondences between Krauss's centrifugal movement of artworks, and Kristeva's diagonal axis of interdisciplinary research, evoke compelling pedagogical possibilities for museum education. Considering museums historical regime of collecting, preserving, and exhibiting works of art, the centrifugal movement of museum pedagogy has the potential of complementing learners' memories and cultural histories. Bearing in mind the cultural dislocations and disparities of modern and contemporary cultural life, intersections of learners' private narratives and museums' public narratives are necessary for emerging "prosthetic memory," a new form of public cultural memory, posits cultural historian Alison Landsberg:

> *[P]rosthetic memory* . . . emerges at the interface between a person and a historical narrative about the past, at an experiential site such as a movie theater or museum. In this moment of contact,

> an experience occurs through which the person sutures himself or herself into a larger history . . . the person does not simply apprehend a historical narrative but takes on a more personal, deeply felt memory of a past event through which he or she did not live. The resulting prosthetic memory has the ability to shape that person's subjectivity and politics. (Landsberg 2004, 2)

According to Landsberg, the transformation of subjectivity, which is made possible through prosthetic memory, is predicated on transgressing cultural and disciplinary boundaries. As Gilles Deleuze and Félix Guattari suggest, by transgressing boundaries, learners *deterritorialize*; their familiar cultural understandings shift and connect with the cultural memory of the museum (Deleuze and Guattari 1987, 9). These scholars characterize the slippage of deterritorialization as a "disjunctive synthesis" (Deleuze and Guattari 1983, 12–13), which, as I have been arguing, is the process whereby prosthesis resists closure, a mutable connectivity that enables learners to suture, as Landsberg claims, their personal memories and cultural histories to the historical narratives of artworks as well as the narratives that constitute the museum as a whole. The deterritorializations and mutable connectivities of prosthesis correspond with literary theorists Peter Erickson and Clark Hulse's conceptualization of cross-disciplinarity, which they maintain "arises not from a transcendence or even a blurring of discipline, but from an embracing of the dynamic and self-transformative quality of intellectual work, which is characterized . . . by a happy convergence and intersection of a variety of disciplinary logics" (Hulse and Erickson 2000, 13).

The interface between the personal and public narrative of Landsberg's prosthetic memory, and the disjunctive synthesis of Deleuze and Guattari's deterritorializations were evident in artist/curator Fred Wilson's exhibition, *Mining the Museum*, at the Maryland Historical Society in Baltimore in 1992–93. For this exhibition, Wilson borrowed artifacts from the Historical Society's collection and juxtaposed text panels that created an alarming awareness of the institution of slavery. In one installation labeled *Metalwork, 1723–1880*,[3] he placed a set of Baltimore repoussé silver goblets, urns, and decanters adjacent to rusted shackles that were once used to enslave African Americans. In another, he installed a punt gun, an extremely large shotgun, that was used for bird hunting and aimed its barrel directly at a wooden doll portraying a black man, suggesting a correspondence between "the sport of duck hunting and the tracking of runaway slaves" (Stein 1993, online). According to art critic Judith E. Stein, *Mining the Museum* raised the historical consciousness of visitors and "revealed to people of color how they have fared in the world of museums. . . . [In doing so, the exhibition] exposed the racist threads that are an integral part of our historical fabric, a reality often skirted in institutional contexts" (Stein 1993). The many viewers who experienced *Mining the Museum* expressed a profound shift in understanding about the institution of slavery. Having been shaken by the mocking, transgressive narratives in Wilson's exhibition, viewers felt the injustices of slavery on a deep, personal level, which was constituted by the transformative power of prosthetic memory. Cultural theorist Elizabeth Wilson writes about the interdependency between transgression and transformation in challenging oppressive representations:

> We transgress in order to insist that we are there, that we exist, and to place a distance between ourselves and the dominant culture. But we have to go further—we have to have an idea of how things could be different, otherwise transgression ends in mere posturing. In other words, transgression on its own leads eventually to entropy, unless we carry within us some idea of transformation. It is therefore not transgression that should be our watchword, but transformation. (Wilson 1993, 116)

Ron Jones's claim that transformative embodiment is the result of curricular and pedagogical practices that expose, examine, and critique disciplinary and cultural biases, corresponds with the multivalent characteristics of Wilson's *Mining the Museum*. Jones identifies four disciplinary forms of practice-based research in art and design that can be applied to museum education. The first, *monodisciplinarity*, consists of the academic stronghold of a single, originary discipline; second, *multidisciplinarity*, consists of differing disciplines that parallel, yet do not necessarily impact or intersect each other. In his third and fourth examples of practice-based research Jones places greatest worth on the risk of *interdisciplinary* failure, without which *transdisciplinary* knowledge is not possible.

> Innovative design education places greater and greater emphasis on interdisciplinary practice-based-research—it has become ubiquitous at university and design schools—but studies tell us that interdisciplinary and transdisciplinary practices are subject to failure rates higher than conventional monodisciplinary or multidisciplinary practices. If this makes failure inevitable, could it become an advantage? (Jones 2009, online)

The answer to Jones's question is in the affirmative. The risk of transgressive failure is an advantage as it inspires a charged, dialectical relationship between disciplinary depth and breadth.

Considering the preponderance of *atychiphobia*, our fear of failure, the question that Jones asks, whether failure can become an advantage, is a provocative one for museums and academic institutions to consider.

Like Jones and Rendell, Hal Foster questions the willingness of current art practice and academic debate to undergo "rigorous and reflective, creative and critical" risk. Foster makes no concessions to either disciplinarity or interdisciplinarity. Instead, he argues that interdisciplinarity must not preclude discipline-specific research because it is imperative that the relationship between depth and breadth of knowledge remain dialectically charged and argumentative.

> To be interdisciplinary you need to be disciplinary first—to be grounded in one discipline, preferably two, to know the historicity of these discourses before you test them against each other. Many young people now come to interdisciplinary work before they come to disciplinary work. As a result they often fall into an eclecticism that does little work on any discipline; it is more entropic than transgressive. (Foster 1998, 162)

The dialectical relationship between disciplinary and interdisciplinary research insisted by Foster corresponds with Jones's (2008) "T" coordinate system, which is constituted by a vertical and horizontal axis. According to Jones, the vertical coordinate of the "T" represents disciplinary depth, while the horizontal coordinate represents disciplinary breadth (Figure 5.3). Similar to Foster's imperative for a disciplinary/interdisciplinary dialectic,

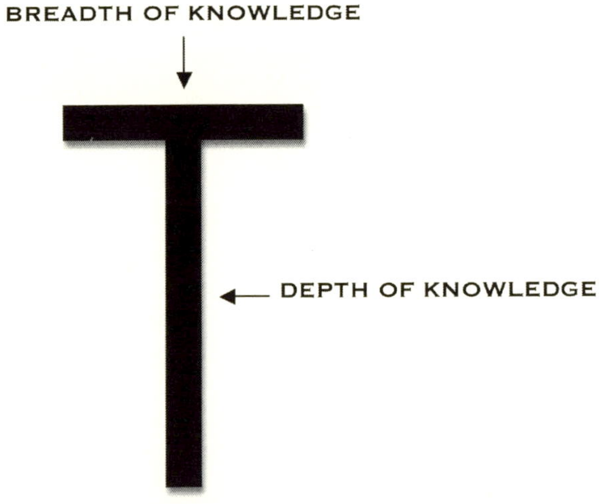

Figure 5.3. The "T" of interdisciplinarity, 2011 (Courtesy Charles Garoian).

Jones argues that interdisciplinarity, and the possibility of transformation, is predicated on the willingness to risk failure, when reaching out from one's discipline-based knowledge to others that are abjectly unfamiliar and seemingly undesirable. The complementarity that Jones seeks with his "T" coordinates is constituted by the betweenness of Kristeva's diagonal axis, both scholars arguing the willingness to risk failure as an advantage to creative and intellectual agency. Thus, quoting author/poet Samuel Beckett (1992, 101), Jones declares: "fail again, fail better" (2009, online).[4]

In their representation of failure as an advantage, artists Dorothy Schultz and Louise Barry parody the presumption of essentialized artifacts, authoritative knowledge, and truth in museums in their installation *Museum of Mistakes*, 2008 (Figures 5.4 and 5.5). Schultz and Barry's installation at The Islip Art Museum in Islip, New York, consisted of several storerooms, which they filled with mis-taken, mis-understood, and mis-represented artifacts. In one part of the installation there is a countertop with typewritten information on age-discolored note cards pinned on the wall above it. Atop the counter there is a beetle fossil, which was found in Sihetun, China, in the same 120 million-year-old volcanic sediments in which the miniature winged dinosaur Sinosauropteryx was discovered. Until recently, the beetle fossil was mistakenly believed to be part of the Sinosauropteryx. The test

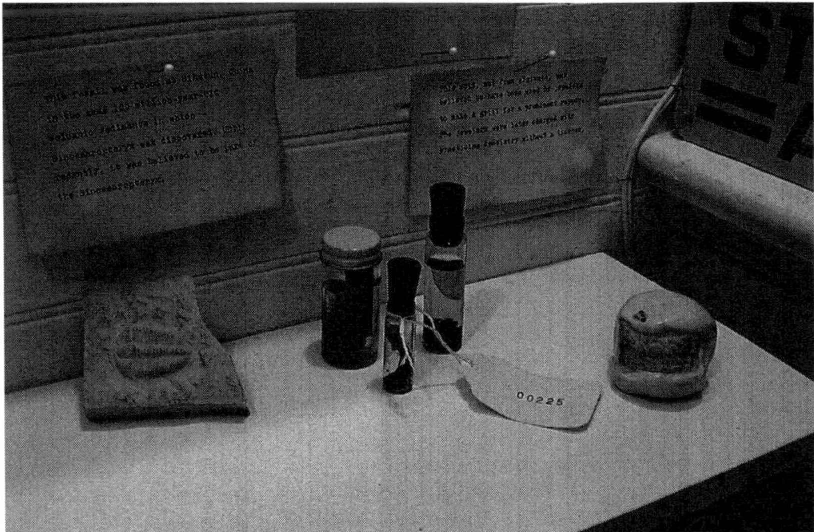

Figure 5.4. Dorothy Schultz and Louise Barry, *Museum of Mistakes*, 2008 (Courtesy the artists).

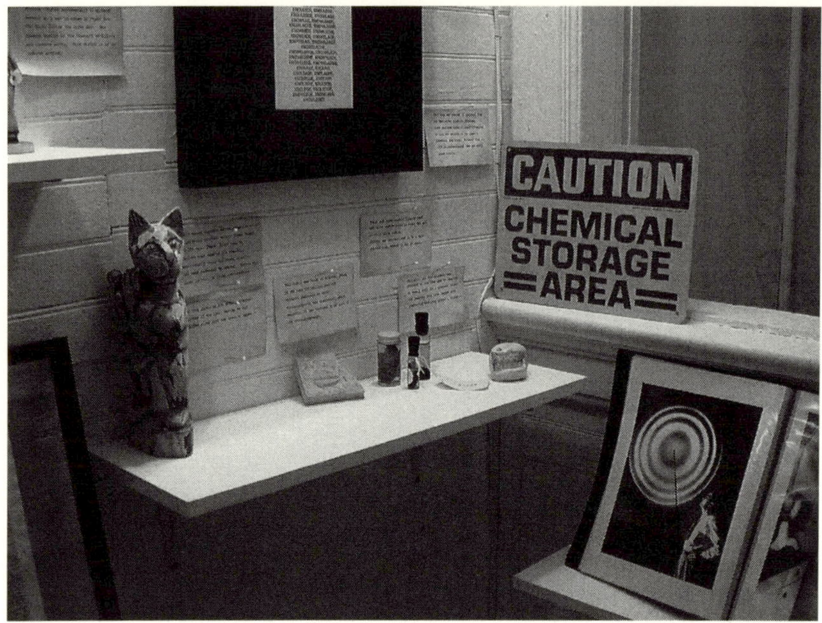

Figure 5.5. Dorothy Schultz and Louise Barry, *Museum of Mistakes* (detail), 2008 (Courtesy the artists).

tubes in the center of the countertop contain insects that are usually misidentified as rare, but are actually quite common. And the item tagged #00225 was once believed to be a rare spotted slug, though the species has no evidence of spots. In addition to these examples there were numerous other mistaken artifacts in Schultz and Barry's installation, including the storerooms, ironically misrepresented as galleries in the artists' mistaken museum. In the exhibition catalog, the artists write about the slippages of meaning intended in their installation:

> The *Museum of Mistakes* celebrates the imperfect process of discovery and the mutable boundaries of human knowledge. While the project explores the excesses of human error, it is also essentially about our relationship to the past. Mistakes are only mistakes in retrospect. The Museum's collection of found objects, informative documents, and obvious forgeries creates a makeshift commentary on the inherent fragility and inconsistency of what we know and what we believe. The *Museum of Mistakes* disregards the moral imperative of "truth," and instead becomes a world in itself, one which imitates our uncertain experience of reality. (2008)

Apropos the oppositional character of parody, Schultz and Barry's *Museum of Mistakes* constitutes an "authorized transgression" given that it mocks museums while it reinforces the institutional conventions of museums. As literary theorist Linda Hutcheon argues, the reflexive criticality that ensues through such transgressions of parody, in the present, "reframes or 'recontextualizes' the past" (Hutcheon 1985, 26, 75, 111). Thus, like Kristeva's diagonal axis of interdisciplinarity and Krauss's centrifugal energy of a work of art, the slippages and disequilibrium of parody represent prosthetic pedagogy whose perturbations expose interstitial, in-between spaces where preexisting frameworks are challenged, extended, and reorganized.

Having argued the slippages of meaning that can occur through prosthetic pedagogy in museums, I now end this writing with a prosthetic memory of a museum experience that I had several years ago. I will begin where I ended my introductory narrative for this paper. In doing so, I will give an example of how the cultural experiences in the vineyard during my youth connected with those that occurred in an art museum setting later in my adult life. As you, the reader, will recall, I previously told of my art teacher encouraging me to paint my parents' recollections of the Genocide, and how that experience transformed my understanding of the cultural dislocations of my life into an associative, prosthetic relationship.

A decade after that classroom experience, I was honored with a one-person exhibition at the San Francisco Museum of Modern Art, along with five other young artists from the Bay Area of California who received the same honor. Considering the importance of this achievement, I invited my parents to drive up from the vineyard in Fresno and to attend the reception that the museum held in our honor. Upon arrival, having had virtually no art museum experience, my parents were astonished by the large crowd of more than five hundred people who were in attendance at the reception to honor me, their son, and my other artist colleagues.

The work that I exhibited in my assigned gallery space consisted of photographic documentations of live, collaborative performances that my students and I had presented at Los Altos High School, where I was their teacher. Also in the exhibition were black and white documentations of my personal performance explorations. Since my parents were not aware of the kind of work that I was doing since my college days, they were mystified as to the reason why such an important institution as the museum would install such work, based on the assumption that it was a place for historic works of art. In other words, my work did not look like art was supposed to look. Nevertheless, considering the stature of the museum and the magnitude of the attendance at the reception, my parents conveyed great pride in my accomplishment.

After looking at my work, my father wandered to an exhibition of photorealistic paintings by another artist in the gallery adjacent to mine and hurriedly darted back to inform me that they were so realistic "you could almost touch them." He reminded me that I once used to draw and paint like that, and while the performance work in my exhibition was important, I should not forget how to make realistic art, suggesting, after all that such art was real art. Understanding where my father was coming from, I listened, without speaking, to what he was telling me. I remained respectful and observed his responses to the abstract visual images and ideas in the works that were exhibited by me and the other four artists in the museum.

Approximately fifteen minutes later, at a distance from where my work was exhibited, and where I was conversing with viewers inquiring about my work, I saw my father standing alone in the far gallery, hunched over, with his gaze fixed on one particular artwork, a kinetic sculpture entitled *Pendulumbrella,* 1974 (Figure 5.6) by artist Bryan Rogers. A mechanical representation of a play on the words "pendulum" and "umbrella," *Pendulumbrella* consisted of a geared mechanical device that opened and closed an umbrella, as it swung back and forth like a pendulum in five-second cycles (Rogers 1976, 267).

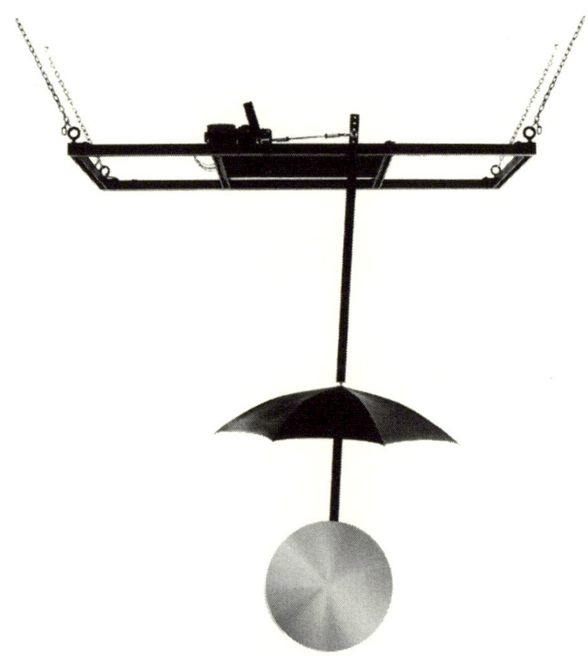

Figure 5.6. Bryan Rogers, *Pendulumbrella,* 1974 (Courtesy the artist).

Considering that my father was transfixed by that particular artwork by Rogers, I figured he was beginning to understand and appreciate the visual and conceptual abstractions of art. Curious about his thoughts, I walked over to him and asked why he found it so fascinating. At first he did not hear me due to his intense concentration on *Pendulumbrella* and the din of conversations among all the people at the reception. When I raised my voice to repeat my question, he quickly turned his head to shush me.

"Sh-sh-sh," he said, "sh-sh-sh, look at this," as he pointed to the geared movement of the mechanical device. "I can use this, I can use this on the vineyard tractor," he said. As he pointed and moved his index finger in synch with the swinging motion of *Pendulumbrella*, he repeated, "see this, I can use this, on the tractor." In that moment of my astonishment, when my father made a connection, between his tractor and Rogers's kinetic sculpture, between the vineyard and the art museum, I was reminded of my roots, of the playful appropriations and improvisations of my youth; I was reminded of my college art teacher encouraging me to explore and express both sides of my cultural identity through art; and, I was reminded of the disequilibrium and slippages of meaning that first roused my creative anxiety and political agency as a young art student. This all happened *with-in* the prosthetic space of a museum.

SIX

~~DRAWING BLINDS~~

Art Practice as Prosthetic Visuality

> The possibility of making the invisible visible, of giving presence to what can only be imagined, is repeatedly stated as the main function of art.
>
> —Paul de Man, *Blindness and Insight*

> The paradox of seeing is that the more forcefully I try to see, the more blind I become.
>
> —James Elkins, *The Object Stares Back*

> Who are you going to believe, me or your own eyes?
>
> —Groucho Marx, *Duck Soup*

. . . was I there, I was, and . . . and I saw it, saw it . . . witnessed with my eyes, with my own eyes . . . did I see what I, what I was looking at . . . did I see what I, what I thought I saw, had my eyes deceived me . . . did what I see really happen . . . did it really happen and I saw it, but did not see . . . just as I am seeing, yet not seeing the words as I write them, about what I saw . . . just as you, the reader may see what I saw as you read the words that I have written on this page . . . these words prospecting the ineffable . . . blind spots are gaining visibility, vaguely revealing events, flitting as they, as they appear before my mind's eye . . . I was there I tell you, I *am* there and, in the ~~blink of an eye, the blinds are drawn (Figure 6.1) . . . the gaps of memory opened, exposing an outlook, drawing my attention outward, through the window of the back door of our house, a~~

Figure 6.1. Venetian blinds, 2010 (Courtesy Charles Garoian).

~~sightline aimed due east along the Thirty-Sixth Parallel, down the hallway, out the window of the back door, past the mulberry tree next to the patio in the backyard, through the quarter mile row aligned with Thompson seedless grapevines, a straight path directing my gaze toward the hazy skyline of the town of Fresno five miles in the distance, its modest cluster of buildings backlit by the morning sun rising in the east, everything within my view illuminated . . . a compelling visual, captivating and directing my transient observation through the hallway where, despite my ocular itinerary, I am still sitting in a chair, tying my *J.C. Penney's* high-top shoes as father breaks two eggs into the cast iron pan and turns up the flame on the *O'Keefe & Merritt* stovetop to brew his *Maxwell House*, "good to the last drop," hobo coffee in the adjacent kitchen . . . it's 6 a.m. and my awareness is heightened of dawn's early light flooding through the oculus in the back door of our house . . . a spectacular phenomenon, it stares back at me . . . now, the aroma of melting butter, fried eggs, and coffee . . . now, I can just smell the distraction . . . as I write these words, and you the reader is now reading them, I'm convinced of memory's olfactory capacities, the delicious sense of smell as vivid as the rays of the sun returning my gaze through the eye of the back door, with blinds drawn, revealing an east-west orientation of visibility along the Thirty-Sixth Parallel, a latitudinal line 36° 44' 55" to be exact, north of the Earth's equatorial plane connecting my geographical coordinates in the hallway of our house with those along its 25,000 mile trajectory (Figure 6.2) . . .~~

~~. . . California, Nevada, Utah, Colorado, Kansas, Missouri, Illinois, Indiana, Kentucky, West Virginia, Virginia, Chesapeake Bay, Maryland and Virginia again, Atlantic Ocean, Portugal, Spain, Mediterranean Sea, Italy, Mediterranean Sea again, Greece, Aegean Sea, Turkey, Iran, Caspian Sea,~~

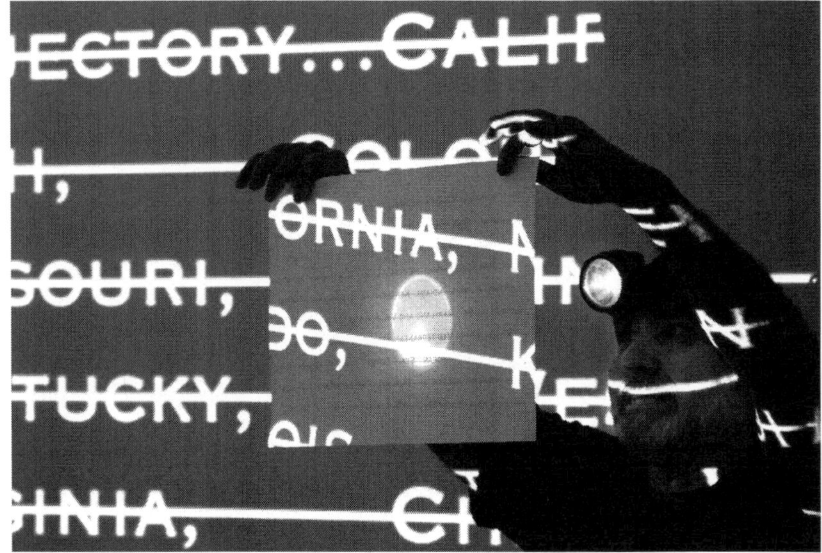

Figure 6.2. Charles Garoian performing ~~*Drawing Blinds*~~, 2009 (Courtesy Rob Martin).

~~Turkmenistan, Uzbekistan, Tajikistan, Afghanistan, Tajikistan again, China, Yellow Sea, North Korea, South Korea, Sea of Japan, Japan, across the Pacific Ocean, and back again through the front door of our house into the hallway where I am sitting, tying my shoes, a perfect constellation, then, then, then (Figure 6.3) . . .~~

FLA-SH-SH-SH

Figure 6.3. FLA-SH-SH, 2010 (Courtesy Charles Garoian).

~~. . . a sudden, unexpected flare, a blast of light blazes through the window of the back door . . . blinding the sun, it overwhelms my seeing . . . BLINK, BLINK . . . blindsided, I'm momentarily disoriented, vertigo, I feel a slight tremor, then in my body, then I hear barking, Prince is barking outside his doghouse, barking repeatedly, I hear him dragging his chain until it stops at its choke collar . . . I BLINK, BLINK, BLINK, as if measuring time and~~

~~space . . . realizing the house is quaking underneath my feet, I BLINK, again and again . . . duck and cover, I fall to the floor, crawl quickly under the kitchen table . . . assuming a fetal position, I shut my eyes and bury my head between my knees and wait, a conditioned response that I learned in grade school at Madison Elementary, in the event of a nuclear attack, to protect my body I was told, to protect my body . . . then, in a moment of stillness, a sudden touch on my shoulder . . .~~ opening my eyes, I see father reaching down to help me up from under the table, to "sit down for our morning meal," he says calmly, "before I leave for work and you walk to school," he says . . . nothing, nothing else was said, yet not saying is saying a lot under the circumstances, not seeing is seeing a lot, not understanding is understanding a lot . . . the aftermath of the "B-B-B-B-Bomb," a wounding, fragmenting perception and memory,[1] averted attention . . . lacunas, blind spots, gaps, aporias, craters of seeing and not seeing remain of the incident at Yucca Flats at 37° 4' 7" latitude, 207.6 miles as the crow flies from where I was sitting tying my shoes . . . like the wound St. Thomas the Apostle probes with his index finger to confirm or refute the immortality of the Christ's body, his survey of that wound in the body of an Other, averting viewers', our gaze, toward and through the focal point of Caravaggio's painting,[2] and through his canvas . . . raising doubt about the veracity of vision and visuality, a questioning of representation that cuts, opens, and folds the historical body of art back onto itself. Similar uncertainty lingered in the hallway as I was tying my shoes next to the kitchen where father was preparing breakfast . . . the less I focus the more I see . . . I'm reminded of my habit of blinking, a tic that coincidently developed back then . . . my eyes stammering, my mouth blinking . . . Jasper Johns's *The Critic Sees*[3] . . . seeing and saying complicated as my eyelids involuntarily oscillate up and down, FLASH-ing fragmentations and discontinuities of perception and memory whenever I get excited or anxious, up and down, open yet shut, enabling a seeing without seeing, a remembering that comes from forgetting, and an understanding from mis-understanding, a FLASH come and gone in the blink of an eye . . .

The narrative that you just read is about a bedazzling spectacle that I witnessed during my youth in the early 1950s. Like novelist José Saramago's (1997) epidemic of "white blindness," the magnitude of the event, 5.0 on the Richter Scale, so overpowered and captivated my attention that all else including my body blurred and receded into the background of my consciousness. "To see is always to see more than one sees," claims phenomenologist Maurice Merleau-Ponty:

> Blindness (*punctum caecum*) of the "consciousness" . . . *what* it does not see it does not see for reasons of principle, it is because it is

> consciousness that it does not see. What it does not see is what in it prepares the vision of the rest (as the retina is blind at the point where the fibers that will permit the vision spread out into it). What it does not see is what makes it see, is its tie to Being, is its corporeity, are the existentials by which the world becomes visible, is the flesh wherein the object is born. (Merleau-Ponty 1986, 247–48)

If "to see is always to see more than one sees," as Merleau-Ponty claims, then why is it that most often we do not see what we are looking at or thinking about? In this chapter I will discuss the significance of lacunas, blind spots, gaps, aporias of perception and memory, those anomalous spaces of learning (Ellsworth, 2005) where collateral discourse (Leverette, 2008) can occur between the visible and invisible in art practice and research. I will argue that slippages of perception in these spaces enable insightful and multivalent ways of seeing and understanding the complexities of alterity, what critical theorist Elizabeth Grosz refers to as "other ways of looking [through art] that may move beyond the mundane and the habitual . . . beyond the [scopophilic] apparatus of [voyeurism] and the gaze" (Grosz 2006, 199). Moreover, I will discuss how the insights and revelations that art practice and research make possible challenge socially and historically constructed ways of seeing and understanding and, in doing so, constitute the immanent and generative[4] learning processes of prosthetic visuality.

About the constructedness of seeing, conceptual artist Robert Morris writes: "Vision is always mediated. We always believe before we look. We always assume (theorize) a wholeness of the visual. We believe to such an extent that we do not 'see' the absences. Can seeing sometimes obscure dark reason?" (Morris 2008, 45). On that morning my absorption was so profound that the depth and breadth of what I had previously seen, thought, and understood seemed to disappear. I was so stunned by what I witnessed along the Thirty-Sixth Parallel running through the hallway of the house, that its FLASH did not register, it seemed void of signification in and of itself.

From then on, "seeing" for me, became a "forgetting the name of the thing one sees," which is how art writer Lawrence Weschler (1982) characterizes the perceptual investigations of artist Robert Irwin's contingent and ephemeral installations, and their positioning of viewers reflexively perceiving themselves perceiving (Irwin 1985). In Irwin's 1968 *Untitled* light installation,[5] "the eye spends time trying to understand what it sees—what is nearer and what is farther, what is solid and what is immaterial light, or even light's absence" (MOMA.org, online). Similarly, in describing the intertwining of corporeal presence (*ecstasis*) and absence, philosopher Drew Leder writes, "The body conceals itself precisely in the act of revealing what is Other" (Leder 1990, 22). In other words, seeing, representing, and understanding the *Other* in *other* than socially, historically, and teleologically determined ways.[6]

Only on occasion do certain stimuli—tying shoes, aromas of breakfast, eating grapes, flashes of intense light, and the morning sun—bring that moment on the thirty-sixth parallel mnemonically to mind; like flashbacks they offer visibility to the invisibility of what remains Other from that morning with my father. Writing about the body's response to and repression of powerful images, art historian David Freedberg claims, "They have the potential to affect even (or perhaps especially) the youngest of viewers, and affect them not just emotionally, but in ways that have long-term behavioral consequences" (Freedberg 1989, 5). The intensity of that FLASH, like the visual power of art, empurpled my seeing and understanding and, in doing so, confounded, complicated, and transformed my perception of reality. Like a FLASH of lightning, that blinding ironically opened my eyes and my mind to other than what I had already seen and pondered, to other ways of seeing and thinking. Like the FLASH that I witnessed on that morning, lightning represents the "perfect congruence" between what is apparent and hidden in flashes of intuition during expression, according to philosopher Wlad Godzick. In his introduction to philosopher Paul de Man's treatise *Blindness and Insight*, Godzick writes:

> Lightning cannot be said to be hidden from its manifestation, but rather it expresses itself . . . fully in the instant of its illumination. In fact, it suspends the difference between the manifest and the manifesting, producing in its instantaneity a moment of perfect presence. However, the punctual brevity of its flash is such as to displace its significance away from itself onto the surrounding darkness whose internal composition it reveals. Even if the eye were to train itself on the flash, and were it able to predict the exact moment and place of its occurrence, it would remain unseeing, for it would be blinded by the force of the light, so that it is not lightning itself that we wish to see but what its flash reveals, the inner configuration of the surrounding landscape and the forces at play within it. The eye remains trained on the darkness knowing it to hold a secret that the flash will disclose. The flash is not the secret but the occasion of the moment when all is in the light; the reward for peering into the dark. (Godzick 1983, xx)

Godzick's correlative between lightning and darkness during moments of insight corresponds with the existential visuality of art research and practice, which paradoxically *reveals* while it *conceals* meaning.[7]

Land artist Walter De Maria's *The Lightning Field* (1997),[8] in the high desert of western New Mexico, corresponds with the revelation and concealment that Godzick ascribes to insight. De Maria installed four hundred highly polished stainless steel poles in a grid pattern measuring one mile in one direction and one kilometer in the other. Each of the poles measures 2" in diameter, standing 20' 7" in height, and 220' apart from the others. Their solid tips come to a share point and, together in the grid, they constitute a horizontal plane. Given the frequency of storms in that region of New Mexico, De Maria's artwork attracts lightning activity to the grid, revealing and concealing its existence in the dark desert landscape.

In yet another example of the visible and invisible in art practice and research, new media artist Gene Cooper lies on a hospital gurney with a set of sensors whose acupuncture needles are inserted into his body. Jacked into an adjacent computer, the sensors' wires are linked through the Internet to the Web site of the National Lightning Detection Network (NLDN) where lightning strikes in the United States are electronically detected and recorded. In this interactive installation and performance entitled *Ghost Lightning* (Figure 6.4), Cooper diverted lightning detection to his body via Transcutaneous Electro Neuro Stimulators (TENS), revealing a dynamic relationship between the electrical system of his body and that of the earth.

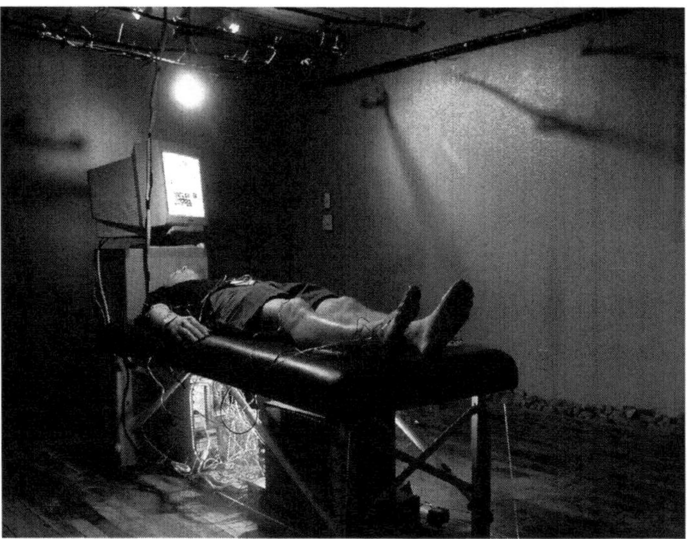

Figure 6.4. Gene Cooper, *Ghost Lightning*, 2003 (Courtesy the artist).

> These sensors reveal the invisible flow of energy within Cooper's body and the simultaneous echoing of lightning as it pulses through his system. Falling from above are small bursts of rain released with each lightning strike. As the pattern of lightning moves across the landscape, a corresponding pattern of rain falls within the gallery. In the background, we hear the voices and sounds of others' interpretation of the ghostly residual energy experienced by all of us, whether it involves deja-vu, past life experiences, hidden memories from the past, or mysterious connections. (Cooper, online)

Similarly, "A light bulb in the dark cannot show itself without showing you something else too" (Rauschenberg Spring 1963, 29). Rauschenberg handwrote this aphorism in pencil between the fragments of a photo collage entitled *Random Order* (ca. 1963),[9] suggesting that a work of art, like a "light bulb," reveals itself as it shows something else; the something else being exposed through the viewer's process of meaning-making. In other words, having introduced the text of the aphorism, Rauschenberg calls our attention to the betweenness of the photo collage fragments where seeing of the yet unseen, yet unknown possibilities of meaning and understanding are "reward[ed] for peering into the dark" of its interstitial spaces, which Godzick describes in similar ways about darkness and lightning. This complementary, interdependent relationship between the revealing and concealing capacities of a work of art, a "showing something else," something in excess of itself, constitutes prosthetic visuality.

Conceptual artist Christo Javacheff refers to his wrapping quotidian objects, architectural monuments,[10] and stretches of landscape as "revealing an object by concealing it." In other words, by concealing what is obvious and self-evident about visual phenomena, Christo's projects reveal excess, more than is assumed, taken for granted, thus supplementing its visual, conceptual, and signifying characteristics, which would otherwise remain hidden and invisible. This paradox of concealment and revelation corresponds with *différance*, Derrida's neologism where the *difference* between seeing and not seeing resists the synthetic closure of the Hegelian and Marxist dialectic, which constitutes perception as forever deferred or postponed. As in the double-coded title of this chapter, ~~Drawing Blinds~~, the slippages and multiplicities in-between visibility and invisibility in art research and practice correspond with the deferral of *différance*, which Derrida hypothesizes in the following two ways:

> Here is a *first hypothesis*: the drawing is blind, if not the draftsman or draftswoman. As such, and in the moment proper to it, the operation of drawing would have something to do with blindness,

> would in some way regard blindness [*aveuglement*]. In this abocular hypothesis (the word *aveugle* comes from *ab oculus*: not from or by but without the eyes), the following remains to be heard and understood: the blind man can be a seer and he sometimes has the vocation of a visionary. Here is the *second hypothesis* then—an eye graft, the grafting of one point of view onto the other: a drawing of the *blind* is a drawing *of* the blind. Double genitive. (Derrida 1993, 2)

Abocular, yet another Derridian neologism representing *différance,* suggests that drawing, and art practice in general, is constituted by the ironic play between "drawing blinds" (concealment) and "blind drawing" (revelation), similar to philosopher Hans-Georg Gadamer's to-and-fro ontology of art, which "renews itself in constant repetition" through a process of deferral (Gadamer 2006, 105).

To resist a binary, reductive understanding of this complex ontology, critical theorist Stephen Barker explains "the *abocular hypothesis* is not merely a matter of a dyad, concealment *or* revelation, but rather of the elision of concealment *and* revelation, a parabolic telling [parable] that *does not* tell, a showing forth that *does not* show" (Barker 2003, online). In describing an example of this "double blindness," art historian James Elkins writes: "At the instant a drawing is begun, the artist is often looking at the paper, so that . . . [s/he] sees neither the model nor the drawing that does not yet exist" (Elkins 1996, 234). Hence, through omission the parabolic process of the *abocular hypothesis,* in perpetual slippage, generates something else, something in excess of itself, something that is not assumed, that is, the valuing of the unseen, of otherness.

Here I want to clarify that the blindness to which I am referring in art practice and research differs from the historical depictions of physical blindness from which Derrida (1993) developed his theory of the visible and invisible. While Derrida's *abocular hypothesis* is important to my argument, his conceptualization of blindness as a phenomenon that is exterior to art differs from what I am describing as the unseen, unknown possibilities, the immanence *within* artworks, which according to art historian Jane Blocker, is the outcome of "sightlessness." Blocker cites artists such as Bruce Nauman and others whose installations "involve intense lights and disorient and blind rather than bring enlightenment to their viewers" (Blocker 2007, online). For example, the intense green lighting of Nauman's *Green Light Corridor* (1970)[11] alters viewers' vision and disorients their bodies as they pass through its tight, narrow space. After having acclimated to seeing green and their bodies compressed during passage, upon exiting the corridor their seeing gradually turns pink at the same time that they feel a gradual expansion in their bodies.

> As a result of . . . immanence, accepting the premise of the blind man means that these [light] installations and the philosopher-artists who inhabit them are engaged in the task of contemplating the very conditions of art's possibility, particularly in a theoretical moment that continues to debate the nature of representation and the real and in a technological age in which such categories have been destabilized. (Blocker 2007, online)

Blocker's characterization of sightlessness can be extended to other examples of art practice and research where seeing and representation are at issue, and where viewers are confounded with the "the very conditions of art's possibility." Moreover, the destabilization of categories to which she is referring corresponds with the slippages of prosthetic visuality.

The immanence of sightlessness—showing that comes from not showing—is evident in Diego Rodriguez Velázquez's painting *Las Meninas* (Figure 6.5). What we, the viewers, see and imagine exists in what Velázquez shows and does not show us. While the backside of his large canvas is in view, the image that he is painting on its front side is not. We see the artist peering

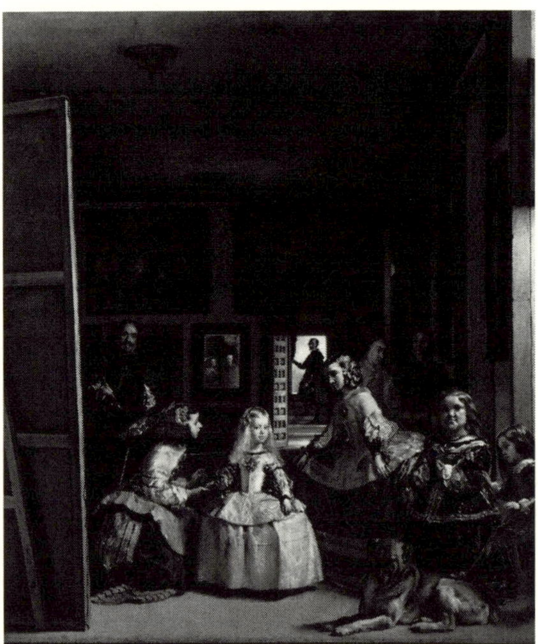

Figure 6.5. Diego Velázquez, *Las Meninas*, 1656, Oil on canvas, 318 x 276 cm. Museo del Prado, Madrid, Spain (Courtesy Scala/Art Resource, NY).

out from the canvas and looking in our direction, yet we are uncertain of the object of his gaze. The presumption, that it is we who are the object of his study, is brought into question by the faint image of a couple on the back wall. Is it a painting or is it a mirror reflecting whoever the artist is looking at?

To complicate showing and not showing further, Velázquez has painted an open doorway in the background with a stairway leading up and away from the foreground of the painting. A figure, with its body in opposing directions, is standing on the stairs with right arm reaching forward, away from the foreground, to draw open a blind and allow in light, while looking back through the doorway, across the span of the room, and beyond the picture plane onto the space where we, the viewers, are positioned. That doorway emitting light like the pupil of an eye, and the dual positioning of the figure reaching forward yet looking back and returning viewers' gaze, suggests the room as an ocular chamber, an in-between orbit of visibility and invisibility, with viewers positioned at its optic nerve. Writing about the parody of perception in *Las Meninas*, Michel Foucault excavates and examines the archeology of double invisibility in Velázquez's painting:

> The painter is looking, his face turned slightly and his head leaning towards one shoulder. He is staring at a point to which, even though it is invisible, we, the spectators, can easily assign an object, since it is we, ourselves, who are that point: our bodies, our faces, our eyes. The spectacle he is observing is thus double invisible: first, because it is not represented within the space of the painting, and, second, because it [the spectacle] is situated precisely in that blind point, in that essential hiding-place [between looking and seeing] into which our gaze disappears from ourselves at the moment of our actual looking. (Foucault 1973, 4)

Velázquez's spectacle suggests that works of art enable us to probe, stir, and call into question the opacity and density of our mediated vision to expose and challenge the cultural assumptions that occlude our seeing and understanding. The resistance of art to concrescence and totalizing assumptions enables a plurality of visual and conceptual associations, speculations, and an ambivalent hybridity of seeing and understanding. The prosthetic visuality of art practice challenges the body's normative perception by exposing and foregrounding, mnemonically, what is ordinarily hidden in the recesses of imagination and memory. As such, the representation of what is unseen through art practice constitutes excess, a multiplicity that supplements and challenges the body's mediated seeing and understanding.

Following Velázquez's and Foucault's double invisible, and de Man's claim in the first epigraph, that art evokes the visible in the invisible, at the beginning of this chapter, here I am arguing that art's ability to give presence to what can only be imagined, constitutes prosthetic visuality, which is mnemonically constituted. That is, works of art enable us to probe, stir, and call into question the opacity and density of our mediated vision; to expose and challenge the cultural assumptions that occlude our seeing and understanding in other than the ways we have been taught to see and understand. The resistance of art to concrescence and totalizing assumptions enables a plurality of visual and conceptual associations, and an ambivalent hybridity of seeing and understanding. The prosthetic visuality of art practice and research challenges the body's normative perceptions by exposing and foregrounding, mnemonically, what is ordinarily hidden in the recesses of imagination and memory. As such, the representation of what is unseen through art research and practice constitutes excess, a multiplicity that supplements the body's extant seeing and understanding. My process of researching and writing the narrative about the event in the hallway in my house functioned in this way. As Derrida claims, the images and ideas came to me only as I wrote in the dark.

I was so blinded by the anomalous FLASH of light that morning that forcing memory to make sense of it, to put into a context that I could understand, only kept me further in the dark, as Elkins (1996) suggests about the paradox of seeing in the second epigraph of this chapter. It was only after I stopped trying to remember and averted my focus to this writing project that the nuances of what I witnessed that day came to mind. Compared with momentary recall, or flashback, the research and writing process ironically took my mind off the event and, in doing so, it brought forth a depth of experience that had long been buried . . .

Contrary to the exteriority of the longitude/latitude world grid, the path of the hallway where I was tying my shoes aligned with the window in the back door functioned as an observatory channeling the intensity of the FLASH onto my body and searing memory. Lacking any knowledge about Cartesian perspective or the metaphysical interiority of camera obscura at such an early age, it was through direct observation that I saw what I saw that morning, a seeing that art historian Jonathan Crary refers to as "subjective vision" (1988, 35). Crary identifies a shift away from previous dominant and universal paradigms of seeing as anomalous scientific investigations into perception increased in the first half of the nineteenth century. An example of such inquiry is poet/philosopher Johann Wolfgang von Goethe's *Theory of Colours*, in which he conceptualizes the body as the ground for visual morphology.

The reflexive scientific preoccupation with vision was so profound back then, according to Crary, that "three of the most celebrated students of vision of this period went blind or permanently damaged their eyesight by repeatedly staring at the sun: David Brewster, who invented the kaleidoscope and stereoscope; Joseph Plateau, who studied the so-called persistence of vision; and Gustav Fechner, one of the founders of modern quantitative psychology" (Crary 1988, 34). Legend has it that a contemporary of these scientists, the painter Joseph Mallard William Turner, was known to have strapped himself to the bow of a ship while at sea during an intense storm so that he could more directly experience and represent its force on his body in his paintings.

As Turner's painting *Shade and Darkness—Evening of the Deluge*, 1843 (Figure 6.6) shows, the regulated symbolic vision of perspectival space and camera obscura have been supplanted by the piercing light of the sun, the blasting force of the wind, and the mystery of darkness, in tension with one another. Unlike symbolic representation, the intensity of light and movement that Turner depicts in this painting, an allusion to Goethe's color

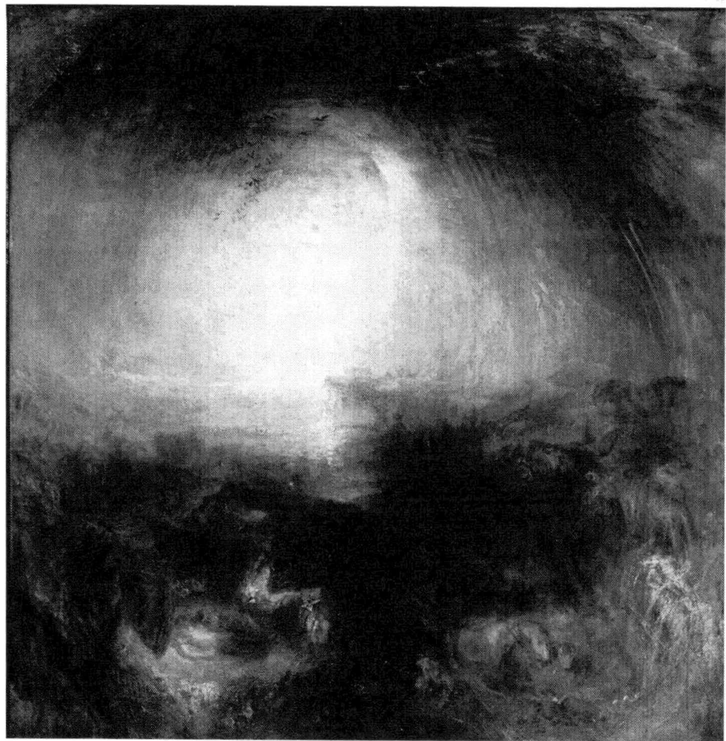

Figure 6.6. Joseph Mallard William Turner, *Shade and Darkness—Evening of the Deluge*, 1843. Oil on canvas. Tate Gallery, London, Great Britain (Courtesy Tate, London/Art Resource, NY).

theory, constitutes the blurring complications of seeing and interpretation witnessed through an empirical, direct observation of an elemental phenomenon. The painting's narrative blur is both seen and unseen. While it consumes the picture plane it also disappears beyond its framing edge. Art historian Nicolas Mirzoeff writes: "Rather than forcing Turner's painting into one experimental classification or another, it might be preferable to see it as a struggle with visuality . . . challenging vision and visuality alike by its refusal of clarity" (Mirzoeff 2006, 62).

Turner's frenzied application of paint on canvas, devoid of symbolism, creates a blurring in the viewer whose gaze is caught in the whirling eye of a painterly storm. Ironically, what may appear confusing in *Evening of the Deluge* clearly represents visual complexity and contradiction; lucid ambiguity and incompleteness that enables a plurality of seeing and interpretation. Mirzoeff suggests that Turner's "refusal to adjudicate" between what is seen and unseen in the painting constitutes "double visuality . . . a tension [slippage] within vision that effectively displaces [the imperialistic gaze of] visuality" (Mirzoeff 2006, 65). He characterizes double visuality: first, as the academic, institutional, and corporate narrative of "commerce, science and industry [whose] formation of a coherent and intelligible picture of modernity . . . culminated in Taylor[ist] and Ford[ist] systems"; and second, "that picturing of the self or collective that exceeds or precedes that incorporation into the commodification of vision by capital and empire" (66).

Hence, the two modes of Mirzoeff's double visuality, like Barker's parabolic elision of concealment *and* revelation, and Derrida's *différance*, are not confined to a dyad or binary system of visuality but "operate in deconstruction, as a relation of difference that is always deferred. . . . In this sense, visual culture would be the product of the collision, intersection and interaction of Visuality 1 and Visuality 2, between capital's picturing of the world and that which cannot be commodified or disciplined" (Mirzoeff 2006, 66). What cannot be commodified represents the excess, the ambiguous and undecideable picturing of Visuality 2, its heterogeneous visuality, which complicates and resists the totalizing spectacle of the world by capital. How, in particular, does the undecideability of Visuality 2 rub against the grain of the totalizing spectacle of Visuality 1? Mirzoeff provides two possibilities: *Inverse visuality* and *veiled visuality*.

> Inverse visuality is any moment of visual experience in which the subjectivity of the viewer is called into question by the density or opacity of what he or she sees. These flickering, excessive, hyperreal, overlaid, pixilated, disjunctive and distracting moments are spectral dust in the eyes of visuality that cause it to blink and become momentarily unsighted. Veiled visuality performs a similar

function by dividing visuality into two by means of the veil that is both visible and invisible at once. (70)

Within the historical context of art practice and research, veiled visuality is evident in the Eduard Manet's Realism, Claude Monet's Impressionism, Paul Cézanne's Postimpressionism, and Pablo Picasso's Cubism. While these artists' empirical research of visual phenomena enabled them to revisit and rethink preexisting systems of visual representation, they did so within the frame of art. In other words, while their works critique previous systems of painting, they are nonetheless framed, or veiled by the canon art. By comparison, inverse visuality reconsiders art from outside of its social and historical context. In doing so, all expectations of art are "momentarily unsighted" as viewers are presented with a conundrum. Marcel Duchamp's readymades, and the disjunctive collage, montage, assemblage, installation art, and performance art narratives of the twentieth century, practices that continue in the twenty-first century, certainly qualify as examples of inverse visuality as they call into the question the retinal preoccupation of historical art. In fact, Duchamp referred to the inverse visuality of his readymades as a "delay"[12] in seeing and understanding, which corresponds with and predates Derrida's *différance*. Regarding the question that conceptual art raises, aesthetician Harold Osborne writes: "When the Impressionists aroused opposition and ridicule nobody doubted that they were painting. It was the way in which they painted that aroused disapproval. . . . Today we are often called upon to decide whether something comes within the category of art at all" (Osborne 1980, 10–11).

Hence, prosthetic visuality emerges at the border, in-between our personal ways of seeing (Visuality 2), and seeing that is socially and historically constructed (Visuality 1). Within this contested space the personal is sutured into a larger, academic, institutionalized, and corporate visuality, and their differences are continually deferred, thus initiating "the rhetorical move that at once destabilizes and reifies the medium [of visuality], opens up communication, slices it, cleaves it (to deconstruction)" (Leverette 2008, 16). Through this suturing and deferral process, prosthetic visuality enables learning that is not solely limited to exposing, examining, and critiquing its scopic regime, but opening "paths of scattering thoughts, angles of linkages, and trajectories of potential alignments," the experimental journeys of art practice that education theorist Elizabeth Ellsworth claims provide "alternative understandings of pedagogy" (2005, 13). Accordingly, prosthetic visuality is constituted in the following ways:

1. Prosthetic visuality is transgressive; a border-crossing trope, its complementary process enables seeing and un-seening, knowing

and un-knowning, understanding and mis-understanding in mutual relationship, and an expansion of one's own perceptual parameters by linking with those of others.

2. Prosthetic visuality is transformative; it enables creative and political agency as its destabilizing/reifying process defers easy interpretations and, in doing so, provides excess, a plurality of ways of seeing and understanding, which resist binary and stereotypical representations.
3. Prosthetic visuality is constituted by art practice and research; its perceptual connectivity enables seeing through the eyes and expressed form and content of others, gaining a deeper appreciation of their social and historical differences, and a deeper understanding of the human condition.
4. The blindspots, aporias, and gaps of prosthetic visuality constitute liminal, anomalous spaces where oppressive perceptions and representations can be exposed, examined, and critiqued, and where a critical, reflexive pedagogy is possible.

Given that I started this chapter with a perceptual wounding, the eye blast that occurred on the Thirty-Sixth Parallel, through the oculus in the back door, and along the hallway where I was sitting on that day, and after having considered the evocative artworks of Caravaggio, Velásquez, Rauschenberg, Irwin, Christo, and others, I would now like to end with yet another artist's parabolic representation of prosthetic visuality. In 2008, artist Janine Antoni was invited to create and install an artwork in the Lower Ninth Ward, one of the areas in the city of New Orleans that was hardest hit by Hurricane Katrina. In response to the devastation and the devastating lack of response to the victims of the storm by the federal government, Antoni wrapped a heavy industrial, steel wrecking ball with lead (Figure 6.7); swung from a crane, the ball was used to demolish an abandoned building in Pittsburgh. [13] During the demolition process, the lead wrapping on the wrecking ball scarred as it ripped through the building's brick and mortar.

Antoni then shipped the damaged ball, with its steel cable attached, to the Prospect.1 exhibition site in the Ninth Ward Village where a temporary gallery was constructed in an abandoned building that had been battered by the hurricane. She installed the wrecking ball, with its shank of steel cable lying on the floor on one end of the gallery while on the opposite wall she projected an eleven-foot video image of her eye (Figure 6.8), which she had recorded in advance by using a video camera attached to a head-restraining

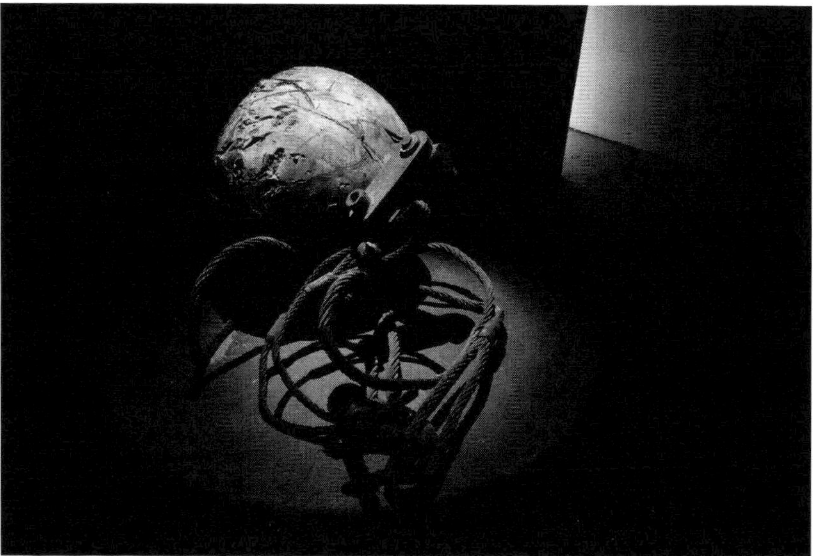

Figure 6.7. Janine Antoni, *TEAR* (detail #1), 2008 (Photo courtesy the artist).

device in order to capture its gaze and its blinking movements. As viewers entered the silent, darkened space of the installation they found themselves in an anomalous space, in-between the stationary wrecking ball on the floor and the video projected motions of her eye. When, at random intervals, the large eye blinked, the loud, violent, demolition sounds of the wrecking ball exploding through brick and mortar projected into the installation space and blasted viewers.

Having titled her installation TEAR, Antoni prefers that its letters are spelled aloud, rather than pronounced, to ensure its double meaning: a *tear* \tir\, alluding to a drop of salty liquid secreted by the eye, and a *tear* \ter\, alluding to the destruction of the wrecking ball. Visual and conceptual dissociations are revealed and concealed as viewers turn from the wrecking ball to the blinking eye, from one image to the other, from one idea to the other, from the visible to the invisible. Obvious associations with the eye and wrecking ball notwithstanding, Antoni's installation destabilizes and reifies their visual and conceptual differences, and through a process of deferral it evokes a plurality of less obvious connections and possible understandings that are seen and unseen: the wrecking of the lead ball, with the reckless, wrecking gaze and surveillance of the eye-ball, with the wrecking spectacle of the media, with the reckless indifference of the federal government, with the calm yet wrecking eye of the hurricane, with the wrecking

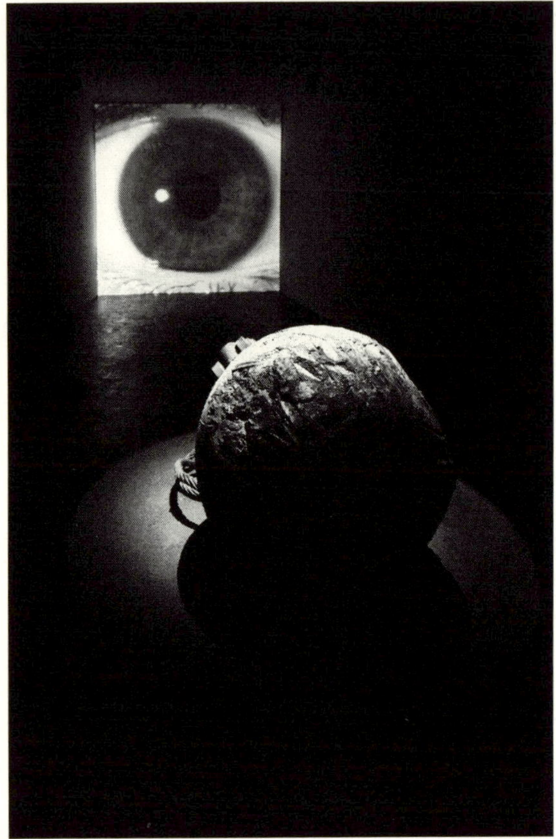

Figure 6.8. Janine Antoni, *TEAR* (detail #2), 2008 (Photo courtesy the artist).

of perception and of the body, with the wrecking of reckless assumptions, clichés, and stereotypes, again and again . . . like the bedazzling light that blasted, lightning-like, through the window in the back door of our house, its allurement of the eye forever affecting my ways of seeing and understanding, the FLASH-es of perceptual plurality that Antoni's *TEAR* affords is the reward for ~~drawing blinds~~, peering into the invisible, into the darkness through the prosthetic visuality of art practice.

SEVEN

ART-IN-THE-FLESH

The Materiality of Sensation and Embodiment

> The body is our general medium for having a world.
>
> —Maurice Merleau-Ponty, *Phenomenology of Perception*

> Things, perception, and thought are in a reciprocal movement into and out of each other and themselves.
>
> —Brian Massumi, *Parables for the Virtual*

> Between the cultural pattern, the body, and the brain, a positive feedback system was created in which each shaped the progress of the other.
>
> —Clifford Geertz, *The Interpretation of Cultures*

There are times in our lives when extraordinary experiences stir our sensate bodies to such an extent that we are jarred out of complacency. To make sense of these strange embodied stirrings, to render them familiar, requires our willingness to extend and expand the parameters of what we already know and understand. On one such an occasion, I witnessed an unusual news report on YouTube that actually affected my breathing and caused some anxiety and slight discomfort throughout my body.

The report, which originated in the April 15, 2009, issue of the Russian newspaper *Komsomolskaya Gazeta* was about a man, Artyoum Sidorki, who was rushed to a hospital emergency room after complaining of extreme pain in his chest, difficulty breathing, and coughing up blood. After ordering X-rays of Sidorki's lungs and finding what appeared to be a tumor, doctors, concerned that it was cancerous, immediately scheduled him for surgery. However, before removing a large portion of his lungs, a biopsy was conducted to investigate the area where the tumor was located. It was then that doctors discovered what was actually causing his infirmity: a 5 cm tree, a fir tree had germinated and was growing in Sidorki's lung, which doctors later deduced was the result of him having unknowingly inhaled a seed, the seed of a fir tree, during the natural course of breathing.

After having seen the images and experienced the news of Sidorki's tree-implanted lung in my own body, I was reminded of an event that took place in a high school art class that I had taught several years earlier. As I recalled, it was around 2 p.m. when Sara passed the plate of oatmeal cookies for her classmates and me to enjoy. Their freshly baked aroma having *whetted* our appetites for a midafternoon snack, each of us grabbed one eagerly and began taking small bites, politely munching, to savor sweet flavor as I asked Sara the whereabouts of her art project. We were in the middle of a critique session where instead of presenting her research and creative work for discussion, she casually offered cookies (Figure 7.1). As Sara calmly listened, and was considering my question about her assignment, the rest of us nibbled, chewed and, while we waited for her response, our salivary glands released their watery contents *wetting*, mixing, and lubricating morsels

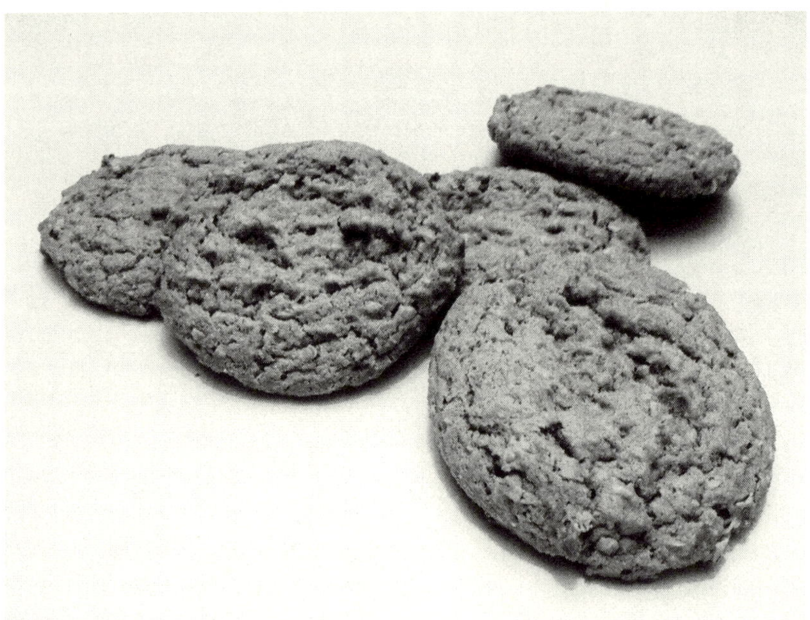

Figure 7.1. Plate of cookies, 2011 (Courtesy Charles Garoian).

of cookie in our mouths, to ease swallowing, and for peristalsis to work the resulting kneaded mass effortlessly down our esophagus into our stomach cavities.

We were in the process of studying the representation of metamorphosis and transformation in art for which I had provided each student with a clean, freshly milled 2" x 4" x 12" length of white pine lumber (Figure 7.2). The assignment was to use up the piece of wood, to alter its rectangular composition and transform its physical appearance. I asked that nothing of the white pine was to be wasted; that its material was to be consumed in its entirety for the solution to the research problem that I had posed.

What preceded the snack that Sara offered on the day of the critique were other students' compelling solutions to the problem. One student brought a white pine tree stump to class into which he had carved an exact 2" x 4" x 12" hole and buried the 2" x 4" x 12" lumber that I had given him, hence representing the paradox of a successful albeit failed attempt at returning the length of wood to its "natural" context. Another student used a chop saw to cut the lumber into small geometric shapes, which she

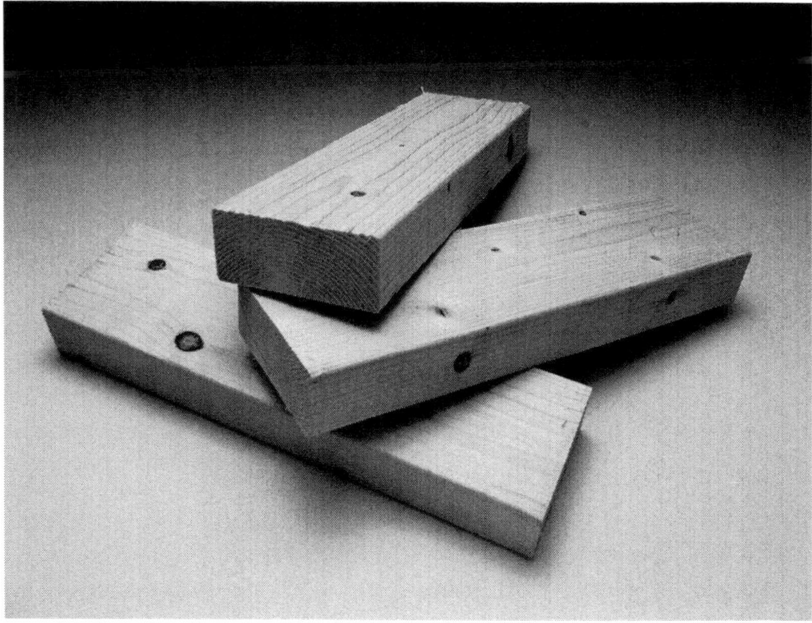

Figure 7.2. 2" x 4" x 12" pine lumber, 2011 (Courtesy Charles Garoian).

had glued together into a miniature representation of a human head that recalled the multivalent perceptual facets of analytic Cubism. It was clear from the several students' various solutions and our discussions that the pieces of white pine had undergone a process of metamorphosis; that while the wooden material still existed in its entirety, a physical and conceptual transformation had been achieved.

The only exception in the class was Sara, whose assignment was nowhere to be seen. Then, as she passed the plate of cookies around the room, she began a dispassionate explanation that initially sounded like an excuse, suggesting the snack as dispensation for having failed to deliver her assignment. Nevertheless, as we willingly munched our delicious pastry, we listened as Sara casually described how she had spent the previous three evenings in the basement of her home operating her father's power sander. Sara explained how she carefully pressed the 2" x 4" x 12" length of white pine lumber against the sander's rotating disk; how its grit milled a fine dust, a powder that emptied into an attached collection bag.

Sara further explained how, after the entire piece of lumber had been sanded down, she mixed the following materials:

1 cup softened butter
1 cup sugar
1 cup brown sugar
2 eggs
1 teaspoon vanilla extract
1 cup all-purpose flour
1 teaspoon baking soda
1 teaspoon salt
2 teaspoons ground cinnamon
3 cups quick cooking oats
1 cup sawdust from a 2" x 4" x 12" length of white pine lumber

Sara continued to describe how she mixed the two kinds of sugar with the softened butter, beat in the two eggs, and stirred in the vanilla extract. She then added the flour, the dust from the 2" x 4" x 12" length of white pine lumber, baking soda, salt, and cinnamon, stirring those ingredients into a velvety mixture. After stirring in the quick cooking oats, she chilled the resulting dough for an hour. Finally, while preheating her mother's oven to 375° F, Sara rolled the dough into small balls, placed them on a greased cookie sheet, baked them for ten minutes, then allowed them to cool on a wire rack.

As we ate and digested the cookies, Sara described the details of how she addressed the metamorphosis assignment. As she spoke, the rest of us started making sense of what was going on. We slowly but surely realized that we had actually ingested the length of white pine lumber that I had given to her. By consuming and absorbing its wooden material into our bloodstreams and the flesh of our bodies, we had unknowingly participated and were physically and conceptually implicated in and complicit with Sara's persuasive representation of metamorphosis. During the critique that ensued a number of students raised questions and expressed concern about the health and safety issues in Sara's solution to the assignment. Experiencing no ill affects from having eaten one of her "wooden cookies," the discussion quickly moved to students' hypotheses about the absorption of culture that occurs through art research and practice as *art-in-the-flesh*.

While in the narrative that you just read, I characterize the research problem that I assigned to my art students as representing "metamorphosis," Sara's ingenious solution, and her classmates' ingestion of her sawdust-laced cookies, raises ontological questions about dichotomous, subject/object representations of the body, and suggest that the exteriority and interiority of the body are inseparable and always already *intertwined* and conterminous. Question: Is it not that what is outside the body actually on the outside, and what is inside the body actually on the inside? While on the surface the answer to this question may seem obvious, at a deeper level it challenges the border-logic of binary representations, those immutable socially and historically constructed assumptions that impede a diversity of creative and intellectual associations and understandings, which are essential in art research and practice. Hence, at a deeper level, was it not that Sara's 2" x 4" x 12" length of white pine lumber was already *enfleshed* with our bodies prior to our having ingested its material in cookie form? For that matter, was it not that we had consumed the cookies prior to actually eating them?

Merleau-Ponty has written extensively about embodiment; how our bodies perceive, understand, and represent their relationship with the external world. The intertwining and enfleshment of the body, its perceptual openness to the world, that eating Sara's cookies evoked, originated with Merleau-Ponty. In characterizing the intertwining of the body's two properties, its interiority and exteriority, as the "chiasm," he writes:

> Our body is a being of two leaves, from one side a thing among things and otherwise what sees them and touches them . . . that it unites these two properties within itself, and its double belongingness to the order of the "object" and to the order of the "subject" reveals to us quite unexpected relations between the two orders. It cannot be by incomprehensible accident that the body has this double reference; it teaches us that each calls for the other. (Merleau-Ponty 1968, 137)

Contrary to rarefied, oppositional understandings and representations of binary logic in which the body is understood and represented as subject *or* object, the subject *and* object of the body are intertwined, one calls for the other, according to Merleau-Ponty. While the former suggests a first-person/third-person ontology of the body as mutually exclusive and absolute, the latter constitutes the body as the nexus in-between its lived subjectivity and as a living being in the world. As such, the *flesh of the body* and the *world perceived as flesh in the body* are bound together in a continuum, simultaneously perceived as the "same flesh" (Merleau-Ponty 1968, 248–50). The body experiences its flesh and the flesh of the world as one. Philosopher Evan Thompson describes this "body-body" nexus as "the relation between one's body as one subjectively lives it and one's body as an organism in the world" (Thompson 2007, 244). Hence, considering that the materiality of our bodies and that of the 2" x 4" x 12" length of white pine lumber were already enfleshed through sensation prior to our ingesting Sara's cookies, we were unknowingly introduced to the hypothetical possibility of Merleau-Ponty's theory through her artwork.

The ingestion of Sara's white pine sawdust cookies, and Merleau-Ponty's concept of enfleshment, recalls philosopher Mortimer J. Adler's analogy about embodiment, where he compares the omnivorous reading, "ownership," and absorption of a book to consuming a beefsteak.

> There are two ways in which one can own a book. The first is the property right you establish by paying for it, just as you pay for clothes and furniture. But this act of purchase is only the prelude to possession. Full ownership comes only when you have made it a part of yourself, and the best way to make yourself a part of it is by writing in it. An illustration may make the point clear. You buy a beefsteak and transfer it from the butcher's icebox to your own. But you do not own the beefsteak in the most important sense until you consume it and get it into your bloodstream. I am arguing that books, too, must be absorbed in your bloodstream to do you any good. (Adler 1940, 1)

Adler describes several devices that readers can use to treat books like beefsteaks, to absorb them into the body's bloodstream: "underlining or highlighting . . . vertical lines at the margin . . . star, asterisk, or other doo-dad . . . numbers in the margin . . . numbers of other pages in the margin . . . circling or highlighting of key words or phrases . . . writing in the margin, or at the top or bottom of the page" (3). These marking devices constitute the biting, chewing, and digestion of text and the book in which it is printed, a process of embodiment that Adler argues enables readers to connect and discourse with authors' writings, to consume and incorporate the text and the book with their lives.

Apropos Adler's concept of embodiment and interconnectivity, Deleuze and Guattari describe a book as a "body without organs," an assemblage of disparate, heterogeneous elements moving across multiple contexts via multiple lines of flight and interconnecting with those of other books, other things, and resisting intellectual closer and sedimentation (Deleuze and Guattari 1987, 4). The correspondences between Sara's sawdust cookies being absorbed into our bloodstreams and passing through our bodies, Adler's analogy of embodied reading, and Deleuze and Guattari's book as body without organs suggest compelling ways to understand and negotiate the idiosyncrasies and complexities of alterity; namely, how bodies interconnect with and incorporate the materiality of art practice, cultural artifacts, and other bodies in the world.

Taking my initial cue from Merleau-Ponty, in this chapter I explore and conceptualize art research and practice with regard to his "double reference" of the body as a binding, the enfleshment of its subject with its object as a continuum. In doing so, I argue that this "double belongingness" constitutes *art-in-the-flesh*, a double-coded figure of speech, a trope that suggests that the existential liveness of art, its ability to arouse and agitate the senses, to evoke and provoke thought, occurs simultaneously in the *flesh of the body* and in the *world perceived as flesh in the body*. Based on their mutuality, Merleau-Ponty compares the body to a work of art in that both are a "nexus of living meanings" (1962, 150–51). Similarly, "the artwork is alive,"[1] asserts performance theorist Adrian Heathfield (2004, 8). This notion that sensate bodies and stirring artworks are interwined and enfleshed through liveness also suggests that they are mutually constructed. In other words, bodies make artworks just as artworks make bodies. Likewise, during her Nobel Lecture in 2009, novelist Herta Müller described the liveness of the art of writing and its mutuality with the body in the following way:

> The more that which is written takes from me the more it shows what was missing from the experience that was lived. Only the words make this discovery, because they didn't know it earlier. And where they catch the lived experience by surprise is where they reflect it best. *In the end they become so compelling that the lived experience must cling to them in order not to fall apart.* (Müller 2009, online; emphasis added)[2]

The exteriority of the body as object, a "thing among things" intertwined with the interiority of the body as subject, "what sees them [things] and touches them," corresponds with philosopher Brian Massumi's conception of a coextensive and cooperative relationship between the body and prosthesis. "The thing, the object, can be considered *prosthesis* of the body—provided that it is remembered that the body is equally a prosthesis of the thing" (Massumi 2002, 95). Consequently, exteriority is the prosthesis that extends interiority extends exteriority, and again. In other words, one augments the other in reciprocity. Given that neither Massumi nor Merleau-Ponty specifies what a "thing" represents, in this writing I assume that all things including materials, objects, artworks, and bodies are extensions of each other, and that body/art enfleshment, or *art-in-the-flesh*, represents *prosthetic* embodiment. To be specific, my use of the prosthesis trope is based on its etymological origins in classical Greece as a literary device that supplements and *ex-tends* language. Similarly, philosopher Gaston Bachelard claims that "poetic space, because it is expressed, assumes values of expansion. It belongs to the phenomenology of those words that begin with 'ex' "; hence, *ex-pression* as the prosthetic ex-tension and ex-pansion of embodied language (Bachelard 1969, 201). Thus, I will argue that the prosthetic enfleshment of the subject with the object of the body is made apparent through art research and practice. As the materiality of the body engages the corporeality of materials, tools, and objects through art making, manifold sensations, associations, and understandings extend one to another prosthetically. In other words, the sensate embodiment of art precedes and enables understanding embodiment *across* bodies, disciplines, and cultures.

Massumi's conception of the body as prosthesis corresponds with critical theorist N. Katherine Hayles's posthuman characterization of the body "as the original prosthesis we all learn to manipulate, so that extending or replacing the body with other prostheses becomes a continuation of a process that began before we were born" (Hayles 1999, 3). Accordingly, prosthesis is a perceptual predisposition that the body learns to use as it engages the corporeality of the world. "The body" in this sense is always already an object, a tool, and cultural artifact; an ontological medium that we use to extend into the materiality of the world.[3] Related to Hayles's prosthetic characterization of the body, Massumi argues against metaphysical, oppositional dualities that compartmentalize complex and contradictory experiences and understandings of embodiment. Instead, he claims that a true duality is constituted by a "processual rhythm" of embrace where subject and object (body and prosthesis) come together as they move in and across contexts through a process of "continuity and discontinuity" (Massumi 2002, 217). Such coming together, and moving in and across contexts, constitutes a process of reciprocal encroachment that hurls the subject out of phase with the object and, by continually blurring their boundaries, enables manifold sensory experiences of the body that, in turn, enable a multiplicity of possibilities for imagining, interpretation, and understanding.

Massumi further characterizes the coexistence and coalescence of these opposing forces as "the virtual," a "lived paradox" that is felt in the body "immediately abstract as it is concrete; its activity and expressivity extend, as on their underside, into an incorporeal, yet perfectly real, dimension of pressing potential" (Massumi 2002, 30–31). He warns against simply equating the "virtual" in the sensate body with the virtual in digital technology, which "confuses the really apparitional [imaginings of the body] with the [systemization and simulation of the] artificial" (137).

The virtual, lived paradox of continuity and discontinuity to which Massumi refers corresponds with Deleuze's conception of "the event," a happening where the body's knowledge from the past (corporeality) and what is yet unknown in the future (incorporeality), conjoin in a disjunctive relationship, thus constituting time in the present out of joint. According to Deleuze, "In its impassibility and inpenetrability, [the event] has no present. It rather retreats and advances in two directions at once, being the perpetual object of a double question: What is going to happen? What has just happened?" (Deleuze 1990, 63). This unhinging of time in the present, "freed from the events which made up its content [from the past], its relation to [continuous] movement overturned" (Deleuze 1994, 88) disrupts time that has been previously established and measured, leaving it an empty form within which the unity of the subject is never complete but in continual state of becoming other. In characterizing this temporal paradox of the event, Deleuze juxtaposes historically embodied experiences (Chronos) with those that are yet to be embodied from the future (Aion). "Whereas Chronos expressed the action of bodies and the creation of corporeal qualities, Aion is the locus of incorporeal events and of attributes which are distinct from qualities. . . . Whereas Chronos was limited and infinite, Aion is unlimited, the way that future and past are unlimited, and finite like the instant" (Deleuze 1990, 165). Hence, the paradoxical, processual rhythm of corporeality and incorporeality of the event constitutes a temporal disequilibrium, a crisis in time that arouses and agitates an existential liveness in the body, a generative condition of time that allows for the unexpected, the unknown, and an indeterminate potential that presses the future to emerge.

In describing the phase cycle of continuity and discontinuity that constitutes the virtual potentialities of the body, Massumi cites the processual rhythm of its bipedal locomotion through walking (Figure 7.3):

> It is a contemporary proverb that walking is controlled falling. Continuity embraces discontinuity as walking includes falling. The momentum of walking is the excess of its activity over each successive step. The ongoing quality of walking is that trans-step momentum. Each next step is momentous, in its own little way:

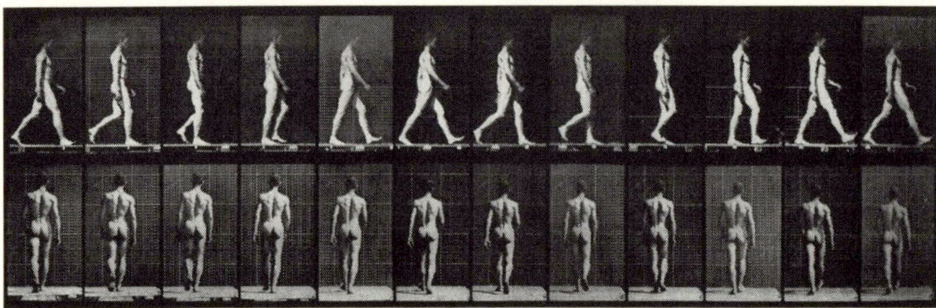

Figure 7.3. Eadweard Muybridge, *Walking man at ordinary speed*, ca. 1883–86 (Courtesy University of Pennsylvania Archives).

> it is the event of a caught fall. The catch renews the walking's functional context. The rhythm of falling and catching organizes an indefinite series of varying contexts for the walking event's continuation. (Massumi 2002, 217–18)

As the continuity of walking includes the discontinuity of falling, the subject-body embraces the object-body prosthetically in a reciprocal relationship. Like the controlled fall of walking, the exploratory, experimental, and improvisational movements of art practice are similarly constituted as continuity embraces discontinuity, a processual rhythm of engagements that are out of phase with disengagements, conjunctions out of phase with disjunctions, where the body's control of materials includes a relinquishment of control to those very materials.[4] The former, the control of materials, is constituted by the body's collection of previously experienced affects, movements, and habits. As control is relinquished, the materiality of the body and those of art practice coexist, coalesce, and connect, thus enabling an excess[5] of potentially unknown and indeterminate affects, movements, and habits to occur. Hence, the wonderment of the imagination that is inspired by the meandering and wanderlust of art research and practice finds its parallel in the "unstructured, associative thinking" that occurs during walking, "which suggests walking as not an analytical but an [exploratory, experimental, and] improvisational act" (Solnit 2001, 21).

Massumi's walking proverb evokes Dewey's characterization of the temporary equilibrium between the live creature and its environment:

> Life itself consists of phases in which the organism falls out of step with the march of surrounding things and then recovers unison with it—either through effort or by some happy chance. And, in

> a growing life, *the recovery is never mere return to a prior state, for it is enriched by the state of disparity and resistance through which it has successfully passed.* . . . Life grows when a temporary falling out is a transition to a more extensive balance of the energies of the organism with those of the conditions under which it lives. (Dewey 1934, 14; emphasis added)

What Dewey describes as falling out of phase in life corresponds with the precarious, yet generative characteristics of prosthetic embodiment in art research and practice where slippages between existing knowledge and life's uncertain, indeterminate experiences open virtual spaces where recoveries and transitions toward more extensive and expansive imaginings and understandings can occur.[6]

Massumi's and Dewey's notions correspond with those of Deleuze and Guattari, who associate controlling experiences with the "actual body" and control that is relinquished with the "virtual body." Referring to the latter, the virtual body as a "body without organs," Deleuze and Guattari describe its opening to extensive possibilities; "to connections that presuppose an entire assemblage, circuits, conjunctions, levels and thresholds, passages and distributions of intensity, and territories and deterritorializations" (1987, 160). Like Merleau-Ponty's double referencing, the body without organs suggests a liminal, in-between space of corporeality where indeterminate affects, movements, and habits occur through manifold conjunctions between the inside of the body and those of cultural bodies outside. Accordingly, the exploratory, experimental, and improvisational processes of art practice represent performances of subjectivity that enable the making oneself a body without organs, a processual rhythm of becoming that is activated by virtual, unforeseen, manifold potentialities.

The actualization of potentialities occurs through conjunctions of the sensate body's interiority and its exteriority, as it intertwines with the potentialities of other bodies as *art-in-the-flesh.* Massumi characterizes this interconnectedness as a network ostensibly separated by the membrane of the skin. Unlike Euclidian three-dimensional understandings of skin as an enveloping membrane, the body also exists in the fourth dimension as its porous, open membrane of skin and other orifices enable a branching and diffusion between its interior and exterior. Understood as a permeable membrane, the body is not closed according to Massumi: "It folds in at the mouth, ears, nostrils, eyes, anus, urethra, vagina, and pores. This is one leaky 'box' . . . [which suggests that] we live between dimensions" (2002, 202–203). Such profuse permeability suggests the body's perceptual opening is all encompassing and coextensive prosthetically with other bodies, the environment, and the world.

Lyotard conceptualizes *art-in-the-flesh* as the body's libidinal economy in similar ways as Massumi. Lyotard questions the necessity for transgression considering that the libidinal body is always already borderless; that the immensity of its "great ephemeral skin," unlike a frame, is compelled by desire, the libidinal drive to interconnect with the other, with the world. To elicit such openness, Lyotard argues for incompossible intensities of expression, the creation of tension in-between disjunctive images and ideas that enable manifold associations, interpretations, and understandings to occur. As such, the libidinal body

> is made from the most heterogeneous textures, bone, epithelium, sheets to write on, charged atmospheres, swords, glass cases, peoples, grasses, canvases to paint. All these zones are joined end to end in a band which has no back to it, a Moebius band which interests us not because it is closed, but because it is one-sided, a Moebius skin which, rather than being smooth, is on the contrary . . . covered with roughness, corners, creases, cavities, which when it passes on the "first" turn will be cavities, but perhaps on the "second," lumps. But as for what turn the band is on, no-one knows nor will know, in the eternal turn. The *interminable* band with variable geometry (for nothing requires that an excavation remain concave, besides, it is inevitably convex on the "second" turn, provided it lasts) has not got two sides, but only one, and therefore neither exterior or interior. (Lyotard 2004, 2–3; emphasis added)

The incompossibility in Lyotard's narrative is constituted by corporeal incompatibilities inside and outside the body. The heterogeneous textures that he identifies may not belong together according to conventional thought, yet when Lyotard initiates an embrace between bone and epithelium, and swords and glass cases, interstitial spaces open, corners, creases, cavities, and lumps where the continuities of body's inside intertwine with the discontinuities of its outside. The interminable composition of Lyotard's Moebius skin is evident in how the continuities of academic, institutional, and corporate knowledge embrace the discontinuities of art practice and art education. Given these corporeal incompatibilities, an excess of potentially unknown and indeterminate affects, movements, and habits are made possible through art making.

In her collage work on paper, *President: #4* (Figure 7.4), artist Sherrie Levine has created an experience of visual tension between the outside of a Lincoln penny profile and its inside, which contains an image of a fashion model gazing out at viewers. As viewers' attention shifts through a processual rhythm of continuity and discontinuity, to-and-fro from one context

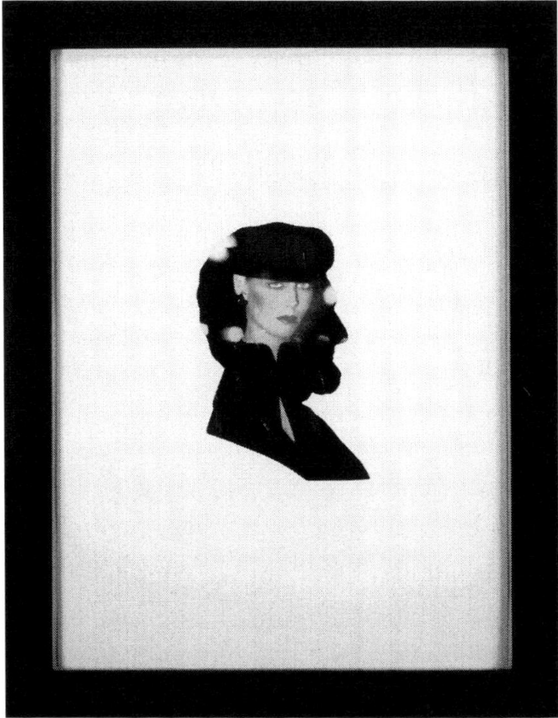

Figure 7.4. Sherrie Levine, *President: #4*, 1979, ©Sherrie Levine (Courtesy Paula Cooper Gallery, New York).

to the other, from Lincoln penny profile to the fashion model, diffusion occurs, as each image is perceived through the other and both as themselves as Massumi suggests in the epigraph at the beginning of this chapter. In other words, the separation of inside and outside, of subject and object, are brought into question and implicated in each other prosthetically. This contextual shift is then intensified as viewers return the brazen, arresting gaze of the fashion model thus implicating them in the same act. While shifts of attention between the Lincoln penny and the fashion model suggest the exchange economy of seduction and desire that constitutes commodity fetishism, Levine's collage corresponds with and supports Merleau-Ponty's double belongingness of enfleshment and the Moebius skin of Lyotard's libidinal body. That is, the exteriority and interiority of her two images are rendered inseparable by way of their interconnectedness with each other and with viewer's bodies.

Such embodiment is analogous to artist Marcel Duchamp's concept of an "aesthetic echo," the emotional abandon and receptivity that is similar to religious belief or being in love. Duchamp argues that compared with aesthetic taste, which "presupposes a domineering onlooker who dictates what he [*sic*] likes and dislikes, and translates it into 'beautiful' and 'ugly' [binary] . . . the 'victim of an 'aesthetic echo' is in a position comparable to a man [or woman] in love or a believer who dismisses automatically his demanding ego and helplessly submits to a pleasurable and mysterious constraint" (SFAI, online; Tompkins, 368–69). While Duchamp's use of "victim" and "submission to constraint" is problematic, what he is suggesting corresponds with Massumi's processual rhythm of engagements, and the continuities and discontinuities of the body's abandon and receptivity of tools, materials, and techniques during art practice.

Like Duchamp's aesthetic echo, the push and pull of seduction and desire in Levine's collage is further eroticized in *Crash*, the controversial novel by J. G. Ballard in which the author explores the interpenetration of the body's exteriority and interiority with technology as his guiding metaphor. Conceptual shift is evident in the continuities and discontinuities of Ballard's narrative structure, which critical theorist Jonathan Crary refers to as "delirious description" and a "promiscuity of forms" (Crary 1986, 162, 165). Ballard's syntactical formations of technology and the body in *Crash* suggest a collision and diffusion of machine and meat. In describing the protagonist's attempt at purging his erotic obsession with automobile wreckage and wounded bodies, Ballard writes:

> Vaughan devised a terrifying almanac of imaginary automobile disasters and insane wounds—the lungs of elderly men punctured by door handles, the chests of young women impaled by steering-columns, the cheeks of handsome youths pierced by the chromium latches of quarter-lights. For him [Vaughan] these wounds were the keys to a new sexuality born from a perverse technology. The images of these wounds hung in the gallery of his mind like exhibits in the museum of a slaughterhouse. (Ballard 1973, 13)

As in the ambiguities and incompleteness of art experience, the contextual shifts in Ballard's narrative blur the boundaries of Euclidian space to such an extent that the incompatibilities of body and environment, body and technology interpenetrate through wounds and orifices. This becoming one flesh is further exemplified by the protagonist's observation of his wounded body after being rescued from an automobile disaster: "As I looked down at myself I realized that the precise make and model-year of my [wrecked] car could have been reconstructed by an automobile engineer from the pattern of my wounds" (Ballard 1973, 28). Crary further claims that such "innumerable modes of conjunction" in *Crash* provide an unrestricted openness and excess "capacity of a subject to conjoin with any object or surface" (Crary 1986, 162). Pertaining to *art-in-the-flesh*, the premise of this chapter, incompatibilities in Ballard's writing, like Merleau-Ponty's enfleshment and Lyotard's libidinal economy, correspond with the processual rhythm of disjunction and conjunction of bodies, tools, materials, and objects during art research and practice. As disjunction and conjunction yield one to the other, prosthetic protractions and adjunctions yield unfettered affects, movements, and habits as a "constellation of epiphanies" (Crary 1986, 165). Hence, the prosthetic embodiment of art practice occurs at the chiasm, the intersection where the materiality of the sensate body of the artist and the corporeal materiality of clay, paint, stone, ink, paper, canvas diverge yet encroach upon each other, where each is seen through the other, and are mutually constituted in manifold ways.

The out-of-phase processual rhythm of the body's materiality with the corporeality of art materials, tools, and objects, evokes Heidegger's characterizations of the body's association with technology: *present-at-hand* and *ready-to-hand* (Heidegger 1962, 54–55). A tool is present-at-hand, that is, foregrounded, when its familiar function or use value has been disrupted, of which Heidegger cites a broken hammer as an example. The hammer's breakage creates a shift in context, from a familiar to an unfamiliar one, which enables a re-conceptualization and re-presentation of its use value. In marked contrast, a tool is ready-to-hand when its function is familiar, assumed, and taken for granted. In other words, there is no question about a hammer's purpose during its routine use as a hammer. Nevertheless, Heidegger's two conceptions of tool use are reciprocally implicated, one in the other, as the continuity of its familiar condition embraces the discontinuity of its unfamiliar condition. Related to art practice, this out-of-phase processual rhythm of handedness between the body's familiar and unfamiliar affects, movements, and habits constitutes prosthetic embodiment, which enables exploration, experimentation, and improvisation with materials, tools, and objects.

In his one-minute sculpture *Untitled (from the series "One-minute sculptures")*, 1997 (Figure 7.5), Austrian artist Erwin Wurm stuffed every orifice in the head of his collaborator with office supplies: 35 mm plastic film canisters fitted into his eye orbits, long thin grease penciles poked into his ears, thick felt tip markers stuck into his nostrils, and a stapler jammed into his mouth. Are the office supplies thrusting into the man's body or thrusting outward? Is he seeing with or without the film canisters; listening with or without the long grease pencils; breathing in or breathing out the thick felt markers; and, eating or vomiting the stapler? Is the body's outside, outside

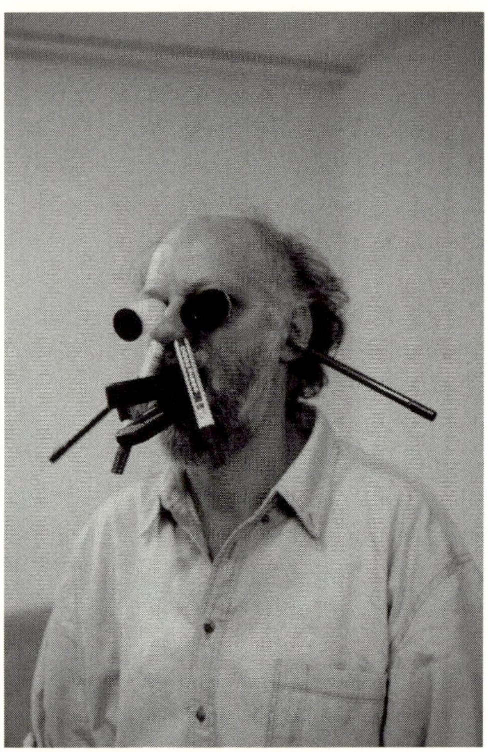

Figure 7.5. Erwin Wurm, *Untitled (from the series "One-minute sculptures")*, 1997. Musée National d'Art Moderne, Centre Georges Pompidou, Paris, © 2012 Artists Rights Society (ARS), New York/VBK, Vienna.

and its inside, inside, or is the body outside in and inside out at the same time? Wurm has complicated the ready-to-hand function of these stationery implements and the man's body through the use of parody. His disjointed performance of embodiment, like Heidegger's broken hammer, shifts the implements' familiar use value to an unfamiliar one. By foregrounding them present-at-hand in this way, contextual movements occur that enable the re-absorption and re-imagination of the implements' and the man's body. In conceptualizing the mutual absorption of body and world as "biodirectional incorporation," Leder writes:

> Ordinarily, many of us are relatively oblivious to our surroundings. Yet there are times when we awaken and the world rushes in, fraught with beauty or significance. At such times, we truly become

> absorbed in our world. That such absorption is a deeply embodied process is suggested by the word itself. It derives from the Latin root *sorbere* meaning to "suck in" or "swallow." When we become deeply absorbed, as in a natural landscape, it is as if we were swallowed into a larger body. At the same time, this landscape is swallowed into our embodiment, transforming it from within. (Leder 1990, 164–65)

Related to enfleshment, the body without organs, body as prosthesis, and the libidinal body, the theories of embodiment that were previously cited, the processual rhythm of continuity and discontinuity in Wurm's *Untitled* one-minute sculpture exposes the presumed boundaries that separate subject and object for examination and critique, thus enabling a mutual "swallowing" and "digestion" of the body's exteriority with its interiority. Hence, as the man's body and the office supplies absorb, one through the other, they incorporate biodirectionally. In doing so, dualistic understandings of embodiment diffuse into and intertwine with multiple imaginings and insights through the incompatibilities in Wurm's art research and practice.

The multivalent, prosthetic imaginings, interpretations, and understandings that I have theorized in this chapter as *art-in-the-flesh*, correspond with Bachelard's concept of "intimate immensity," which occurs in poetic space. While, on the one hand, his juxtaposition of "intimate" with "immensity" constitutes an oxymoron, on the other hand, it suggests an enfolding, interdependent relationship between the body's interiority and exteriority. "Poets," Bachelard writes, "help us to discover within our selves such joy in looking that sometimes, in the presence of a perfectly familiar object, we experience an extension [and expansion] of our intimate space" (Bachelard 1969, 199). This generative, prosthetic characteristic of intimate space, which is unfettered through poetic imagination, constitutes *immensity*, similar to Crary's constellation of epiphanies, as "the two kinds of space—the space of intimacy [interiority] and world space [exteriority]—blend . . . [and] keep encouraging each other . . . in their growth" (Crary 1986, 201, 203).

Like Merleau-Ponty's intertwining of the *flesh of the body* and the *world perceived as flesh in the body* discussed earlier in this chapter, Bachelard's blending of the body's intimate space with the space of the world corresponds in compelling ways with the generative imaginings and interpretations that occurred within the poetic space of Sara's delicious sawdust cookies. After her classmates and I overcame the surprise of having ingested and digested the 2" x 4" x 12" piece of pine lumber into our bodies, ex-tensive conversations and ex-pansive understandings ensued about *art-in-the-flesh* where the intimate, inside space of the body and the world of immensity outside of the body intertwine within the poetic space of art research and practice.

EIGHT

ART RESEARCH AND PRACTICE AS DELEUZOGUATTARIAN EMBODIMENT

(In collaboration with Joseph Julian Jr., MD)

> The genuinely utopian moments are not when you are doing okay . . . but when you are in a deadlock. Then, in order even to survive normally, you are forced to invent something.
>
> —Slavoj Žižek, Interview, 2009

> Don't be one or multiple, be multiplicities!
>
> —Deleuze and Guattari, *A Thousand Plateaus*

> The word/experience of *disabled*/disabled gains extension.
> It intrudes and extrudes, shivers over other words.
>
> —Petra Kuppers, "Toward a Rhizomatic Model of Disability"

INTRODUCTION

Throughout the chapters in this book, I have explored and examined *prosthesis*, the slippages and adjunctive characteristics of the trope, as it applies to creative and intellectual performance in the visual arts. I have focused my writing on the prosthetic pedagogy and epistemology of art research and practice, namely, its enabling of eccentric and ecstatic ways of making and knowing, and its resistance to synthetic closures, totalizing representations, and assumptions that constitute the body as enabled or disabled, normal or abnormal. To avoid confining the concept of prosthesis to a binary stricture,

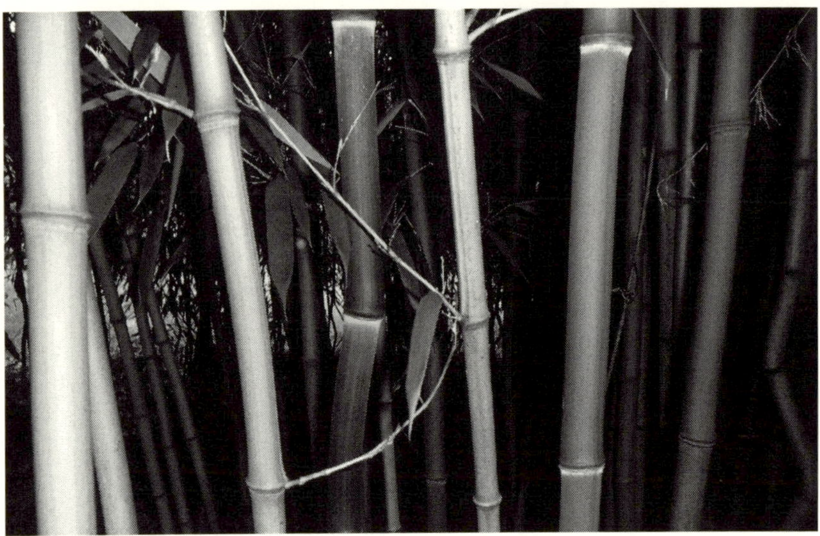

Figure 8.1. Bamboo patch, 2011 (Courtesy Charles Garoian).

between its originary, etymological function as a linguistic supplement and its subsequent reconstitution as a compensatory metaphor signifying lack and replacement in the body, I have assumed that all bodies are always already physically dislocated and fragmented based on the liminal, contingent, and ephemeral circumstances of living and learning in the world.

Contrary to the dynamic, oppositional tension between thesis and antithesis, I have argued that the ambiguities and incompleteness of art research and practice, in resisting synthesis and totalization, enable an escape from dialectics toward extensive and expansive ways of experiencing and understanding alterity and otherness. In doing so, the research and practice of art as prosthesis corresponds with what Deleuze and Guattari (1987, 32–33) characterize as *multiplicities*, *assemblages*, *rhizomes*, and *bodies without organs*. In what follows I will conceptualize the creative and political agency that is enabled through the prosthetic pedagogy of art in terms of Deleuzoguattarian embodiment. I will invoke the writings of these two philosophers as well as those of disability scholars who, in theorizing the body, have challenged the institutionalization and exclusivity of disability politics by arguing for an inclusive politics based on *impairment*, which advocates for the creative agency of all bodies regardless of their differences. Furthermore, I will discuss the creative research and practice of artist Chuck Close and artist/scholar Petra Kuppers whose respective modes of addressing disability and impairment correspond with the rhizomatic assemblage of Deleuzoguattarian embodiment. I will then end the chapter with excerpts of an interview with Joseph Julian Jr., MD (1986), whose creative teaching and rehabilitation accomplishments serve as an example of the rhizomatic assemblage of Deleuzoguattarian pedagogy. As a young neurologist, Dr. Julian spent one and a half years (1981–82) building and administering a comprehensive rehabilitation program for disabled Cambodian refugees at Khao I Dang, the largest of the Cambodian refugee camps on the Thai-Cambodian border.

So, the question is not whether bodies are lacking, but whether they are capable of living fully integrated and productive lives because of their differences and peculiarities. As I have indicated in the previous chapters, my concern has been that positioning art practice solely within a compensatory framework risks underestimating and undervaluing the creative and political agency of all bodies regardless of their differences. My purpose in conceptualizing prosthesis in this way is not to suggest cultural relativism that simply diminishes and homogenizes difference, or cultural pragmatism that isolates, stereotypes, and maligns difference, but a contingent, *critical pragmatism*, which according to curriculum theorist Cleo H. Cherryholmes "is realistic because it begins with what is in place . . . and relativistic because it is relative to what is in place" (Cherryholmes 1988, 185–86). Cherryholmes's conception of critical pragmatism constitutes a differential space that is both realistic and relative; where disjunctive bodies coexist in contiguity and through their interactivity, interconnectivity, and interdependence challenge and resist socially and historically constructed assumptions, representations, and sedimentations that "shatter the integrity of the individual body, the social body, the corpus of human needs, and the corpus of knowledge" (Lefebvre 1991, 52). Hence, a contingent, critical pragmatism of impairment is realistic because it advocates for the removal of social barriers, as well as medical, art, and all other therapies that pathologies of the body require; and, relativistic because it advocates an interdependent understanding of all bodies within differential space.

Concern for the individual and social body's integrity has been at the core of recent criticisms that have been leveled at the Social Model of the British disability movement, which was organized and institutionalized in the 1970s. According to disability scholars Tom Shakespeare and Nicholas Watson, the impact of the British model was twofold. First, "rather than pursuing a strategy of medical cure, or rehabilitation" (Shakespeare and Watson 2001, 11), it exposed disabling social barriers and politicized disablement as a strategy for social change. Second, it replaced the medical view of the body's disability with social oppression so that "people were able to understand that they weren't at fault: society was" (11). Shakespeare and Watson argue that while the radical rhetoric of the movement was highly effective in politicizing disability, evaluating and conforming all bodies to its ideology constituted a "denial of difference" (14); in other words, "Disability cannot be reduced to a singular identity: it is a multiplicity, a plurality" (19).

In critiquing the metanarrative and exclusivity of the Social Model, Shakespeare and Watson contend that its social politics constitutes a binary that overarches, brackets, and levels all dimensions of disability and in doing so overlooks *impairment* as the causal role of individual bodies. In their advocacy for a broader and more inclusive conception of disability, they point to the differences and peculiarities of impairment, which includes all bodies due to their imperfections, inconsistencies, and morbidities. They maintain, "An embodied ontology would argue . . . that there is *no qualitative difference between disabled people and non-disabled people, because we are all impaired.* Impairment is not the core component of disability (as the medical model might suggest), it is the inherent nature of humanity" (Shakespeare and Watson 2001, 24; emphasis added).[1] This differential ontology of impairment, which corresponds with my previous assertions that all bodies are dislocated and fragmented, destratifies, complicates, and enables re-imagining reductionist binaries (abled/disabled and normal/abnormal) that constitute the body as an organism, as an organizational totality; and that essentialize and brand bodies as lacking.

DELEUZOGUATTARIAN EMBODIMENT

By invoking the word *impairment*, Shakespeare and Watson create a discursive anomaly by way of parody, a semantic play that destratifies socially and historically constructed, rarified representations of disability.[2] As parody, their use of the word resonates with Deleuzoguattarian *schizo-analysis*: a process by which preexisting, reductionist assumptions, representations, and systems of analysis are deterritorialized and reterritorialized within rhizomatic structures, assemblage, and *bodies without organs* (BwO); anomalous structures from which heretofore unknown, unforeseen multiplicities of knowing and understanding difference can emerge (Deleuze and Guattari 1987, 18). Deleuze and Guattari's use of the term is not a denial of the seriousness of schizophrenia, but that the deterritorialization and reterriorialization of its complex, uninhibited flow of desire within a discursive assemblage, the rhizome, problematizes and destratifies representations of this and other impairments. As Deleuze scholar Lorna Collins argues: "Schizo-analysis is concerned with founding a new way of thinking desire, which engages with the body and can create a 'place of healing' and restorative sense not only for the schizophrenic but for all of us" (Collins 2010, 243). In the following schizo-analysis, Deleuze and Guattari differentiate between the complexities of *anomaly* and the specificities of *abnormality*.

> It has been noted that the origin of the word *anomal* ("anomalous"), an adjective that has fallen into disuse in French, is very different from that of *anormal* ("abnormal"): *a-normal*, a Latin adjective lacking a noun in French, refers to that which is outside rules or goes against the rules, whereas *an-omalie*, a Greek noun that has lost its adjective, designates the unequal, the coarse, the rough, the cutting edge or deterritorialization. The abnormal can be defined only in terms of characteristics, specific or generic; but the anomalous is a position or set of positions in relation to a multiplicity. (Deleuze and Guattari 1987, 243–44)

Contrary to arborescent, taproot structures such as those of trees (Figure 8.2), which Deleuze and Guattari attribute to the dialectical movement of centralized, hierarchical systems, the nondialectical connectivity of a rhizome (Figures 8.1 and 8.3) consists of a reticulated system of manifold, transversal trajectories, anomalous lines of flight that diverge and converge as assemblage . . . diverge and converge as assemblage . . . and . . . and . . . and . . .

> A rhizome has no beginning or end; it is always in the middle, between things, interbeing, *intermezzo*. The tree is a filiation, but the rhizome is alliance, uniquely alliance. The tree imposes the

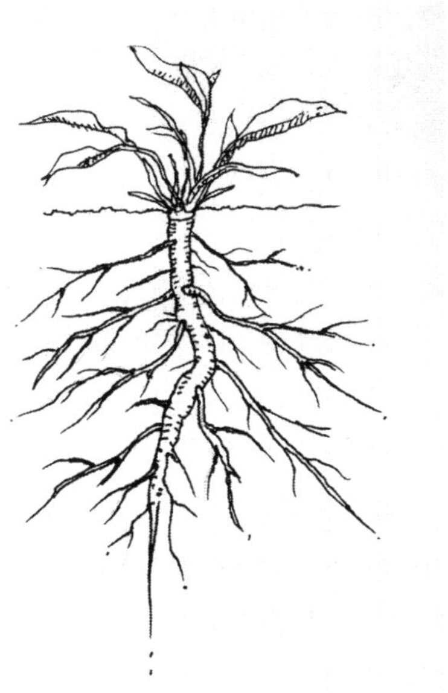

Figure 8.2. Taproot system, 2011 (Courtesy Charles Garoian).

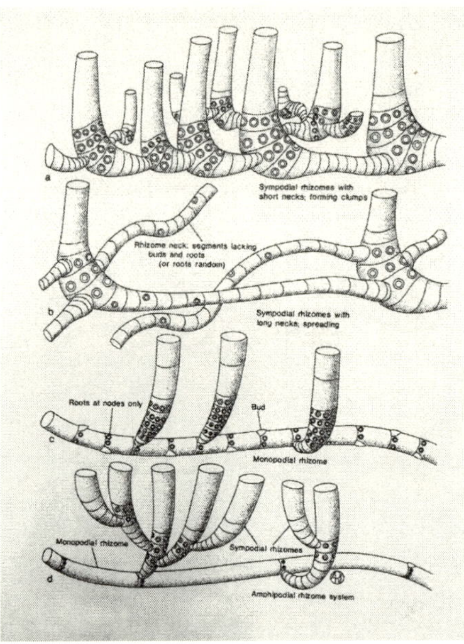

Figure 8.3. Rhizome root system (Courtesy The Missouri Botanical Garden, Annals 1983).

> verb "to be," but the fabric of the rhizome is the conjunction, "and . . . and . . . and . . ." This conjunction carries enough force to shake and uproot the verb "to be." (Deleuze and Guattari 1987, 25)

As rhizomatic lines of flight deterritorialize, converge, and reterritorialize, their constellations constitute multiplicities, indefinite assemblages that resist over coding and concrescence. Given its "principle of asignifying rupture . . . a rhizome may be broken, shattered at a given spot, but it will start up again on one of its old lines [of flight], or on new lines" (Deleauze and Guattari 1987, 9). As the discrete, disjunctive, and unattributable organs of assemblage approach organizational synthesis, the BwO[3] dismantles its organizational strata making totalization and wholeness impossible. The BwO is "nonstratified, unformed, intense matter, the matrix of intensity, intensity = 0, but there is nothing negative about that zero, there are no [binaries] negative or opposite intensities" (153). In other words, the nonstratifed, zero ontology of the BwO is "opposed to the organism, the organic organization of the organs" (158). It is at the zero, unformed, unassuming, and unconditional—the n-dimension of Deleuzoguattarian research and practice, that the creative and political agency of all bodies is possible regardless of difference because through the persistent conjunctive, "and . . . and . . . and . . ." logic of the rhizome, ontology is overthrown, foundations done away with, and endings and beginnings are nullified (25). Thus, as subjects in process, nonstratified bodies exist in a boundless state of becoming at the zero degree; where impairments and other assumed failings and limitations of the body are perceived as opportunities for ceaseless exploration, experimentation, and improvisation.

This n-dimension of the rhizome, assemblage, and the BwO is interstitial; it constitutes an in-between, liminal and contingent space of agency: (1) where explorations, experimentations, and improvisations through art research and practice reach their emergent potential; (2) where fragments, convergences, and slippages of social and historical meanings and understandings constitute a prosthetic pedagogy of art; (3) where students' playful, improvisational learning processes, complimented by teachers' playful, improvisational pedagogies, resist and nullify normative formulations; and (4) where the lived experience of impairment nullifies totalizing assumptions about ability/disability and normality/abnormality to such a degree that all differential bodies have potential in becoming-limitless as creative agents.

Hence, these characteristic movements within Deleuzoguattarian n-dimension constitute "becoming-intense," a concept of incorporeal embodiment that enables getting "outside dualisms . . . to be-between, to pass between, the intermezzo . . . never ceasing to become" (Deleuze and Guattari 1987, 277). In that sense, becoming-intense is becoming-limitless. For example, rather than assuming that the body is compromised by the morbidities of aging, Deleuze and Guattari describe the becoming-intense of aging in the following way: "Knowing how to age does not mean remaining young; it means extracting from one's age the particles, the speeds and slownesses, the flows that constitute the youth of that age" (277). Thus, becoming-intense within the n-dimension suggests that all bodies are capable of creative and political agency as they extract their differing and particular movements. In doing so, the focus is always on the limitless potentialities of the body: what it can do rather than what it cannot do.

CHUCK CLOSE BECOMING-INTENSE

Leonardo da Vinci, Michelangelo Buonarroti, Francisco de Goya, Honoré Daumier, Claude Monet, Edgar Degas, Vincent Van Gogh, Frida Kahlo, Robert Rauschenberg, Mark di Suvero, Chuck Close are but a few artists who extracted movements of creative production from their impaired bodies and, in doing so, their work challenges cultural assumptions that stereotype, marginalize, and ostracize impairment. Tenaciously, they refused to conflate the stereotypes of disability and impairment with what they wanted to say, do, and become through art practice.

Contemporary artist Chuck Close (Figure 8.4), for example, has *prosopagnosia*, a rare impairment of face perception and recognition that is often referred to as "face-blindness." He describes the phenomenon as follows:

> I have a great deal of difficulty recognizing faces, especially if I haven't—if I've just met somebody, it's hopeless. I will never remember them again unless it's reinforced over and over and over, and even people that I know very well, if I haven't seen them for a while. It's like a bucket with a hole in it—[perceptual] information is coming in, but it's pouring out the bottom just as fast, I'm often losing information. (Close 2010, online)

Close goes on to describe his process of seeing and recognizing as an extraction of his art practice.

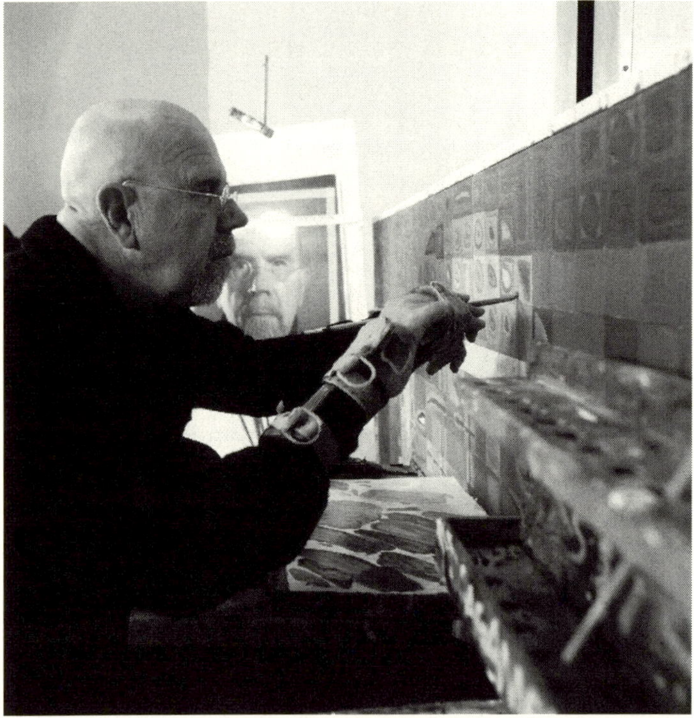

Figure 8.4. Artist Chuck Close, the subject of Marion Cajori's documentary *Chuck Close*, working in his studio on *Self-Portrait*, 2004–05 (Photo by Michael Marfione/ Courtesy the artist and Pace-Wildenstein, New York).

> Because in real life if you move your head a half an inch, to me it's a whole new face I've never seen before. But if we flatten it out—I have and I take photographs—I work from photographs and make flat things called paintings and prints. I have virtual photographic memory for anything that is flat, so it's not an accident that I only do images of people who matter to me—family, friends, other artists. There are no commissioned portraits. These are images that really matter, and I want to commit them to memory and the only way I can really do that is to flatten them out, scan them . . . make these drawings and paintings and prints. And then they enter my memory bank in a different sort of way. (Close 2010, online)

Close's extraction, his mining of facial recognition, corresponds with the Deleuzoguattarian n-dimension of becoming-intense, which is evident in the meticulous way that he creates his paintings. Since the 1960s the artist has gridded photographic portraits that he then scales to large canvases. By replicating whatever visual information is contained in each grid unit on the flat surface of the photograph onto its adjacent unit on the canvas, Close *builds* the faces incrementally, one grid unit at a time; a protracted schizo-analytic process that enables him to commit the faces to memory while creating a unique visual experience.

As viewers position themselves near the paintings' surface, they see the artist's grid structure and the painterly information contained within (Figure 8.5). At that proximity, what is painted in each grid unit appears as a distinct miniature abstract painting within the larger abstract painterly field of the grid. Then, as viewers' distance from the painting's surface, a gestalt occurs as the contiguous grid units merge and emerge a recognizable face, a portrait. Paradoxically, notwithstanding the recognition of a whole face that is greater than the sum of its gridded units, viewers' to-and-fro movements enable them to experience perceptual slippages in Close's paintings; a push and pull against the grain of socially and historically constructed visuality; a schizo-analytic process of becoming-perceptive that resists visual and conceptual absolutes through the artist's seeing and understanding in a "different sort of way" that enabled him to overcome the problem of comprehending something as a whole (Ravin and Odell 2008).

Close experienced yet another physical complication, a spinal artery collapse brought about by a blood clot that left him paralyzed from the upper body down in 1988. During his rehabilitation process at The Rusk Institute of Rehabilitation Medicine in New York City, an occupational therapist arranged for a basement studio space where Close could continue his creative practice. It was during his work in that basement studio that his hand functions returned. By holding a brush with a splinted right hand

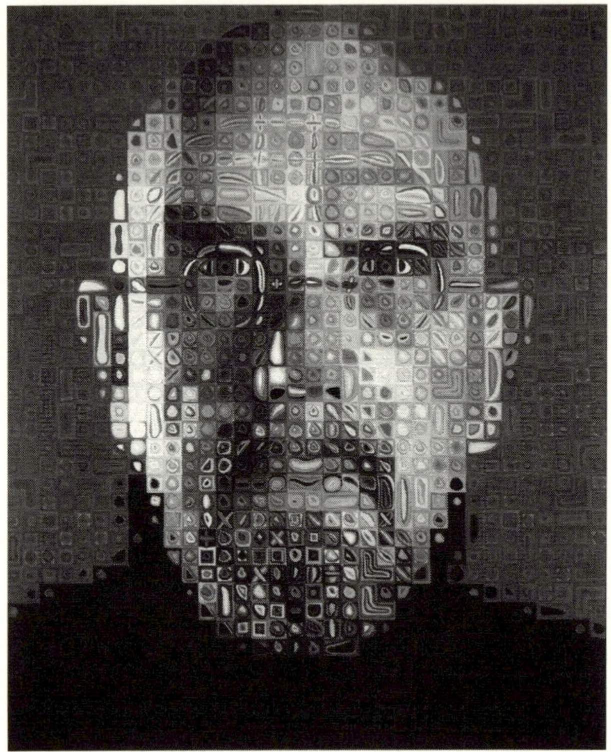

Figure 8.5. Chuck Close, *Self-Portrait (Image #2)*, 2004–05 (Courtesy The Pace Gallery, New York).

and with motors that moved his large canvases he was able to paint from his wheelchair (Christopher and Dana Reeve Foundation, online).

Close's art research and practice in the n-dimension of impairment corresponds with that of the BwO insofar as it constitutes *minoritarian* embodiment, a Deleuzoguattarian neologism not to be confused with disenfranchised, marginalized, or lacking bodies. Instead, minoritarian poverty exists in relation with codified, *majoritarian* systems in order to approach them "from above or below instead of positioning oneself with [them]" (Deleuze and Guattari 1987, 104). This nondialectical process of operating[4] contiguously within dominant systems sidesteps and nullifies distinctions that end in ontological syntheses by initiating a treatment whereby dominant assumptions are deterritorialized; subtracted and placed in continuous variation, to constitute "a becoming minor of the major language" (104). In doing so, "Minor languages do not exist in themselves: they exist only in [contiguous] relation to a major language and are also investments of that language for the purpose of making it minor" (105).[5]

Minoritarian embodiment corresponds with Close's research and practice in two ways: first, his uncompromising drive and relentless pursuit of seeing, recognizing, and enablement through art because of his face blindness and quadriplegia, subtracts from and places major, dominant assumptions and practices about disabled bodies in continuous variation; second, his differentiated way of seeing and painting deterritorializes dominant assumptions and stylizations of painterly art in the majoritarian art world. For Close, the research and practice of art enables *becoming-intense*: extending and expanding his body's extant abilities in manifold ways through multiple lines of flight and assemblage; destratifying artistic categorizations and ontologies of disablement; and, always already open to immanent possibilities of becoming-other, and moving beyond what disability politics assumes he can or cannot do. As such, his subjectivity is mutable, in a continual process of becoming. Related to Deleuze scholar Inna Semetsky's (2006, 6) concept of the "subject-in-process," Close's desire is not to become *the* other of disability, but to become-other within the differential, in-betweenness of rhizomatic assemblage: a virtual, incorporeal space where contiguous bodies can affect[6] and be affected by others.

PETRA KUPPERS'S RHIZOMATIC MODEL OF DISABILITY

In problematizing the extrinsic politicization of the body's disability by the social model, and the intrinsic, abnormal categorization of the medical model, Kuppers proposes a third, minoritarian model of disability based on the Deleuzoguattarian rhizome whereby the social and medical are juxtaposed in contiguity within a differential, heterogeneous space of lived experiences.[7] In Kuppers's *rhizomatic model* the social and medical

> mix and merge, as they do in my own physical and psychical being when I am in pain, and cannot walk up the stairs and wish for a painkiller, and take pride in my difference (what choice do I have?), and unable to speak of the nature of my discomfort, cannot find the words, but find comfort in the company of others whose pain might be different, but who somehow feel sympatico. (Kuppers 2009, 225–26)

It is the space in-between the known socially and historically constructed assumptions, codes, and stereotypes of disability, and the unknown lived experiences of the other, where Kuppers locates her art and scholarly practice. This liminal and contingent space, which she refers to as a "scar . . . a locus of memory and of bodily change" (Kuppers 2007, 1), is the cutting edge of deterritorialization mentioned previously; where the knowing self exists and interconnects with the unknown lived experience of disabled others; an unassimilable space of repetition and difference between the known and unknown that resists concrescence; an interstitiality where creative and political agency is always immanent; and, where community between and among others is possible. In characterizing the vulnerability and mutability of the scar and its connectivity with the world, Kuppers writes: "The scar moves matter into a future of a new flesh: a different subject emerges, a re-creation of the old into the new, into a repetition that holds on to its history even as it projects itself into an unpredictable future" (19). Here, Kuppers's suggestion of a scar's repetition and difference corresponds with Deleuze's way of thinking about time as a wounding, an incorporeal event where time is unhinged, out-of-joint; that is, "always and at the same time something which has just happened and something which is about to happen; never something which is happening" (Deleuze 1990, 63). This undecidability of the scar as event constitutes a disruption and delay of time, which "eschews the unity of the subject" (Reynolds 2010, online).

By situating her impairment within the rhizomatic enunciation of art research and practice, Kuppers destratifies and complicates "pain and pleasure" and "pride and shame" binaries to create multiplicities of meanings and understandings of disability. Through her performances and writings she "allow[s] for an immanent transformation, a coming into being of a state of life in this world, one that is constantly shifting and productive of new subject/individual positions" (Kuppers 2007, 226). Being a woman and disabled, Kuppers understands that her body is always already double-coded; a double discrimination of gender and impairment, which she juxtaposes with other contiguous poetic modalities to initiate the schizo-analysis[8] of rhizomatic assemblage; to create differential, in-between spaces where complex and contradictory discourses about bodies as multiplicities can flourish interminably. Where "poetry and disability become machines together . . . [they enable Kuppers] to think of words as productive machines, holding simultaneity, tension and agency" (Kuppers 2009, 229–30).

The becoming-community that Kuppers aspires to with her rhizomatic assemblage is constituted by the "desiring-machine"[9] of Deleuzoguattarian thought; where "desire" is not about acquisition and compensation for something lacking in the body, but ceaseless immersion and alliance with multiplicities, assemblages, and differential productions (Deleuze and Guattari 1983, 36). These manifold characteristics of becoming-community correspond with philosopher Jacques Rancière's concept of "symbolic montage" as heterogeneous, disjunctive "little machines" that work to establish proximity, familiarity, and co-belonging as compared with the clashing, disruptive and divisive characteristics of "dialectical montage" (Rancière 2007, 56–57). By creating alliances and community through her little, desiring machines of poetic assemblage, Kuppers's cultural work functions as minoritarian language that deterritorializes, reterritorializes, and complexifies reductive dialectical denunciations of majoritarian assumptions about disability.

By advocating for a poetic usage of the word *disability*, Kuppers suggests that her rhizomatic model corresponds with the unbounded possibilities of becoming-other through art research and practice in general, and, through disability culture poetry in particular. As her epigraph at the beginning of this chapter suggests, her poetry "charts a lyrical exploration, a space-making, but one that veers into the absurd with its juxtaposition between the word or concept *disabled* and multiple subjects not usually in tactile relations with the [lived] experience of disability or the word *disabled*" (Kuppers 2009, 230). Hence, for Kuppers, ontologies of identity and subjectivity are not fixed, but in perpetual motion within the rhizome, continually destratifying, becoming minoritarian through multiple lines of flight and the contiguous, familiar-strange juxtapositions of her poetic assemblage.

JOE JULIAN'S PROSTHETIC PEDAGOGY

Deleuzoguattarian schizo-analysis and minoritarian language also describe Dr. Julian's pedagogical processes in Cambodia. Considering that much of his rehabilitation efforts at Khao I Dang were dedicated to jury-rigging and teaching volunteer refugee workers how to make and repair simple prostheses (artificial limbs), orthoses (braces), wheelchairs, and other rehabilitation devices for disabled Cambodian refugees at the rehabilitation hospital, Julian's minoritarian research and practice destratified the majoritarian social, political, and economic circumstances that he found when he first arrived in Cambodia.[10] Faced with the limitations of his Western rehabilitation expertise within the rudimentary conditions of living and working in a war zone hospital, he initiated *prosthesis*/prosthesis—rhizomatic pedagogy similar to Kuppers's *disabled*/disabled poetic assemblage. In other words, in the process of destratifying his own medicalized assumptions about rehabilitation, he created a liminal and contingent space between the word *prosthesis* and the living with and making of prostheses in a war zone. In doing so, the word/experience of *prosthesis*/prosthesis "gains extension . . . it intrudes and extrudes, shivers over other words," as Kuppers suggests (230).

In the conversation that follows,[11] Julian talks about the shocking predominance of children and young adults at Khao I Dang who lost their limbs from the thousands of landmines that were indiscriminately planted by the Khmer Rouge and other fighting factions along the Thai-Cambodian border. Faced with a large population of maimed and traumatized children and adult patients who were in immediate need of medical attention, and an insurmountable bureaucratic medical system that was socially, politically, and economically stymied when he arrived at Khao I Dang, Julian, together with his small expatriate staff of rehabilitation professionals and trained refugee workers (some of whom were former patients), explored, experimented, and improvised multiple ways of addressing their impairments, mobility, and agency by improvising tools and equipment from indigenous materials and processes at the hospital site. There was urgency for a *prosthetic*/prosthetic process where bodies and communities that were torn apart by the regime's butchery could be reassembled and restored. Julian's ingenuity and creativity in meeting that urgency head-on, in collaboration with the trained refugee workers that apprenticed in his workshop, constituted Deleuzoguattarian embodiment and the prosthetic pedagogy of art.

CG: Joe, let's begin our conversation with some background story. What had happened in Cambodia before you arrived there?

JJ: Between nineteen seventy and nineteen seventy-five there was civil war in Cambodia. General Lon Nol had disposed of Prince Norodom Sihanouk through a military coup in nineteen sixty-nine and nineteen seventy. Lon Nol then ended up running a military government, which was opposed by Sihanouk and the Khmer Rouge. The civil war lasted about five years, which the Khmer Rouge won in nineteen seventy-five when they took over Phnom Penh, the capital of Cambodia. The Khmer Rouge under the communist dictator Pol Pot had a very strong philosophical stance: to return Cambodia to a simple agrarian society based on the production of rice, and that it was going to be untainted by the influences of other cultures, especially Western cultures. So, the Khmer Rouge emptied the cities, including the capitol, Phnom Penh, and they systematically tried to eliminate any outside influences. They killed off teachers, bureaucrats, lawyers, doctors, nurses, and ex-soldiers, and they took away money, took away personal possessions, and they drove the populace en masse out into the countryside to live in communal farms and grow rice.[12] Their rule lasted about five years to around nineteen seventy-nine when Viet Nam invaded and drove the Khmer Rouge, along with several hundred thousand civilians, toward the western border that Cambodia shares with Thailand. It was there that all the activity I will be discussing took place.

CG: How did you get involved in the Cambodian work and what did you find when you arrived in the country?

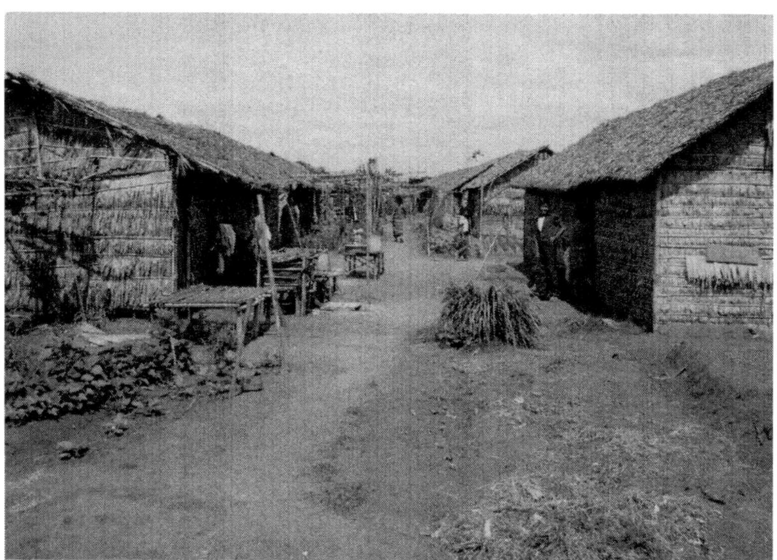

Figure 8.6. Refugee camp at Khao I Dang, 1981–82 (Courtesy Joseph Julian Jr., MD).

JJ: In nineteen eighty-one, which was the United Nations "Year-of-the-Disabled," Catholic Relief Services (CRS), the largest private relief organization in the world, hired me as a neurologist on a one-year contract. When I arrived at Khao I Dang refugee camp, I found survivors from the horrific ten-year period of civil war and the murderous policies of the Khmer Rouge. Many of them were disabled in one way or another due to starvation, lack of medical care, and trauma . . . at this time, the border was a war zone where you had a large civilian population without adequate resources in water, food, and shelter . . . there were amputees, victims of landmines, which had been planted by the differing factions in the region . . . everybody set landmines, the Vietnamese set landmines, the Khmer Rouge set landmines . . . and, while the Khmer Rouge were fighting the Vietnamese, they were also fighting the Khmer Serei, or Free Khmer, who were noncommunists who had been fighting against the Khmer Rouge in a kind of guerrilla war . . . so, basically there were three major fighting factions. . . . The civilians were caught between a rock and a hard place in this region where landmines were frequently sowed and then forgotten or left unmarked . . . landmines functioned as an effective deterrent, an inexpensive way to protect territory . . . a cheap way to protect from being attacked . . . also knowing that there are landmines in your area certainly has an emotional impact . . . seeing your buddy have his legs blown off has a lasting psychological impact . . .

CG: Considering the physical and emotional trauma of the patients at Khao I Dang, what resources did you have at your disposal for rehabilitation?

JJ: We started with a small expatriate staff of rehabilitation professionals, but as we trained refugees to become nurses, therapists, prosthetists, and brace makers, our staff at the rehabilitation facility grew to more than one hundred . . . what existed grew organically, things changed all the time . . . one day I would find out that twenty of our workers were being resettled to Australia . . . one day I received a phone call, "Your budget's been cut in half, call me by this afternoon and cut your budget in half" . . . so, when I talk about a staff of one hundred, at one point in time we did have a staff of more than one hundred, but at any given time it might have been eighty-five or whatever . . . at one point, we had staff of ten expatriate professionals from the Philippines, from Thailand, from the United States . . .

CG: Describe the health and rehabilitation circumstances of the children and young adults at the rehabilitation hospital. What was the extent of their afflictions and impairments?

JJ: The children in the hospital had grown up most of their lives without any medical care, with very poor starvation-level nutrition, they were born during a period in which there was no maternal-child healthcare, and so a lot of them were suffering from that lack of care, not to mentioned lack of proper medical treatment for things like malaria, polio, and all the childhood infectious diseases that they were not vaccinated for, and so among the survivors there were children with residual problems related to that lack of care . . . there were a lot of children and adults who, who just didn't survive . . . we were working with the hearty survivors, those who despite the horrific circumstances survived . . . it's not clear, but it is estimated that during the Khmer Rouge horror as many as one to three million Cambodians died in a total population of seven to eight million . . . there are those who argue that that estimate is too high, I don't know, but a significant number of people did not survive to even get to the border or beyond . . .

CG: What was the process at Khao I Dang whereby patients could seek medical care? Did patients go to the doctor or the doctor to the patients?

JJ: The four hundred bed hospital complex served both the camp population of up to one hundred and thirty thousand as well as the border area where two hundred to three hundred thousand more refugees existed precariously in a war zone . . . patients in the camp came to the hospital and its outpatient facilities . . . seriously ill patients from the border were trucked into the camp for hospitalization or surgery . . . we drew our rehab patients from the surgical, medical, pediatric, leprosy, and tuberculosis wards of the hospital as well as from the border camps . . .

CG: Given the basic conditions of the hospital and the camp environment, what philosophical changes did you have to make in your thinking to best serve the patients?

JJ: When we first started building the program we tried to recreate what was familiar to us, a classic university hospital rehab unit with all the standard comprehensive programs . . . very specialized with all the "bells and whistles" . . . as I became more conscious of the unique environment and its unique demands, as I learned from the staff, the patients, the accumulated experiences we all had, I realized the wisdom of simplicity not complexity . . . our basic approach was to become less specialized and more generalized . . . refugee medicine demanded flexibility and a deep appreciation of the fluidity and uncertainty inherent in the work we were doing . . . the key to success was our being "appropriate" in our response to an at times overwhelming set of problems . . . a pre-packaged Western template often was not appropriate to meet these demands . . .

CG: By simplify, I'm assuming that you mean that your approach at the hospital shifted from prescriptive to an organic process where you learned as much from the patients and the culture of Khao I Dang as they received medical help from you. Please elaborate on what you mean by a simpler and less complicated approach.

JJ: It's basically the old saw, when you're dropped into a situation like refugee medicine, you tend to apply a prescriptive approach, solutions in search of problems . . . I mean if I did this again, the trajectory of building this program would be so different . . . the value to me is all the mistakes that were made and learned from . . . it was trial and error, but, unfortunately, there's a cost to that . . . there's a cost to patients . . . while we are learning, they are not getting optimal care . . . optimal care is a combination of understanding where they came from, where they are now, and where they are going . . . understanding about what resources are available for each patient, and what timeframe is available to provide treatment, and a real appreciation for unintended consequences, that every time you do something there are consequences, for example, when I arrived some well meaning people had spent several thousand dollars to order Western braces made in Bangkok . . . these arrived eight months later and the patients for whom they were measured had long since gone and were not traceable . . . they had been either resettled to countries of second asylum, or repatriated back to the border camps in Cambodia . . . so that money was basically wasted, a couple of thousand dollars was a lot of money . . . the problem wasn't necessarily access to modern technology, it was the fact that it was an impractical way of providing the kind of care these patients needed . . . because of several factors . . . a modern prosthesis, a modern orthosis, it's expensive, it takes time to fabricate, once it's fabricated its durability for these kinds of conditions may not be good, it's been devised for city life, not for war zones . . . once it breaks, or a part wears out, parts are not available, the kind of technicians that are required, or materials that are required to fix it or replace it are not available, the patient has gotten used to a [professionally manufactured] very beautiful, well-designed, functional device, and will not be satisfied with something that doesn't look as nice and is not as functional . . .

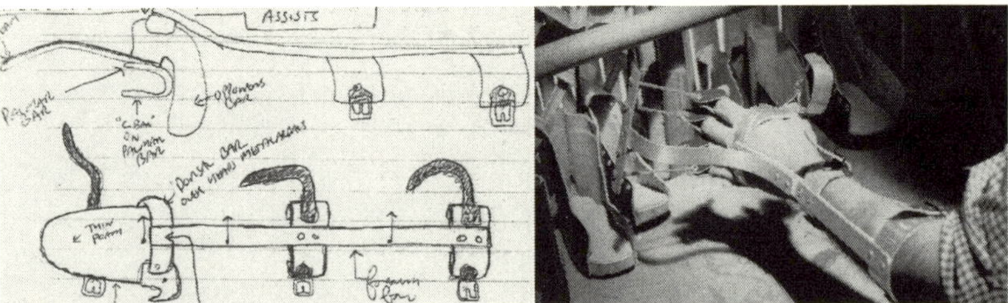

Figure 8.7. Arm brace made of aluminum and leather, 1981–82 (Courtesy Joseph Julian Jr., MD).

CG: Was your decision against accommodating the patients with modern prostheses and orthoses yet another example of simplifying the rehabilitation process at the hospital? What was the basis for that decision?

JJ: I would not allow those kinds of Western devices anywhere near our patients, because if they saw a beautiful prosthesis made of plastic, and a nice functional joint, and a beautiful foot, they wouldn't wear the kind of things we made at the hospital, or if they did wear them, they'd feel cheated because they know what's available to other people in affluent parts of the world . . .

CG: Considering the impracticality of industrial prostheses and orthoses from the outside, what decisions did you make to provide the patients with rehabilitation?

JJ: Our goal was to train refugee workers to make simple but sturdy and useful orthoses, prostheses, and other mobility aids that would not only meet the injured patients' present needs by making them more functional, but prevent the kinds of complications that might hinder them in the future . . . for example, if you lay around and don't move your leg, you'll get a contracture, if you're up walking, even if it's on a primitive peg leg, you're going to buy some time as contractures won't develop, muscles won't wither from disuse . . . it's an uncertain future the amputees are going into, but we can hope that it will be a future in which more sophisticated devices and care may be available, and the patient will not have lost so much ground that they are unable to benefit from more sophisticated devices . . . we'll train them so that they'll be ready to take the next step, if that is available, to a modern prosthesis or orthosis . . . also there was a byproduct to our training refugee staff . . . we originally trained refugee workers to be rehabilitation assistants so that the work could be done . . . rehabilitation is very labor-intensive and the handful of expatriate rehabilitation professionals could never have treated the hundreds of patients that were seen every day . . . but, as we saw how quickly and successfully and creatively the refugee workers took to the rehab process, our goals expanded to include the hope that some of our staff, when repatriated back to Cambodia, would continue to make and repair artificial limbs and braces and wheelchairs, etc. . . . and would be able to make a living doing this . . . they might even begin to train

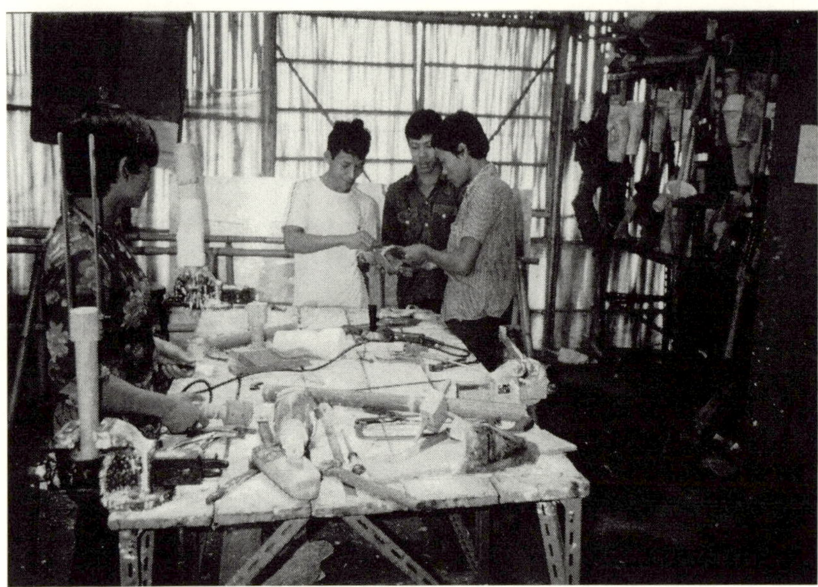

Figure 8.8. Refugee workers in rehabilitation workshop, 1981–82 (Courtesy Joseph Julian Jr., MD).

assistants to help them, so that we would in effect be "training the trainers" . . . in this way our work might continue to have some lasting value even beyond the time we were in direct contact with the refugees . . .

CG: From what you have described, the teaching and collaboration that you initiated with the refugee workers and former patients, to include them in creative efforts to meet theirs and others rehabilitation needs, was based on exploration, experimentation, and improvisation.

JJ: Exactly! We had to improvise once we arrived at the camp, and adapt to the circumstances that we found . . . initially our energies went into replicating a comprehensive Western-style rehab center, but what I eventually came to was a much simpler philosophy, in fact, I'm sure that . . . my philosophy, if I had been as knowledgeable when I started as I was when I ended a year and a half later, would have been *less is more* . . . deciding what worked and what didn't work required time, trial and error, lots of mistakes, but learning from those mistakes . . . we learned a lot . . .

CG: So, the mistakes you made enabled you to adjust your efforts, to re-imagine Western rehab assumptions by developing processes that were specific to the cultural environment of the refugee camp.

JJ: One has to learn from experience what works and what doesn't work . . . and, we certainly had a ton of experience . . . at one point we were seeing over three hundred patients a day . . . the gadgets, devices that we replicated were in some way what you might find in a Western hospital, but ours were made of bamboo or some other locally available material . . . I mean, we replicated as best we could what we knew from past experience but with the materials at hand . . . replicated devices that we had been familiar with in a Western rehab hospital . . .

CG: Talk more about the indigenous materials that you and the patients worked with, especially bamboo. What difference did it make that bamboo is prevalent in that part of the world. Did the patients have an understanding about the properties of bamboo that was useful in constructing prostheses and other rehabilitation equipment?

JJ: People in this region are so extraordinarily innovative with bamboo . . . it's a marvelous material, which they use every day of their lives . . . bamboo is cheap and readily available . . . over the generations it has been used in many different ways in constructing buildings and the making of objects . . . we had access to not only the raw material but to refugees who were knowledgeable and skilled

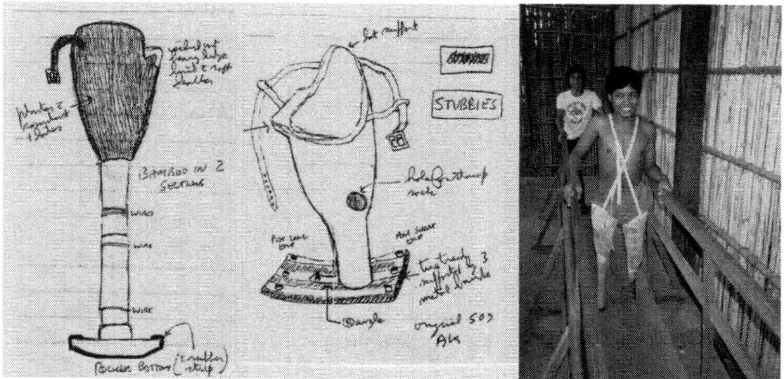

Figure 8.9. Patient with prosthesis, 1981–82 (Courtesy Joseph Julian Jr., MD).

in using it in ways that were readily adaptable to the making of rehab devices and equipment . . . if you talked to Western rehab professionals and told them that you were going to train refugee workers and assistants with no previous medical background to be rehab nurses, physical and occupational therapists, prosthetists, orthotists, and rehab "engineers," they would say it can't be done without a long training period of maybe years . . . visiting professionals would marvel at the fact that people with no medical background . . . how quickly they learned the principles of rehabilitation therapy and the construction of rehab devices and equipment . . . their ability to problem solve in creative and inventive ways that *taught us* . . . the predominant use of locally available materials that they already knew how to use certainly enhanced their comfort in working with and adapting these materials to new uses . . .

CG: After having experienced the success of collaborating with your staff, refugee workers, and patients, and their resourcefulness

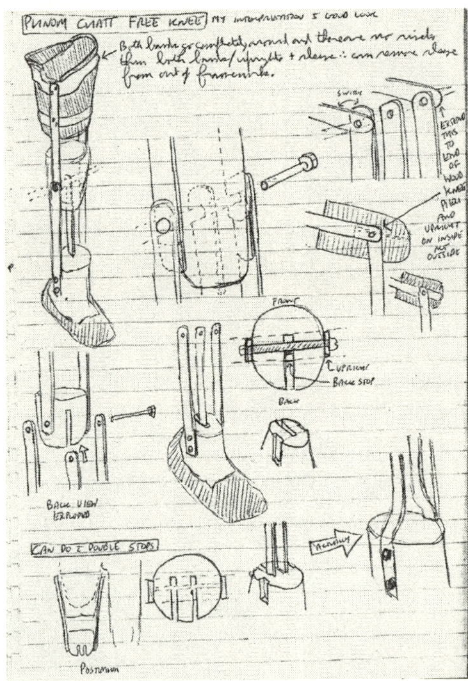

Figure 8.10. Drawing and notes for a prosthetic device, 1981–82 (Courtesy Joseph Julian Jr., MD).

and creative initiative, did modern prostheses and orthoses ever reenter your thinking?

JJ: Whenever we received shipments of used prostheses and orthoses from abroad, which were sent over as though they were gifts . . . the unintended consequences of their use would have been unfortunate if I hadn't just refused to accept them . . . some of my assistants tried to jury-rig some of those devices, but philosophically I was strongly against it . . . those prostheses and orthoses were *closed systems* . . . making things out of bamboo and wood, stainless steel and leather, and other materials that were readily available on the open market in the region was an *open system* . . . people could get into that system and do their thing, and grow, and learn, and feel very comfortable in working with these materials, and expanding their usefulness . . . they would have been so intimidated by Western technology that they would have been shut off from any creative opportunity and effort . . .

CG: If you could, please elaborate on how your non-Western rehab process evolved. What was the nature of that process and how was it based on a more simple approach?

JJ: When we first started, we tended to initiate various rehabilitation programs and make devices and equipment that replicated those we had been comfortable with back home, we recreated, even if it was in bamboo, what we already knew . . . we did not necessarily see the medical issues and functional problems in the light of the unique demands and unique culture of refugee life, and we tried to bend the materials available to us to our will, rather than letting them speak to us about what they could and could not do . . . We brought with us a tool box of solutions, which we then used to deal with whatever problems came our way . . . whether that was the most appropriate way of doing it or not . . . there was growth, the maturation of the program over time, but it was like a Darwinian evolutionary process . . . it may look thoughtful and carefully planned out, but it doesn't come from multiple intended causal events . . . through trial and error, a lot of things were made and what worked was then selected . . . there was this creation of multiple options, and then, the key thing, the thing I'm most proud about is that we didn't continue to make the same error over and over again . . . we selected those things that were functional, those things that worked . . . those things that resulted in some advantage were kept, and those things that were disadvantageous, dysfunctional, or problematic were dropped . . . it really was a Darwinian process . . .

CG: I'm curious about your Darwinian analogy regarding the generative and emergent process that you initiated at Khao I Dang. What specifically about that theory are you referring to?

JJ: I'm talking about the "Darwinian two-step,"[13] the creation of a lot of different variants, and then the crucial second step, which is the selection of certain variants because they provide some kind of advantage . . . so, I'm saying we created a lot of variations, we tried them, we saw what worked and didn't work, we grew, we learned, we started to see the bigger picture, and through that, started selecting certain variants, and I think the program progressed because of that . . . eventually we had to be honest with ourselves and say no matter how good our intentions much of our labor did not work . . .

CG: What do you mean much of your labor did not work? From what you have described until now, your simplified rehab process was beneficial to the patients at Khao I Dang. You seem dissatisfied by the results. Why?

JJ: There's no point in making something unless . . . and, this is also true for things that were actually biomechanically sound, and technically appeared to be good solutions . . . but, there's no point in spending time in making something if people aren't really going to use them when you're not around . . . I mean, I can't tell you how often I went out to the border, I used to go out to the border encampments, on occasion, and I would take time trying to find former patients and visit them . . . I would see their prosthesis or their brace hanging on a wall like a souvenir . . . the devices were more trouble than it was worth to them . . . the issues are, How does it look? . . . people are vain, they're not going to wear something that targets them as disabled, targets them as different . . . they're not going to wear something that promises some future preventive benefit if at the moment it inhibits them, or hinders them, or makes them less functional . . . aesthetics are really important because the issue is not that the patient makes me feel good because he's wearing my brace while he's on the rehab unit under my control . . . the issue is, when I'm not there, when he's faced with the issue, Should I wear this thing or not? What will be his decision? Because if his decision is "I don't like the way it looks," "I don't like the way it hinders me," "I don't understand that it's providing any value," "I will not wear it," then I've wasted his and my time, and I've wasted valuable resources, which are limited . . .

CG: Was that level of criticality useful to your efforts? Did it lead to cynicism or persistence in designing and re-designing, constructing and re-constructing functional prosthetic and orthotic devices that would be beneficial and valued by the patients?

JJ: I don't want to mislead you . . . we weren't doing "research" there . . . we were trying to provide a service to people in the best way we could under extremely difficult circumstances . . . the one constant in such a situation is change . . . the camp itself, the rehab program, the patients, and staff were in constant flux . . . the "philosophy" I'm speaking about evolved, emerged, if you will, from the process of being there and trying to do the work . . . being honest with ourselves about what was working for the patients' benefit, and what was not, was critical . . . limited resources in time, money, materials, and trained staff forces you to make such decisions . . . some of the major lessons of this experience for me was an awareness of having to be a "good steward" of resources and also of being appropriate . . . "appropriate" to me means achieving some balance between what *can* be done, as if you were in an ideal situation and had unlimited resources, and what *should* be done, given the time available, the resources at hand, the culture and environment one finds oneself in and the "opportunity costs" (i.e., If I spend time and money doing this one thing, will I not be able to meet other needs later?) . . . it became very clear that the best way to be appropriate, to steward limited resources, to provide the greatest value was not to impose our "pre-packaged" Western top-down medical and rehabilitation models on this unique situation, but to engage in ongoing dialogue with the staff, the patients, even the materials we were using so that all "voices" were heard and respected and valued . . . in this way, we were all both students and teachers . . .

CG: Considering that the design and construction of the devices was a constant, evolving process, did you ever reach a point of satisfaction and repeated production?

JJ: Absolutely! It would have been the worst kind of folly to be constantly changing just for the sake of change . . . there was work to be done, patients to be treated, refugee workers to be trained in making the devices . . . at some point in the design of the mobility aids, a decision had to be made that this was a "good enough solution" . . . if I had been aware of the saying "the ideal is the enemy of the good," it would have been on a sign hanging on my wall . . . our first feeble efforts at making shoes and braces, for example, were quickly obvious to everyone to be far from "good enough solutions" . . . pressing on with better designs was an easy decision . . . later, when the designs showed themselves to be functional, acceptable to the patients, cost effective to make and repair, easy to teach construction to our staff, then there was a resistance to further changes . . .

CG: Describe the contents of your rehabilitation workshop. What construction equipment, materials, and processes did you and your assistants use in making prosthetic and orthotic devices for the patients?

JJ: The overall rehabilitation program had many mothers and fathers. Too many to mention and give them all their due. It was truly a collaborative "team" effort. Since you are particularly interested in the making of devices, I must credit two people who were instrumental in developing specific areas. Those would be Jean-Baptiste Richardier, from France, in prosthetics and Jimmy Miranda, an occupational therapist from the Philippines, in orthotics. Our resources were limited to indigenous materials and simple hand tools . . . for example, the Thai military would not allow us to have welding equipment, so most of what we constructed were made of bamboo, wood, nails, screws, bolts, glue, sawdust, stainless steel, aluminum, etc. . . . the first generation lower extremity prosthesis were made of bamboo, Plaster of Paris, sawdust, latex glue, and baked in the sun . . . these were very crude prostheses and were replaced in time by a succession of more sophisticated designs . . . but they were still useful later as training prostheses . . . they would be fitted to the amputee's stump and then as he walked on it, the stump would shrink, it would "mature" . . . this process would be repeated two or three or four times before the amputee's stump would be ready for the final prosthesis, which would be of a more sophisticated design such as the ones in which buffalo leather was carefully formed over a positive mold of the stump . . . we took plaster bandage molds of the stump, closed it off, filled it with plaster, and made a positive plaster cast of the patient's stump, then shaped this cast . . . you shape the plaster to accommodate the stump . . . there are areas

> where you want to relieve pressure and areas where you want to have weight bearing . . . then you take wet leather and put that over the cast, and you rub it with a stick . . . rub it and smooth the leather socket into which the stump will eventually be placed . . . wet leather . . . the heat and pressure of that rubbing and shaping is what formed the leather into a well-fitting socket . . . the leather socket was then attached to a metal and wood framework to form the prosthesis . . . subsequent iterations included a "foot" rather than a "peg leg" configuration . . .
>
> CG: Can you describe how you were affected personally and professionally by working in the rudimentary conditions of the hospital?
>
> JJ: Some of the things I was taught by the difficult environment, the staff, the patients, and the materials that we used, became part of a core philosophy that has informed both my professional and personal life to this day . . . I've already mentioned the importance I found of becoming an aware, conscientious steward of resources as well as the issue of "appropriate" care . . . I was originally taught in the traditional top-down medical model, but since this experience, I learned the value and the wisdom of listening first and doing later . . . I shifted from valuing knowledge (facts) to valuing understanding, which meant respecting the opinions, concerns, and values of the whole therapeutic community (the staff, the patients, families, etc.) . . . I shifted my role from being the "expert," to being part of a "team" . . . I found greater satisfaction in being a facilitator and communicator for the work and wisdom of others rather than doing it all myself . . .

The correspondences between the Deleuzoguattarian rhizome, and the predominance of and reliance on bamboo, a rhizome, have not been overlooked in this chapter. The coincidental associations between *a learning theory of bamboo* and *living and learning from bamboo* emerged as Julian discussed the schizo-analytic characteristics of his (*prosthesis*/prosthesis) pedagogy at Khao I Dang, which, due to the unavailability or impracticality of external resources, relied on the prodigious supply of indigenous bamboo, and any other locally available materials. Equally important was the cultural valuing of bamboo by Julian's patients and assistants; their indigenous knowledge of living and learning from bamboo. Considering the impracticalities of his Western medical expertise at Khao I Dang, Julian threw caution to the wind and initiated a process of exploration, experimentation, and improvisation to create prostheses and orthoses together with his assistants and patients. In doing so, the rhizomatic assemblage of his pedagogy consisted of multiplicities whose lines of flight interconnected and constituted a dynamic interdependent community consisting of Khao I Dang's children and adult patients, Julian, his colleagues and assistants, bamboo, sawdust, plaster, leather, wood, nails, screws, bolts, metal parts, the hospital, the war zone, their memory and history of the war, their wounds of genocide, and, and, and . . . interconnected and engaged in an interminable process of becoming-intense, becoming-limitless, becoming-other, which are the characteristics of the prosthetic pedagogy of art research and practice advocated in this book.

NOTES

CHAPTER ONE. INTRODUCTION

1. R. Barry, *Frieze*, 80. [online]. Available: http://www.frieze.com/magazine/.

2. Lefebvre's characterization of interstitiality as a "lethal zone" and "mixed space" correspond with critical theorist Carol Becker's *Zones of Contention* (1996, 38, 43) where creative and political agency are possible through art practice.

3. In *Parables for the Virtual* (2006), Massumi describes the embodied processual rhythms of continuity and discontinuity (217), which corresponds with Lefebvre's rhythmic oscillation.

4. Massumi (2006) refers to liminal space as "virtual" from which parabolic possibilities of art emerge (30–31, 137).

5. See J. Roberts, *The Intangibilities of Form: Skill and Deskilling in Art after the Readymades* (London: Verso, 2007).

6. The concept of "delay" should not be confused with somnambulation or hibernation. On the contrary, it is an alertness of mind and a tarrying for imagination while in the process of work. In regard to the necessity for "lingering," John Dewey writes: "The crucial educational problem is that of procuring the *postponement of immediate action* upon desire until observation and judgment have intervened" (1938, 69; emphasis in original). Such postponement affords contemplation, seeing, and transformational becoming through art research and practice.

7. Anthropologist Claude Lévi-Strauss (1966) describes the process of ethnographic representation as similar to that of a *bricoleur* (21–22).

8. Herbert Read (1955, chapter 1) describes the eidetic visuality of the cave painters who possessed a keen ability to *see*, *project*, and *render* images of bison in great detail as if giving them virtual life on cave walls long after actually seeing and hunting them in the field.

9. See the discussion of Robert Rauschenberg's bridging of various processes of art making and combination of found visual and material culture in chapter 2, "Verge of Collapse."

10. "Feet of clay" is a euphemism from the Book of Daniel, which is used to indicate "a fundamental weakness in someone supposedly of great merit" (*Oxford English Dictionary*, online, 4c); "Thou, O king, sawest, and behold a great image . . . his feet part of iron and part of clay . . . And as the toes of the feet were part of iron, and part of clay . . . so the kingdom shall be partly strong, and partly broken" (King James Version, Daniel 2:31, 33, and 42).

11. Lefebvre's differentiation between "representations of space" and "representational spaces," corresponds with de Certeau's (1988, 117) distinctions between "places" and "spaces."

12. According to cultural theorists Chomsky and Herman (1988), this negative operation within abstract space represents the "manufacture of consent" by corporate power (302).

13. Mouffe's critique of capitalism in museums.

14. See Koestler's "bisociation" (1975, 178–79) and Rothenberg's "Janusian thinking" (1979, 256), where ideas and images coexist and correspond in the same space of the mind.

15. Such interventions to counter the commodification of art by corporate capitalism were first proposed by Duchamp, who in the early 1960s declared, "the great artist of tomorrow will go underground."

CHAPTER TWO. VERGE OF COLLAPSE

This chapter was previously published in Spring 2008 in *Studies in Art Education: A Journal of Issues and Research in Art Education* 49, no. 3: 218–34. It is reprinted here with permission from the National Art Education Association www.arteducators.org.

1. Poff, C. (2005, February 24). Survival rates higher among recently wounded troops in Iraq, Afghanistan. Online. Available: http://www.international-reportingproject.org/.

2. Hambling, D. (2006, September 4). Instant expert: Weapons technology. Online. Available: http://www.newscientist.com.

3. Globalization 101.org: A project of the Carnegie endowment. (July 14, 2003). Technology changes news coverage of war. On-line. Available: http://www.newscientist.com.

4. Moniz, D. (2005, April 28). Female amputees make clear that all troops are on front lines. *USA Today*. Online. Available: http://www.usatoday.com/news/nation/2005-04-28-female-amputees-combat_x.htm.

5. See example of Feininger's photograph at *Gallery* M. Online. Available: <http://www.gallerym.com/default.cfm, and *David Gallery*. Online. Available: <http://www.en.wikipedia.org/wiki/Main_Page.

6. Derrida's discussion about the hierarchy of speech over writing is found in *Of Grammatology* (1976, 8).

7. See *Artnet*. Online. Available: http://www.artnet.com/, and *Artsjournal*. Online. Available: http://www.artsjournal.com/artopia/.

8. See examples of Chicago's artworks. Online. Available: http://www.judy-chicago.com/.

9. See examples of Ringgold's artwork. Online. Available: http://www.faithringgold.com/.

10. See examples of Colescott's artwork. Online. Available: http://kravetswe-hbygallery.com/.

11. See examples of Ukeles's artworks. Online. Available: http://look.gvsu.edu:8000/pony/78.

12. See examples of Sherman's arworks. Online. Available: http://www.cin-dysherman.com/.

13. See photograph of installation in Springgay, 2004, 63.

14. See example of Dyer's installation in Sullivan, 2005, 134.

CHAPTER THREE. THE PROSTHETIC PEDAGOGY OF THE IGNORANT SCHOOLMASTER

This chapter was previously presented in November 2007 as a keynote lecture at II Congrés d'Educació de les Arts Visuals: Creativitat en temps de canvis (II Congress of Visual Arts Education: Creativity in Changing Times), Edifici historic de la Universitat de Barcelona. Barcelona, Spain.

1. See M. De Certeau, *The practice of everyday life*. (Berkeley: University of California, 1988). 117.
2. Ibid.
3. Bhabha (1994) cites Derrida's cumulating function of the supplement as *double entendre* that "intervenes or insinuates itself in-the-place-of . . . ," 154.
4. B. Aune (1998). Plato's objections to mimetic art. Online. Available: http://www.umass.edu/philosophy/PDF/Aune/plato_on_art.pdf.
5. See film still of Charlie Chaplin's *Modern Times* (1936). Online. Available: http://www.mds975.co.uk/Content/charlie_chaplin.html.
6. "The essence of mimesis is somatic, visceral, a shared psychic element wherein we feel the action, the wounding, the marking of a body, in our own being" (Slattery 2000, 13).
7. See Robert Frank's *My Father's Coat* (2001). Online. Available: http://www.pacemacill.com/.
8. See Leonardo's *Vitruvian Man* (1487). Online. Available: http://en.wikipedia.org/wiki/Accademia.

CHAPTER FOUR. PRECARIOUS LEANINGS

As of this writing, a version of this chapter is in press in C. Stout, ed., *Teaching and Learning Emergent Research Methodologies in Art Education* (Reston: National Art Education Association).

1. This was a story that I remember Rudolf Arnheim telling in the context of an invited lecture on the relationship of play and art. The lecture was held in the School of Education at Stanford University when I was a doctoral student there in the late 1970s.
2. See Jerome Bruner citation, the second epigraph of this chapter.
3. Cultural theorist Celia Lury (1998) suggests an adjunctive, supplementary relationship where public memory is prosthetically constituted and challenged by personal memory.
4. Lefebvre's (1991) description of *social space* corresponds with the in-between spaces of prosthesis conceptualized in this chapter. According to Lefebvre, social space has a dual nature that constitutes and positions the identity of the body within society on the one hand, while on the other hand serving "an intermediary or mediating role . . . [that] offers sequences, sets of objects, concatenations of bodies—so much so . . . that anyone can at any time discover new ones, forever slipping from the non-visible realm into the visible, from opacity into transparency" (182–83).
5. See John Roberts's (2007) characterization of Duchamp's readymades as artistic production that leads to "a rapid opening up of the prosthetic imagina-

tion . . . [a] place of rich experimentation" (73, 156). See Duchamp's readymade, *Fountain* (1917). Online. Available: http://www.sfmoma.org/.

6. Duchamp referred to conceptual play, which he initiated through his unassisted readymades, as *delay*, "the artwork that purposefully defies all its audience's expectations, resulting in its disappearance as an object of contemplation, and (hopefully) reappearance at a later point as an object of reflection" (Roberts, 37).

7. The fusion-resistant bisocations about which Koestler refers correspond with Wills's (1995) indeterminacy of prosthetic juxtaposition where "every relation is a relation to difference" (42).

8. See also Sullivan's "Framework of Visual Arts Research" in which "conceptual borders help to define areas of interest . . . [while serving as] permeable barriers that allow ideas to flow back and forth" (2005, 94).

9. The hidden "folding" of *Exquisite Corpse* as used in this writing functions in two ways: first, the strange, unfamiliar associations between the disjunctive components in each exercise; and second, the "folding" of lesson #1 into #2 into #3 and into #4.

10. The collaborative process of *Exquisite Corpse* research occurs in these exercises as the performing students' classmates explore, experiment, and improvise manifold associations, speculations, and understandings within the contingent and liminal spaces of the disjunctions performed. In other words, rather than mere passive spectators, classmates' interventions in these spaces constitute participation and collaboration.

11. Fold #2 assumes that graduate students in art education have had either professional or volunteer teaching experiences that they can draw upon for this exercise.

12. See Magritte's *Ceci n'est pas une pipe* (1926). Online. Available: http://www.lacma.org/.

13. In his review of political theorist Ernesto Laclau's *On Populist Reason* (2005), sociologist Oliver Marchart (2005, online) describes Laclau's concept of "democratic horizon" as a site of heterogeneity where, like Foucault's range of similitude, "conditions of possibility and possibility of conditions are inseparably intertwined."

14. The liminal and contingent spaces within which prosthetic associations occur and coexist correspond with Lefebvre's (1991) "differential spaces" where the homogenization and elimination of cultural differences are resisted and their heterogeneous social integrity and diversity is restored and accentuated (52).

15. The hyphenated association of the not-not double negative represents prosthetic contiguity and interconnectivity.

CHAPTER FIVE. THE ANXIETY OF DISEQUILIBRIUM IN THE MUSEUM

This chapter was previously presented in October 2008 as a keynote lecture at Encontro International, Arte/Educação Como Mediação (International Meeting, Art/Education and Mediation), Centro Cultural Banco do Brasil, Rio de Janeiro, Brazil, co-organized by Anna Mae Barbosa, Professor, University of São Paulo and Rejane Coutino, Professor, University of São Paulo.

1. In his introduction to *Reconstruction in Philosophy* (1948), Dewey cited these remarks from a lecture by British biologist C. D. Darlington to characterize the function of pragmatist science.

2. Foucault (1977) writes, "[T]ransgression contains nothing negative, but affirms limited being—affirms the limitlessness into which it leaps as it opens this zone to existence for the first time. But correspondingly, this affirmation contains nothing positive: no content can bind it, since, by definition, no limit can possibility restrict it" (35).

3. See Fred Wilson's, *Metalwork, 1723–1880* (Mining the Museum, 1992). Online. Available: http://mdhs.org/.

4. There exist interesting correspondences between Jones's and Cyborgian (Mentor et al.) epistemologies monodisciplinarity (*thetical*), multidisciplinarity (*antithetical*), interdisciplinarity (*synthetical*), transdisciplinarity (*pro-thetical*), and "fail again, fail better" (*and again*).

CHAPTER SIX. ~~DRAWING BLINDS~~

This chapter was previously presented as the "Studies Invited Lecture" at the 2009 National Art Education Association Annual Conference and later published in Winter 2010 in *Studies in Art Education: A Journal of Issues and Research in Art Education* 51, no. 2: 176–88. Later versions were presented as invited lectures and performances at the University of Wisconsin-Milwaukee, Peck School of the Arts (2010), and the University of Arkansas-Fayetteville (2011).

1. Regarding the impact of the A-Bomb on Jackson Pollock and the Abstract Expressionists see art historian Serge Guilbaut's (1983). *How New York Stole the Idea of Modern Art*, 97.

2. See Caravaggio's *The Incredulity of St. Thomas* (1601–02). Online. Available: http://en.wikipedia.org/wiki/The_Incredulity_of_Saint_Thomas_(Caravaggio).

3. See Jasper Johns's *The Critic Sees* (1964). Online. Available: http://www.nga.gov/.

4. According to educational psychologist Merlin C. Wittrock (1974, 1990), generative learning is "a function of the abstract and distinctive, concrete associations which the learner generates between his[her] prior experience, as it is stored in long-term memory, and the stimuli" (1974, 89). Hence, generative learning occurs in the liminal space between the learner's memory and cultural history, the knowledge that s/he brings to the classroom, and that knowledge imparted by the teacher. Accordingly, the learner is not "a passive consumer of information . . . [but] actively constructs . . . [his/her] own interpretations of information and draws inferences from them" (1990, 348).

5. See Robert Irwin's *Untitled* (1968). Online. Available: http://www.moca.org/.

6. The eighth-century polymath Saint John of Damascus wrote about the concealing and revealing operations of images: "Every image is declarative and indicative of something hidden . . . inasmuch as man has no direct knowledge of the invisible (his soul being covered by a body), or of the future, or of things that are severed and distant from him in space, being as he is circumscribed by place and

time, the image has been invented for the sake of guiding knowledge and manifesting publicly that which is concealed" (quoted in Freedberg 1989, 404–405).

7. Godzick's analogy of insight as the perfect congruence of lightning corresponds with Brian Massumi's "virtual vision" that emerges from the "eventful resolution of the tension" within the relational field of lightning, its electromagnetic activity (2011, 18–20).

8. See Walter De Maria's *The Lightning Field* (1977). Online. Available: http://c4gallery.com/artist/database/walter-de-maria/walter-de-maria.html.

9. See Rauschenberg's *Random Order* (ca. 1963) in B. W. Joseph, *Random Order: Robert Rauschenberg and the Neo-Avant-Garde* (Cambridge: MIT Press, 2007), 28–29.

10. See Christo and Jeanne-Claude's *The Reichstag (Berlin, June 1995)* wrapped in silver fabric. Online. Available: http://www.nga.gov/exhibitions/2002/christo/74fs.htm.

11. See Bruce Nauman's *Green Light Corridor* (1970). Online. Available: http://www.guggenheim.org/.

12. Duchamp's use of "delay" is fully explored by art historian John Roberts (2007).

13. For photo stills and video clip of Antoni's *TEAR* installation see: D. MacCash, "Prospect.1 Artist Janine Antoni Considers Demolition," *The Times-Picayune*, November 2, 2008. Online. Available: http://blog.nola.com/dougmaccash/2008/11/post_8.html.

CHAPTER SEVEN. ART-IN-THE-FLESH

A version of this chapter was previously presented in October 2011 as an invited lecture and performance for the School of Art Visiting Artists and Scholars Lecture Series at the University of Arizona, Tucson, Ariz.

1. Heathfield (2004) characterizes the liveness of the visual arts as a condition that "brings us spectators into a fresh relation: into the now of enactment, the moment by moment of the present" (8).

2. H. Müller, "Every Word Knows Something of a Vicious Circle." The Nobel Foundation, December 7, 2009. Available: http://nobelprize.org/.

3. Hayles further writes, "Writing [and art practice] is a way to extend the author's body into the exterior world; in this sense, it functions as a technological aid so intimately bound up with his thinking and neural circuits that it acts like a prosthesis" (126).

4. Lefebvre (1991) suggests that the space where these phased oppositions and generative rhythms occur is the "body" in relationship with its "counterpart or 'other' its mirror-image or shadow: it is the shifting intersection between that which touches, penetrates, threatens or benefits my body on the one hand, and all other bodies on the other" (184).

5. The noun *excess* as it is used here represents the multivalent imagings, interpretations, and understandings that are made possible through the prosthetic research of art practice, which resist and extend beyond synthetic closure. Similar to Bachelard's (1969) concept of "immensity," which will be discussed later in the chapter, excess "is a 'category' of the poetic imagination, and not merely a generality formulated during [consumption and] contemplation of grandiose spectacles" (198–99).

6. Bruner (1986) describes the meandering wanderlust of the virtual during the act of reading as follows: "As our readers read, as they begin to construct a virtual text of their own, it is as if they were embarking on a journey without maps—and yet, they possess a stock of maps that might give hints, and besides, they know a lot of journeys and about mapmaking. First impressions of the new terrain are, of course, based on older journeys already taken. In time, the new journey becomes a thing in itself; however, much of its initial shape was borrowed from the past. The virtual text becomes a story of its own, its very strangeness only a contrast with the reader's sense of ordinary" (36–37).

CHAPTER EIGHT. ART RESEARCH AND PRACTICE AS DELEUZOGUATTARIAN EMBODIMENT

1. Pertaining to Cherryholmes's critical pragmatism discussed previously, "the ubiquity of impairment is an empirical fact, not a relativist claim" (Shakespeare and Watson, 24).

2. Shakespeare and Watson's "emphasis on the ubiquity of impairment *is a political move*. It is a performative signification that does not take itself 'seriously,' but that acts as a tendential joke, drawing on the humorous absurdity of the normal/abnormal dyad by subverting the latter through radical fabulation" (Sub Specie Aeterni 2010, online).

3. The BwO should not be confused with the "lacking body" mentioned above. While the latter is a loaded, institutionalized term that signifies corporeal deficiencies, the former, BwO, is an incorporeal space where assumptions and codes of bodily lack are destratified, and its becoming-other is constituted limitless within a rhizomatic assemblage. These workings of the BwO correspond with Foucault's (1972) "incorporeal materialism," which occurs as *caesurae* disrupt, thereby "breaking the instant and dispersing the subject [and its assimilated cultural constructions] in a multiplicity of possible positions and functions" (231).

4. "Operating" is used here according to Deleuze's conception of minoritarian practice; art research and practice understood as an operation, "as the movement of subtraction, of amputation, one already covered by the other movement that gives birth to and multiplies something unexpected, like a prosthesis" (Deleuze 1997, 239).

5. As minoritarian embodiment, the multiplicities of impairment disclosed by Shakespeare and Watson operate within majoritarian understandings of disability and in doing so render them minor. Considering that it deviates from the social and medical model of disability, impairment is the "potential, creative and created, becoming" minoritarian of everybody (Deleuze and Guattari 1987, 105–106).

6. "Affect," in the Deleuzoguattarian sense, is not the noun of sentimental feelings and emotions, but the verb, ability, and drive of becoming-other; "an ability to affect and be affected . . . a prepersonal [autonomous] intensity corresponding to the passage from one experiential state of the body to another and implying an augmentation or diminution in the body's capacity to act" (Deleuze and Guattari 1987, xvi).

7. According to Kuppers, "[D]isability is experiential—a lived experience that resists linguistic structuring. The experiential nature of this knowledge stands in a complex relationship to discursive knowledge formations" (2003, 15).

8. Kuppers's epigraph at the beginning of this chapter, in which she juxtaposes the word *disabled* with "disabled" as a lived experience, constitutes Deleuzoguattarian schizo-analysis.

9. Given their antirepresentational stance, Deleuze and Guattari do not use "machine" as a metaphor, but as the literal functioning of bodies within a rhizomatic assemblage. They differentiate between "mechanisms," which they define as closed systems that consist of predefined, specific functions, and "machines" as open systems of continuous connectivity in all aspects of life where bodies affect and are affected by others.

10. I first learned about Dr. Julian's work history through conversations with students in the School of Visual Arts at The Pennsylvania State University. One day, after having shared some preliminary ideas for this book with a few students, two who were enrolled in sculpture classes barged into my office and insisted that I meet "Joe," a returning adult student and a classmate of theirs who formerly designed and constructed prosthetic devices. After retiring from medical practice, Joe had settled in State College, Pennsylvania, and immersed himself in sculpture classes at the university. Considering that I was writing about the prosthesis of art research and practice, and Joe had formerly designed and taught prosthetic construction, I was excited to meet him and to gain his perspective about these seemingly disparate cultural practices. During our ensuing conversations, it became apparent that he had not considered any affinity between making and teaching prostheses and artworks. Nevertheless, in telling his story, it quickly became clear that his immersive process of exploration, experimentation, and improvisation corresponded with the emergent, expansive, and extensive characteristics of art research and practice.

11. All citations in this chapter about Dr. Julian's practice at Khao I Dang are excerpted from a recorded conversation that I had with him in January 2011.

12. Deleuzoguattarian scholar Brian Massumi (1992) characterizes Cambodia under the Khmer Rouge as an extreme example of molarization, a social formation that justified a "murderous fascist-paranoid attack," the genocide of its own people (120).

13. Julian's analogy of the "Darwinian two-step" corresponds with Deleuzoguattarian becoming-molecular in as much as he created a "zone of proximity," an incorporeal pedagogical space where complex and contradictory images, ideas, materials, and processes could coexist and coextend multiple ways in which to rehabilitate his patients (Deleauze and Guattari 1987, 273).

REFERENCES

Adler, M. J. 1940. How to mark a book. Online. Available: http://grammar.about.com/od/60modelessays/qt/adlertip.htm.

Bachelard, G. 1969. *The poetics of space*. Trans. M. Jolas. Boston: Beacon.

Bader, G. 2007. The body politic. *Artforum* XLV, no. 5 (January): 228–31.

Ballard, J. G. 1973. *Crash*. New York: Picador.

Barker, S. 2003. The abocular hypothesis, or "drawing the blind." Online. Available: http://www.derridathemovie.com/comment-1.html.

Barrett, W. 1962. *Irrational man: A study in existential philosophy*. Garden City, NY: Doubleday Anchor.

Barry, L., and D. Schultz. 2008. *Projects '08: New work in the carriage house* (Gallery Catalog). East Islip: The Islip Art Museum.

Barthes, R. 1974. *S/Z: An essay*. Trans. R. Miller. New York: Hill and Wang.

Becker, C. 1996. *Zones of contention: Essays on art, institutions, gender, and anxiety*. Albany: State University of New York Press.

Beckett, S. 1992. *Nohow on*. London: Calder.

Benson, B. K. 1997. Coming to terms: Scaffolding. *The English journal* 86, no. 7(November): 126–27.

Berger Jr., H. 2000. Second world prosthetics: Supplying deficiencies of nature in renaissance Italy. In *Early modern visual culture: Representation, race, and empire in renaissance England*, ed. P. Erickson and C. Hulse, 98–147). Philadelphia: University of Pennsylvania Press.

Berk, L. E., and A. Winsler. 1995. *Scaffolding children's learning: Vygotsky and early childhood education*. Washington, DC: National Association for the Education of Young Children.

Bhabha, H. K. 1994. *The location of culture*. London: Routledge.

Bruner, J. 1986. *Actual minds, possible worlds*. Cambridge: Harvard University Press.

———. 1990. *Acts of meaning*. Cambridge: Harvard University Press.

Buck-Morss, S. 1989. *The dialectics of seeing: Walter Benjamin and the arcades project*. Cambridge: MIT Press.

Butler, J. 2004. *Precarious life: The powers of mourning and violence*. London: Verso.

Caillois, R. 2001. *Man, play, and games*. Trans. M. Barash. Urbana and Chicago: University of Illinois Press.

Chambers, C., D. Donald, and E. Hasebe-Ludt. 2002. Creating a curriculum of métissage. Online. Available: http://www.ccfi.educ.ubc.ca/publication/insights/v07n02/metissage/authors.html.

Cherryholmes, C. H. 1988. *Power and criticism: Poststructural investigations in education*. New York: Teachers College, Columbia University Press.

Chomsky, N., and E. S. Hermann. 1988. *Manufacturing consent: The political economy of the mass media*. New York: Pantheon.

Christopher & Dana Reeve Foundation. 1997. Chuck Close: A portrait in progress. *Paralysis resource center*. Online. Available: http://www.christopherreeve.org/.

Close, C. 2010. Conversation: Chuck Close, Christopher Finch. PBS Newshour, December 14. Online. Available: http://www.pbs.org/newshour/.

Collins, L. 2010. Making restorative sense with Deleuzian morality, art brut. and the schizophrenic. *Deleuze Studies* 4, no. 2 (July): 234–55.

Cooper, G. 2003. Ghost lightning. Online. Available: http://www.pulsecooper.com/artwork_ghost_lightning.php.

Crary, J. 1986. J. G. Ballard and the promiscuity of forms. In *Zone 12: The contemporary city*, ed. J. C. Crary, M. Feher, H. Foster, and S. Kwinter, 159–65). New York: Zone/MIT.

———. 1988. Modernizing vision. In *Vision and visuality*, ed. H. Foster, 29–44. Seattle: Bay Press.

Culler, J. 1982. *On deconstruction: Theory and criticism after structuralism*. Ithaca: Cornell University Press.

De Certeau, M. 1988. *The practice of everyday life*. Berkeley: University of California Press.

De Man, P. 1983. *Blindness and insight: Essays in the rhetoric of contemporary criticism*. Minneapolis: University of Minnesota Press.

Deleuze, G. 1990. *The logic of sense*. Trans. M. Lester. Ed. C. V. Boundas. New York: Columbia University Press.

———. 1993. *The Deleuze reader*. Ed. C. V. Boundas. New York: Columbia University Press.

———. 1994. *Difference and repetition*. Trans. P. Patton. New York: Columbia University Press.

———. 1997. One less manifesto. In *Mimesis, masochism, and mime: The politics of theatricality in contemporary French thought*, ed. T. Murray, 239–58. Ann Arbor: University of Michigan Press.

———, and F. Guattari. 1983. *Anti-Oedipus: Capitalism and schizophrenia*. Trans. R. Hurley, M. Seem, and H. R. Lane. Minneapolis: University of Minnesota Press.

———. 1987. *A thousand plateaus: Capitalism and schizophrenia*. Trans. B. Massumi. Minneapolis: University of Minnesota Press.

Derrida, J. 1976. *Of grammatology*. Baltimore: The Johns Hopkins University Press.

———. 1986. *Glas*. Lincoln: University of Nebraska Press.

———. 1993. *Memoirs of the blind: The self-portrait and other ruins*. Trans. P-A. Brault and M. Naas. Chicago: The University of Chicago Press.

Dewey, J. 1934. *Art as experience*. New York: Minton, Balch.

———. 1938. *Experience and education*. New York: Collier.

———. 1944. *Democracy and education*. New York: Macmillan.

———. 1948. *Reconstruction in philosophy*. Boston: The Beach Press.

Doherty, B. 1998. Figures of the pseudorevolution. *October* 84 ((Spring): 65–89.

Eliasson, O. 2010. The museum revisited. *Artforum* XLVIII, no. 10 (June): 308–309.

Elkins, J. 1996. *The object stares back: On the nature of seeing*. San Diego: Harcourt Brace.

Ellsworth, E. A. 2005. Places of learning: Media, architecture, pedagogy. New York: Routledge.

Erickson, P., and C. Hulse. 2000. Introduction. In *Early modern visual culture: Representation, race, and empire in renaissance England*, ed. P. Erickson and C. Hulse, 1–14. Philadelphia: University of Pennsylvania Press.

Evangelista, C. 2009. Exhibition catalog: *Rule 10 for the* MFA *5+1*. Wilmington: Delaware Center for the Contemporary Arts.

Feininger, A. 1951. *The Photojournalist*. Online. Available: http://www.gallerym.com/default.cfm.

Fisher, W. 2006. *Materializing gender in early modern English literature and culture*. Cambridge: Cambridge University Press.

Foster, H. 1998. Trauma studies and the interdisciplinary. In *The anxiety of interdisciplinarity: de-, dis-, ex-*, ed. A. Coles and A. Defert, 155–68. London: Black Dog.

Foucault, M. 1972. *The archeology of knowledge and The discourse on language*. New York: Pantheon.

———. 1973. *The order of things: An archeology of the human sciences*. New York: Vintage.

———. 1977. *Language, counter-memory, practice: Selected essays and interviews by Michel Foucault*. Ed. D. F. Bouchard. Trans. D. F. Bouchard and S. Simon. Ithaca: Cornell University Press.

———. 1982. *This is not a pipe*. Ed. And Trans. J. Harkness. Berkeley: University of California Press.

———. 1994. *The birth of a clinic: An archeology of medical perception*. New York: Vintage.

Franklin, B. 2008–09. *Fermata: Jesse Owens*. Online. Available: http://www.brianpatrickfranklin.com/fermata_owens.html.

Freedberg, D. 1989. *The power of images: Studies in the history and theory of response*. Chicago: The University of Chicago Press.

Freud, S. 1962. *Civilization and its discontents*. New York: W. W. Norton.

Gablik, S. 1973. *Magritte*. Greenwich, CT: New York Graphic Society.

Gadamer, H. G. 2006. *Truth and method*. Trns. J. Weinsheimer and D. G. Marshall. London: Continuum.

Garoian, C. R. 2001. Performing the museum. *Studies in art education: A journal of issues and research* 42, no. 3 (September): 234–48.

Geertz, C. 1973. *The interpretation of cultures*. New York: Basic Books.

Godzich, W. 1983. Introduction. In P. de Man, *Blindness and insight: Essays in the rhetoric of contemporary criticism*. Minneapolis: University of Minnesota Press.

González, J. A. 1995. Autotopographies. In *Prosthetic territories: Politics and hypertechnologies*, ed. G. Brahm Jr. and M. Driscoll, 133–50. Boulder: Westview.

Gray, C. H. 2002. War, peace, and complex systems. *Borderlands* 1, no. 1. Online. Available: http://www.borderlands.net.au/vol1no1_2002/Gray_complexity.html.

———, H. J. Figueroa-Sarriera, and S. Mentor. 1995. *The cyborg handbook*. New York: Routledge.

Griffen, T. 2010. Postscript: The museum revisited. *Artforum* XLVIII, no. 10 (June): 328–35, 386.

Grosz, E. 2006. Naked. In *The prosthetic impulse: From a posthuman present to a biocultural future*, ed. M. Smith and J. Morra, 187–202. Cambridge: MIT Press.

Guilbaut, S. 1983. *How New York stole the idea of modern art*. Trans. A. Goldhammer. Chicago: The University of Chicago Press.

Haraway, D. J. 1991. *Simians, cyborgs, and women: The reinvention of nature*. New York: Routledge.

Harbison, R. 1977. *Eccentric spaces: A voyage through real and imaginary spaces*. New York: Alfred A. Knopf.

Hayles, N. K. 1999. *How we became posthuman: Virtual bodies in cybernetics, literature, and informatics*. Chicago: The University of Chicago Press.

Heathfield, A. 2004. Alive. In *Live: Art and performance*, ed. A. Heathfield, 6–13. New York: Routledge.

Hedtke, L. and J. Winslade. 2005. *NNN: Narrative network news*. Online. Available: http://www.waikato.ac.nz/php/research.php?mode=parent&doc=Narrative+Network+News.

Heidegger, M. 1962. *Being and time*. Trans. J. Macquarrie and E. Robinson. Oxford: Blackwell.

Huizinga, J. 1955. *Homo ludens: A study of the play-element in culture*. Boston: Beacon Press.

Hulse, C. 2000. Reading painting: Holbein, Cromwell, Wyatt. In *Early modern visual culture: Representation, race, and empire in renaissance England*, ed. P. Erickson and C. Hulse, 140–77. Philadelphia: University of Pennsylvania Press.

Hutcheon, L. 1985. *The theory of parody: The teachings of twentieth-century art forms*. New York: Methuen.

Illich, I. 1976. *Medical nemesis: The expropriation of health*. New York: Pantheon.

Irwin, R. L. 1985. *Being and circumstance: Notes toward a conditional art*. Larkspur Landing: The Lapis Press.

———. 1972. The state of the real, part 1, conversation with Jan Butterfield. *Arts* 46, no. 10 (June): 48.

———. 2004. A/r/tography: A metonymic métissage. In *A/r/tography: Rendering self through arts-based living inquiry*, ed. R. L. Irwin and A. de Cosson, 27–38. Vancouver: Pacific Educational Press.

Jain, S. S. 1999. The prosthetic imagination: Enabling and disabling the prosthesis trope. *Science, technology, & human values* 24, no. 1 (Winter): 31–54.

Jones, R. 2009. Fail again, fail better. Online. Available: http://red-tape.info/Images/LearningMind_Jones.pdf.

———. 2008. Fail again, fail better. Paper presented for the John M. Anderson Lecture Series at the Penn State School of Visual Arts, University Park, Pennsylvania.

Joseph, B. W. 2006. The gap and the frame. *October* 117 (Summer): 44–70.

Julian Jr., J. 1986. Physical rehabilitation. In *Years of horror, days of hope: Responding to the Cambodian refugee crisis*, ed. B. S. Levy and D. C. Susott, 141–46. New York: Associated Faculty Press.

Klee, P. 1920. *Schöpferische Konfession* (1920; *Creative Credo*). Online. Available: http://www.famousquotessite.com/famous-quotes-5035-paul-klee-creative-credo-1920.html (Also see the "Creative Credo," in *Notebooks, vol. 1: The Thinking Eye*, ed. J. Spiller, trans. H. Norden (London, 1961), 78; orig. publ. as "*Schöpferische Konfession*," in *Paul Klee: Das Bildnerische Denken*, ed. J. Spiller (Stuttgart, 1956), pagination the same in German and English editions).

Koestler, A. 1973. *The act of creation*. London: Picador.

Krauss, R. 1974. Rauschenberg and the materialized image. *Artforum* 13, no. 4 (December): 36-43.

———. 1998. Death of a hermeneutic phantom: Materialization of the sign in the work of Peter Eisenman. In *The anxiety of interdisciplinarity: de-, dis-, ex-*, ed. A. Coles and A. Defert, 23–52. London: Black Dog.

Krauss, R. E. 1993. *The optical unconscious*. Cambridge: MIT Press.

Kristeva, J. 1982. *Powers of horror: An essay on abjection*. Trans. L. S. Roudiez. New York: Columbia University Press.

———. 1998. Institutional interdisciplinarity in theory and in practice. In *The anxiety of interdisciplinarity: de-, dis-, ex-*, ed. A. Coles and A. Defert, 2–22. London: Black Dog.

Kuhn, T. S. 1970. *The structure of scientific revolutions*. Chicago: The University of Chicago Press.

Kuppers, P. 2003. *Disability and contemporary performance: Bodies on edge*. New York: Routledge.

———. 2007. *Scar of visibility: Medical performances and contemporary art*. Minneapolis: University of Minnesota Press.

———. 2009. Toward a rhizomatic model of disability: Poetry, performance, and touch. *Journal of literary & cultural disability studies* 3, no. 3): 221–40.

Kuspit, D. 1983. Collage: The organizing principle of art in the age of the relativity of art. In *Relativism in the arts*, ed. B. J. Craige, 123–47. Athens: University of Georgia Press.

Kwon, M. 2008. Francis Alÿs: Hammer museum, Los Angles. *Artforum* XLVI, no. 6 (February): 280–82.

Laclau, E. 2005. *On populist reason*. London: Verso.

Landow, G. P. 1992. *Hypertext*. Baltimore: The John Hopkins University Press.

Landsberg, A. 2004. *Prosthetic memory: The transformation of American remembrance in the age of mass culture*. New York: Columbia University Press.

Leder, D. 1990. *The absent body*. Chicago: The University of Chicago Press.

Lefebvre, H. 1991. *The production of space*. Trans. D. Nicholson-Smith. Malden, MA: Blackwell.

Leverette, M. 2008. By the silent writing of its a: *Différance* and the performance of medium theory. *Journal of communication inquiry* 32, no. 1: 5–21.

Lévi-Strauss, C. 1966. *The savage mind*. Chicago: The University of Chicago Press.

Lingis, A. 2006. The physiology of art. In *The prosthetic impulse: From a posthuman present to a biocultural future*, ed. M. Smith and J. Morra, 73–89. Cambridge: MIT Press.

Lury, C. 1998. *Prosthetic culture: Photography, memory, and identity*. New York: Routledge.

Lyotard, J-F. 1999. *The postmodern condition: A report on knowledge*. Minneapolis: University of Minnesota Press.

———. 2004. *Libidinal economy*. Trans. I. H. Grant. London: Continuum.

Marchart, O. 2007. In the name of the people: Populist reason and the subject of the political. *Diacritics* 35, no. 3 (Fall): 3–19. Online. Available: http://muse.jhu.edu.ezaccess.libraries.psu.edu/journals/diacritics/v035/35.3marchart.html#bio.

Marx, G. Online. Available: http://able2know.org/topic/102071-1.

Massumi, B. 1992. *A user's guide to capitalism and schizophrenia: Deviations from Deleuze and Guattari*. Cambridge: MIT Press.

———. 2002. *Parables for the virtual: Movement, affect, sensation*. Durham: Duke University Press.

———. 2011. *Semblance and event: Activist philosophy and the occurrent arts*. Cambridge: MIT Press.

McLaren, P. 1993. *School as ritual performance: Towards a political economy of educational symbols and gestures*. London: Routledge.

Mead, R. 2008. Eerily composed: Nico Muhly's sonic magic. *The New Yorker*, February 11 and 18, 74–83.

Merleau-Ponty, M. 1962. *Phenomenology of perception*. Trans. C. Smith. London: Routledge.

———. 1968. *The visible and the invisible*. Trans. A. Lingis. Evanston: Northwestern University Press.

Meyer, U. 1972. *Conceptual art*. New York: E. P. Dutton.

Mirzoeff, N. 2006. On visuality. *Journal of visual culture* 5, no. 1: 53–79.

Mitchell, D. T., and S. L. Snyder. 2000. *Narrative prosthesis: Disability and the dependencies of discourse*. Ann Arbor: University of Michigan Press.

MOMA.org. Robert Irwin. Online. Available: http://www.moma.org/collection/.

Morris, R. 2008. Writing with Davidson: Some afterthoughts after doing *Blind Time IV: Drawing with Davidson*. In *Robert Morris, have I reasons: Work and writings, 1993–2007*, ed. N. Tsouti-Schillinger, 41–49. Durham: Duke University Press.

Mouffe, C. 2010. The museum revisited. *Artforum* XLVIII, no. 10 (June): 326–27, 384.

Nietzsche, F. 1957. *The use and abuse of history*. Trans. A. Collins. Indianapolis: Bobbs-Merrill.

Osborne, H. 1980. Aesthetic implications of happenings, conceptual art, etc. *The British Journal of Aesthetics* 20, no. 1 (Winter): 6–17.

Oxford English Dictionary. Online. Available: http://oed.com.ezaccess.libraries.psu.edu/view/Entry/34027?rskey=RWjsyG&result=1&isAdvanced=false#eid9320789.

Pace/MacGill Gallery. Robert Frank: *My father's coat, 2001*. Online. Available: http://www.pacemacgill.com/.

Paz, O. 1978. *Marcel Duchamp: Appearance stripped bare*. Trans. R. Phillips and D. Gardner. New York: Viking.

Perreault, J. 2006. Rauschenberg's combines. Online. Available: http://www.artsjournal.com/artopia/.

Perry, H. R. 2002. Re-arming the disabled veteran: Artificially rebuilding state and society in world war one Germany. In *Artificial parts, practical lives*, ed. K. Ott, D. Smith, and S. Mihm, 75–101. New York: New York University Press.

Pinar, W. n.d. The internationalization of curriculum studies. Online. Available: http://www.riic.unam.mx/01/02_Biblio/doc/Internationalizaton_Curriculum_W_PINAR_(MEXICO).pdf.

———, and M. Grumet. 1976. *Toward a poor curriculum*. Dubuque: Kendall/Hunt.

Rancière, J. 1991. *The ignorant schoomaster: Five lessons in intellectual emancipation*. Trans. K. Ross. Stanford: Stanford University Press.

———. 2007. The emancipated spectator. *Artforum* XLV, no. 7 (March): 271–80.

———. 2007. *The future of the image*. Trans. G. Elliott. London: Verso.

Rauschenberg, R. 1963. Random order. *Location* 1, no. 1 (Spring): 29.

Ravin, J. G., and P.M. Odell. 2008. Pixels and painting: Chuck Close and the fragmented image. *Archives of ophthalmology* 126, no. 8 (August): 1148–51.

Read, H. 1955. *Icon and idea: The function of art in the development of human consciousness*. New York: Schocken.

Rendell, J. n.d. A place between: Art, architecture and critical theory. Online. Available: http://www.eki.ee/km/place/pdf/kp3_14_Rendell.pdf.

Reynolds, J. 2010. Time out of joint: Between phenomenology and post-strucuralism. *Parrhesia* 9: 55–64. Online. Available <http://www.parrhesiajournal.org/.

Roberts, J. 2007. *The intangibilities of form: Skill and deskilling in art after the ready-mades*. London: Verso.

Roda, T. 2008. *Untitled #27*. Online. Available: http://jazno.net/recentwork/2008/03/16/tim-rodas-silent-movies/.

Rogers, B. 1976. The "umbrella series": Static and kinetic constructions. *Leonardo* 9, no. 4: 265–69.

Rothenberg, A. 1979. *The emerging goddess: The creative process in art, science, and other fields*. Chicago: The University of Chicago Press.

King James Version. Online. Available: http://www.biblegateway.com/.

Saramago, J. 1997. *Blindness*. Trans. G. Pontiero. New York: Harcourt Brace.

Schechner, R. 1985. *Between theater and anthropology*. Philadelphia: University of Pennsylvania Press.

———. 1988. Playing. *Play & Culture* 1: 3–19.

Semetsky, I. 2006. *Deleuze, education, and becoming*. Rotterdam: Sense. Online. Available: http://www.sensepublishers.com/catalog/files/90-8790-017-1.pdf.

Serlin, D. 2002. Engineering masculinity: Veterans and prosthetics after world war two. In *Artificial parts, practical lives*, ed. K. Ott, D. Smith, and S. Mihm, 45–74. New York: New York University Press.

SFAI: San Francisco Art Institute Archives. The western roundtable on modern art, 1949. Online. Available: http://www.sfai.edu/special-collections.

Shakespeare, T., and N. Watson, N. 2001. The social model of disability: An outdated ideology? *Research in Social Science and Disability* 2: 9–28.

Shklovsky, V. 1965. Art as technique. In *Russian formalist criticism: Four essays*, ed. L. T. Lemon and M.J. Reis. Lincoln: University of Nebraska Press.

Sidman-Taveau, R., and M. Milner-Bolotin. 2001. Constructivist inspirations: A project-based model for L2 learning in virtual worlds. Online. Available: http://eric.ed.gov:80/ERICDocs/data/ericdocs2sql/content_storage_01/0000019b/80/29/cf/ae.pdf.

Slattery, D. 2000. *The wounded body: Remembering the markings of flesh*. New York: State University of New York Press.

Smith, M. 2006. The vulnerable articulate: James Gillingham, Aimee Mullins, and Matthew Barney. In *The prosthetic impulse: From a posthuman present to a biocultural future*, ed. M. Smith and J. Morra, 43–72. Cambridge: MIT Press.

Sobchack, V. 2006. A leg to stand on: Prosthetics, metaphor, and materiality. In *The prosthetic impulse: From a posthuman present to a biocultural future*, ed. M. Smith and J. Morra, 17–41). Cambridge: MIT Press.

Søby, M. 2005. Collective Intelligence—Becoming Virtual. Online. Available: http://folk.uio.no/mortenso/Collective.Intelligence.html.

Solnit, R. 2001. *Wanderlust: A history of walking*. New York: Penguin.

Sontag, S. 1966. *Against interpretation and other essays*. New York: Farrar, Straus, and Giroux.

———. 2003. *Regarding the pain of others*. New York: Farrar, Straus, and Giroux.

Springgay, S. 2004. Body as fragment: Art-making, research, and teaching as a boundary shift. In *a/r/tography: Rendering self through arts-based living inquiry*, ed. R. L. Irwin and A. de Cosson, 60–74. Vancouver: Pacific Educational Press.

Stein, J. E. 1993. Sins of omission: Fred Wilson's *mining the museum*. Online. Available: http://slought.org/files/downloads/publications/salons/1083.pdf.

Strathern, M. 1991. *Partial connections*. Lanham, MD: Rowman and Littlefield.

Sub Specie Aeterni. 2010. Toward a post-human political theory: Deleuze, Guattari, and disability studies—pt. 1. Online. Available: http://unpresentable.wordpress.com/2010/05/03/toward-a-post-human-political-theory-deleuze-guattari-and-disability-studies-pt-1/.

Sullivan, G. 2005. *Art practice as research: Inquiry in the visual arts*. Thousand Oaks: Sage.

Sutton-Smith, B. 1997. *The ambiguity of play*. Cambridge: Harvard University Press.

Thomson, R. G. 1996. *Freakery: Cultural spectacles of the extraordinary body*. New York: New York University Press.

Tompkins, C. 1996. *Duchamp*. New York: Henry Holt.

Trafí, L., and M. Rifá. 2007. Researching the production of visual narratives in an education project based on the understanding of Robert Frank's photographs. Paper presented at the National Art Education Association Annual Conference, March, New York, NY.

Turner, V. W. 1983. Body, brain, and culture. *Zygon* 18, no. 3: pp. 221–45.

———. 1990. Are there universals of performance in myth, ritual, and drama? In *By means of performance*, ed. R. Schechner and W. Appel, 8–18). Cambridge: Cambridge University Press.

Ulmer, G. L. 1985. *Applied grammatology: Post(e)-pedagogy from Jacques Derrida to Joseph Beuys*. Baltimore: The Johns Hopkins University Press.

Vygotsky, L. S. 1978. *Mind in society*. Cambridge: Harvard University Press.

Weschler, L. 1982. *Seeing is forgetting the name of the thing one sees: A life of contemporary artist Robert Irwin*. Berkeley: University of California Press.

White, A. 1993. *Carnival, hysteria, and writing: Collected essays and autobiography*. Oxford: Clarendon.

Wigley, M. 1991. Prosthetic theory: The disciplining of architecture. *Assemblage* 15 (August): 6–29.

Wills, D. 1995. *Prosthesis*. Stanford: Stanford University Press.

Wilson, B. 2007. A story of visual cultural and pedagogical webs. In *International handbook of research in art education*, ed. L. Bresler, 917–21). Dordrecht: Springer.

Wilson, B., and M. Wilson. 1982. *Teaching children to draw: A guide for teachers and parents*. Englewood Cliffs, NJ: Prentice-Hall.

Wilson, E. 1993. Is transgression transgressive? In *Activating theory: Lesbian, gay, bisexual politics*, ed. J. Bristow and A. R. Wilson, 107–117. London: Lawrence and Wishart.

Wittrock, M. C. 1974. Learning as a generative process. *Educational psychologist* 24, no. 4: 345–76.

———. 1990. Generative processes of comprehension. *Educational psychologist* 11, no. 2: 87–95.

Wood, D. J., J. Bruner, and G. Ross. 1976. The role of tutoring in problem solving. *Journal of child psychology and psychiatry* 17: 89–100.

Žižek, S. 2009. Interview: Democracy now! *Pacifica Radio*, October 15. Online. Available: http://www.democracynow.org/2009/10/15/slovenian_philosopher_slavoj_zizek_on_the.

INDEX

Note: Page numbers in italics indicate illustrations.